IN THE PATH
OF THE
MASTERS

Also by Denise Lardner Carmody

Feminism and Christianity: A Two-Way Reflection
The Oldest God: Archaic Religion Yesterday & Today
Seizing the Apple: A Feminist Spirituality of Personal Growth
Women & World Religions

Also by John Tully Carmody

Ecology & Religion: Toward a New Christian Theology of Nature
The Heart of the Christian Matter: An Ecumenical Approach
Holistic Spirituality
Reexamining Conscience

Co-authored books by Denise Lardner Carmody and John Tully Carmody

How to Live Well: Ethics in the World Religions
Peace & Justice in the Scriptures of the World Religions
Shamans, Prophets, & Sages: An Introduction to World Religions
Contemporary Catholic Theology
Exploring American Religion
Republic of Many Mansions: Foundations of American Religious Thought

IN THE PATH
OF THE
MASTERS

*Understanding the Spirituality
of Buddha, Confucius,
Jesus, and Muhammad*

DENISE LARDNER CARMODY
AND JOHN TULLY CARMODY

University of Tulsa

M.E. Sharpe
Armonk, New York
London, England

First paperback edition, 1996
Published in the United States by M. E. Sharpe, Inc.

Copyright © 1994 by Paragon House Publishers
Reprinted by special arrangement with Paragon House Publishers

Library of Congress Cataloging-in-Publication Data

Carmody, Denise Lardner, 1935–
In the path of the masters : understanding the spirituality of Buddha, Confucius, Jesus,
and Muhammad / Denise Lardner Carmody, John Tully Carmody.
p.   cm.
Includes bibliographical references and index.
ISBN 1-56324-863-8 (pbk : alk. paper)
1. Spiritual life.
2. Religious biography.
3. Religions.
4. Religions—Relations.
I. Carmody, John, 1939–
II. Title.
BL624.C347   1996
291.6′3—dc20
96-11387
CIP

Printed in the United States of America

The paper used in this publication meets the minimum requirements of
American National Standard for Information Sciences—
Permanence of Paper for Printed Library Materials,
ANSI Z 39.48-1984.

EB (p)   10   9   8   7   6   5   4   3   2   1

CONTENTS

PREFACE

In this book we reflect on the legacy of four great religious figures: the Buddha, Confucius, Jesus, and Muhammad. Billions of people have made their way through life following what these figures taught and exemplified. The four founded some of the most influential religious systems the world has known, and their followers continue to think they furnish the wisdom most precious for determining how to live well.

Our interest is the "spiritualities" of these great founders. We focus on the existential, personal, experiential aspects of their messages and wisdoms. After situating them in their historical context, we try to glimpse what they were like personally, hear what they taught, and assess both how they saved their followers from confusion and where their legacy may be imperfect, open to friendly criticism.

The result should be an invitation to approach the Buddha, Confucius, Jesus, and Muhammad as great benefactors of humankind. For either academic or personal purposes, the questions these founders generate and the answers they provide can be enormously stimulating. Each points beyond the obvious to the mysterious—the intriguing foundations of holiness and fulfillment. None backs away from the most challenging of tasks: determining what is realistic, on what human beings can rely, when they seek to ground their lives. So, we believe, each founder remains a great educator. If we can stimulate readers to meditate on the texts and other bequests of these founders, we shall be more than gratified.

Our thanks to Peter Coveny and Jo Glorie of Paragon House, who brought the book to publication.

CHAPTER 1

INTRODUCTION

The Great Religious Founders

When we speak of "the great religions," we mean the traditions that have lasted for centuries, shaped hundreds of millions of people, and gained respect for their depth and breadth. In most surveys of the world's religions, Hinduism, Buddhism, Confucianism, Taoism, Judaism, Christianity, and Islam step forth as candidates for this title. The "founders" of such traditions may be anonymous, legendary, or historical. For example, the founders of Hinduism were anonymous, inasmuch as the seers (*rishis*) usually credited with the Vedas have no names. They were legendary inasmuch as sages such as Yajnavalkya, who appears in the Upanishads, and deities such as Krishna, who appears in the *Bhagavad-Gita*, are mythological more than factual. They were historical inasmuch as one considers the sage Shankara (788–820) or the political holy man Mahatma Gandhi (1869–1948) a "founder" of native Indian religious traditions.

This raises the question, "What do we mean by 'founder'?" Here the word will mean a person who launched a comprehensive religion—a way of dealing with ultimate reality that expanded to touch all of human culture in the geographical areas where it flourished. In effect, this way of defining the term "founder" requires that the candidate be a historical figure—someone we are certain lived in a given period of time, a given geographical space, a given native culture.

One may debate whether any human figure could launch a comprehensive religion. Isn't that something that only God can do? Or, isn't that something at which many human hands would have to labor? In the sense in which we use the term, a single human being can be a

1

founder of a great religion. Such traditions as Buddhism, Confucianism, Christianity, and Islam only came into being through the labors of the Buddha (Gautama), Confucius, Jesus, and Muhammad. Even if we say that many other people shaped Buddhism and Confucianism, it remains true that Gautama and Confucius were the discernible, historical originators of what subsequently became known as "Buddhism" and "Confucianism." Even if we say that God was the reason that Christianity or Islam began, it remains true that Jesus and Muhammad were the prophetic figures who decisively shaped the human beginnings of "Christianity" and "Islam."

Thus far, we have nominated the Buddha, Confucius, Jesus, and Muhammad for inclusion in our study of the spirituality of the great religious founders. Each was a fully historical human being who marked the starting point from which the religion associated with his name began. Even though many of the materials that we must use when studying these four figures are legendary, mythological, or filled with assumptions from religious faith, the figures themselves stand solidly in history. Few if any responsible historians argue that Gautama, Confucius, Jesus, or Muhammad never existed. No one disputes that the religions these men launched have had a momentous impact on history. (In the course of discussing Buddhism and Confucianism, we shall clarify what has been "religious" about them, and what has not, since some observers do not classify them as religions.) What about Taoism and Judaism? Do they have founders we ought to include?

The question is more difficult than it would be if raised for Hinduism, Buddhism, Confucianism, Christianity, or Islam. For those five traditions, we can answer with fair confidence: no, yes, yes, yes, yes. The Hindu candidates are either not fully historical or not the starting point for the religion. The Buddha, Confucius, Jesus, and Muhammad meet all our criteria. Lao Tzu, the best candidate for "founder of Taoism," is shadowy—hard to pin down as a historical figure. Also, it is not clear how decisively he launched "Taoism," because the poetic philosophy of *The Lao Tzu* (the book attributed to him, which also goes by the name *Tao te Ching* [*The Way and its Power*]), begot only part of "Taoism." Another part, equally influential in Chinese culture, is sometimes called "religious Taoism," and it has drawn on traditions of shamans and peasants that predate recorded history in China. Thus, on the grounds of both historical specificity and fullness of responsibility, Lao Tzu does not stand on the same plane as Gautama, Confucius, Jesus, and Muhammad. This does not mean, of course, that Lao Tzu is not worth studying. *The Lao Tzu* is a marvelous work, and it has had enormous influence, especially in East Asia but also in the West. It simply means that, if we want to pare the roster of the founders of the great religious traditions to its bare essence, we can omit Lao Tzu.

Judaism is certainly a wonderful religious tradition, now the best part of 4,000 years old. Christianity derived from it directly, and Islam owes it a great deal, according to secular historians, although many Muslim theologians deny that Islam owes anything decisive to Judaism or Christianity. But there are two problems with admitting a Jewish founder to stand alongside the four figures we have admitted thus far. The first is that there are two candidates for the title "founder," Abraham and Moses.

Abraham, whom we meet in the biblical book of Genesis, is the "father" of the Jews. The Bible credits him with faith in the God who eventually makes Israel a people. Because he believes in this God, and the promises this God makes to him and Sarah, his wife, Abraham stands at the beginning of the progeny that history comes to know as Israelites and Jews. But we know little about the dates or physical details of Abraham's life, and it is hard to know how much religious culture he created. (The depiction of Abraham in the book of Genesis is the product of many centuries of Israelite religious culture.)

Moses, the better candidate, is associated with the Torah, the "Law" that makes Israel the people of Abraham's God, bound to Him in a special covenant. What we know as "Judaism" is unthinkable without this Torah, and because Moses has been known as the great "Lawgiver," he seems to create the critical foundations of the later tradition. Much as there was no "United States" until the American Revolution and Constitution, what we now know as "Judaism" depends crucially on the Torah that God gave through Moses (following the "revolutionary" Exodus of the Hebrews from Egypt under the leadership of Moses). Still, the historicity of the life of Moses, as well as of the giving of the Torah, is questionable. Like Abraham, Moses appears in a literary setting many centuries after his historical life and work. The Bible fits him into categories and roles developed by later periods and useful to the time when the stories about him become canonical (regulative, normative). Thus Moses, too, creates problems, when we try to treat him as a founder.

The second issue, in the case of Judaism, is the size of this tradition. One of our requirements for a "great" tradition is that it has shaped hundreds of millions of people. Certainly Judaism has influenced great numbers of Jews. Over the centuries, they might total 100 million. Furthermore, it has greatly influenced Christianity and Islam, meriting being called their mother. But nowadays there are only about 17.5 million Jews in the world, compared to about 303 million Buddhists, 935 million Muslims, and 1,758 million Christians.[1] If we said that virtually all Chinese, and most other East Asians, were "Confucians" to some degree, we might number this fourth great tradition at over 2,000 million. Any such reckoning is problematic, especially for Confucians but also for Buddhists, Christians, Muslims, and Hindus (who now stand at about 705 million). It is also problematic for Jews, however, because many of them are not religious.

The point, then, is that the numerical "greatness" of Judaism does not stand on a level with that of the other traditions. Needless to say, this numerical fact does not make Judaism less beautiful, profound, or worthy of study than traditions enrolling greater numbers. Not only does quantity not determine quality, Judaism has exerted strong historical influence in a great number of cultures where its members were only a creative minority. It simply means that, when combined with the problems of determining a founder for Judaism to stand alongside the Buddha, Confucius, Jesus, and Muhammad, the symmetry slips and the inclusion of Judaism causes intellectual discomfort. Thus, for a brief study focused on the unarguable core of the matter of "great religious founders," Judaism does not suit our purpose.

Last, it is clear that not all the people in the world are religious. Prior to modernity, most people in the world were religious, but since modernity religion has suffered many setbacks, first in the West and then throughout the rest of the world. As a result, perhaps 1,100 million people today are either nonreligious or atheistic. Still, perhaps three of every four present day people are religious—well over 3,500 million. Of these, the four founders we treat have shaped the solid majority, well over two billion, by the most conservative reckoning, at least 70 percent.[2] Indeed, well over half of all the people in the world owe more of their sense of "reality" to these four men than to any other clearly discernible source (the influence of science and technology is strong, but how does one compare that to the impact of a single historical person?). In dealing with the spiritualities of the great religious founders, then, we are studying some of the most significant ideas and attitudes in today's world, to say nothing of past recorded history.

Spirituality

Granted the significance of the Buddha, Confucius, Jesus, and Muhammad, what does it mean to focus on their "spiritualities"? How ought we to understand this word? In general, here a "spirituality" will be a living, existential religious concern. We focus on what the Buddha taught about how to live, what to think about ultimate reality, how to become dispassionate, what to feel and love. The same for Confucius, Jesus, and Muhammad. In each case, our interest is not so much speculative as practical and personal. What is the path to peace, joy, wisdom, fulfillment, holiness that the founder, the spiritual master, laid out? On what did he want his community to focus? What were the values that any myths and rituals developed by his community ought to have promoted? How did he prompt his followers to interact with the natural world, their fellow human beings, their own selves, and ultimate reality or God? What were the stances in the world, the intellectual and emotional "positions," that Muhammad, or Christ, or Confucius, or Gautama would have applauded? What were the saintly virtues, the praiseworthy options in work and love, prayer and politics, that the life of the founder encouraged?

We could continue to multiply examples of "spiritual" issues, but the point should be clear. We are not pursuing the historical biography of the founders, nor a philosophical analysis of their teachings. Either project would be difficult on textual grounds, but even if we had the sources to allow a critical biography or a full philosophical analysis, that would not be our interest. Rather, we want to suggest how these founders wanted their followers, their disciples, to live. We are in search of the style, the cast of mind and heart, the "spirit" inculcated by the Buddha or Jesus, Muhammad or Confucius. Even when we rush to admit that there is no single style, cast of mind and heart, or spirit in any of the four traditions, we have to say also that something distinctive remains. There is little danger of confusing Buddhists with Christians or Confucians with Muslims. It is this "something distinctive" that intrigues us, serves as our goal. If we can suggest, sketch, give a hint of the lasting imprint of these great founders, the "character" of the ways of life they launched, we shall feel successful. For in suggesting the spiritualities of these four geniuses, we shall have opened many mansions of "religion"—indeed many mansions of simple humanity.

To place this understanding of "spirituality" in the context of contemporary discussions of the term, let us consider two representative uses. The Preface of *The Westminster Dictionary of Christian Spirituality* explains the concerns of this reference work as follows:

"Spirituality" is a word very much in vogue among Christians of our time. French Catholic in origin, it is now common to evangelical Protestants also. A recent course was criticized for lack of "spirituality," meaning that the timetable included few periods for worship. The Orthodox might prefer to speak of "mystical theology," as in Vladimir Lossky's title *The Mystical Theology of the Eastern Church* (where "theology" is the contemplation of God rather than an activity of the discursive reason alone), or simply, as does Alexander Schmemann, of "the Christian life."

In all traditions, and in many non-Christian faiths and philosophies, the underlying implication is that there is a constituent of human nature which seeks relations with the ground and purpose of existence, however conceived. As Job says, "There is a spirit in man." For the Christian, as for Job, this Spirit is "the breath of the Almighty," the Holy Spirit of God himself, and the activity the Spirit inspires is prayer. "We do not even know how we ought to pray, but through our inarticulate groans the Spirit himself is pleading for us" (Rom. 8.26, NEB). But prayer in Christian theology and experience is more than pleading or petition; it is our whole relation to God. And spirituality concerns the way in which prayer influences conduct, our behaviour and manner of life, our attitudes to other people. It is often best studied in biographies, but clearly it shapes dogmas, inspires movements and builds institutions.[3]

For *The Westminster Dictionary of Christian Spirituality*, spirituality centers on the interior life. The interior life flows outward, inspiring doctrines and works, but the crucial spiritual work is prayer, the center of which is contemplating God or being led by the Holy Spirit. The implication for our own slant on spirituality is that where the founders themselves centered, how they themselves dealt with God or what they considered the foundations of human existence, ought to be a major interest.

For example, the New Testament portrays Jesus as a man of prayer. The Qur'an suggests that Muhammad was equally devoted to contacting God, listening for the directions of Allah. The key moment in the Buddha's search for enlightenment came while he was deep in meditation. Determined to solve the problem of suffering, he was flooded with light when he had extinguished all desire, and from this enlightenment came the core of his teaching: the Four Noble Truths.

It is harder to determine the interior experience of Confucius, but a few texts in the *Analects* give us clues. For example, when the Master says that one who hears the Way in the morning can die in the evening content, we sense that the Way was more to him than a dry compendium of how the ancients had looked on nature or politics. Similarly, when the Master says that by the time he was seventy he could do whatever he wished, because his will and the Way had become one, we sense that the passion of his life was making the Way his own—fitting himself to the wisdom of the ancients, letting it form his joints and marrow.

There will be ample occasion to reflect on texts and issues related to these interior matters. By the end of the book, the place of prayer, meditation, trying to make tradition a personal, living nourishment should be clear. Here we need only note the rough, general compatibility of the notion of "spirituality" guiding *The Westminster Dictionary of Christian Spirituality* and the notion guiding our inquiries. With a few changes, to accommodate our wider range of material (four great traditions instead of one), and our more exact focus on the founders of these traditions, the description laid out in this dictionary serves quite well: Spirituality connotes prayer, behavior, manner of life, attitudes to other people, and similar pivotal aspects of an existential commitment, a living pathway through human experience.

Our second instance of present-day usage of the term "spirituality" comes from the Preface to a series of volumes dealing with the spirituality of leading religious traditions. We quote from the first of two volumes on Islamic spirituality, but the sentences apply to volumes on Jewish, Christian, Hindu, Buddhist, and other spiritualities:

> The present volume is part of a series entitled World Spirituality: An Encyclopedic History of the Religious Quest, which seeks to present the spiritual wisdom of the human race in its historical unfolding. Although each of the volumes can be read on its own terms, taken together they provide a comprehensive picture of the spiritual strivings of the human community as a whole—from prehistoric times, through the great religions, to the meeting of traditions at present. . . . In the planning of the project, no attempt was made to arrive at a common definition of spirituality that would be accepted by all in precisely the same way. The term "spirituality," or an equivalent, is not found in a number of traditions. Yet from the outset, there was a consensus among the editors about what was in general intended by the term. It was left to each tradition to clarify its own understanding of this meaning and to the editors to express this in the introduction to their volumes. As a working hypothesis, the following description was used to launch the project: The series focuses on that inner dimension of the person called by certain traditions "the spirit." This spiritual core is the deepest center of the person. It is here that the person is open to the transcendent dimension; it is here that the person experiences ultimate reality. The series explores the discovery of this core, the dynamics of its development, and its journey to the ultimate goal. It deals with prayer, spiritual direction, the various maps of the spiritual journey, and the methods of advancement in the spiritual ascent.[4]

While this description is fuller than that from *The Westminster Dictionary of Christian Spirituality*, it heads in the same interior direction. Spirituality is interested in the core of the person, the deepest center, where he or she makes contact with God, ultimate reality, the holy, what gives life and creation their coherence, beauty, enduring significance. The danger with this description, more than that of the *Dictionary*, lies in its not making clear the links between interiority and exteriority. Especially, one would want to add that any comprehensive spirituality shapes political, economic, artistic, and other realms of external, public culture. Spirituality is existential religion: faith, ultimate commitments, as they move along nerves, direct actions as well as thoughts, feelings as well as votes and disbursements of money. Spirituality is lived, experienced philosophy, theology, wisdom, or whatever else one wants to call people's outlook, *Weltanschauung*, way of proceeding in the world. It is comprehensive because it is deep. It touches all aspects of the person's life, including the person's contributions to the religious or civic community, because it colors if not determines the person's core.

This suggests that in pursuing the spiritualities of the great religious founders we are looking for the core that gives comprehensiveness, the depth that "explains" much of the style, cultural slant, ways of fingering the world that one finds in the tradition that a given founder launched. Spirituality is therefore elusive by definition. It is not something so simple or clear that we can ever nail it down, capture it in words, once and for all. Yet the more we live with a given founder, ponder his words and actions, scan the history of his followers, the more we learn about his lived religion and the more confidence we gather that we are gaining a feel for his values, outlook, formation through dealings with ultimate reality, sense of the sacred—in a word, his spirituality.

Light

We have mentioned that the Buddha came to his wisdom through an experience of enlightenment. Indeed, the name "Buddha" means "the Enlightened One." The Four Noble Truths that constitute the core of Buddhist Teaching (*Dharma*) express what the Buddha saw when the light dawned. The main focus of Buddhist spirituality throughout the ages has stayed fixed on enlightenment. If one gained an experience like that of Gautama, one would understand his Way, appropriate his wisdom, live with a peace, compassion, and detachment like his. Even today, Zen masters urge their students toward the light that will make them whole, counsel letting the light intrinsic to their beings express itself more and more fully. Light is the central metaphor in Buddhist religious experience. It is nearly equally central in many other traditions.

For example, in the Christian *Gospel of John* we read:

> And this is the judgment, that the light has come into the world, and people loved darkness rather than light because their deeds were evil. For all who do evil hate the light and do not come to the light, so that their deeds may not be exposed. But those who do what is true come to the light, so that it may be clearly seen that their deeds have been done in God. (3:19-21)

Here the light in question is twofold. Jesus, whom the author considers the incarnate Word of God, is the light of salvation, come into the midst of human beings to make them whole. The human conscience stands or falls by the degree to which it honors the light, follows the truth, wants to work and live transparently, with no need to lie or hide. The juxtaposition of these two senses of light creates the Johannine understanding of judgment. The worth of people depends on their response to the light that God has given them. If they reject Jesus or dishonor the truths they know in conscience ought to command their allegiance, they have ruined themselves. If they embrace Jesus as God's revealer and savior, they will merit divine approval, be a great success. Darkness is the realm of what opposes God, what ruins human beings.

In the *First Epistle of John*, this conviction dominates how the followers of Jesus ought to live:

> This is the message we have heard from him and proclaim to you, that God is light and in him there is no darkness at all. If we say that we have fellowship with him while we are walking in darkness, we lie and do not do what is true, but if we walk in the light as he himself is in the light, we have fellowship with one another, and the blood of Jesus his Son cleanses us from all sin. (1:5-7)

Certainly, Christians have developed other metaphors for the spiritual life, as Buddhists have spoken of more than light. But light shines down the Christian ages as a primal symbol. Not to live in the light, love the light, want one's whole life to be transparent to God's truth is, for Christian tradition, to be in mortal peril—serious opposition to God and so a contradiction of Jesus.

Light may not be so central in Islam as it is in Buddhism and Christianity, but all Muslims (especially the mystics) would deem it important, if only because it figures in one of the most beautiful verses of the Qur'an. In *surah* (Chapter 24), which is named "Light," we read:

> Allah is the Light of the heavens and the earth. The similitude of his light is as a niche wherein is a lamp. The lamp is in a glass. The glass is as it were a shining star. (This lamp is) kindled from a blessed tree, an olive neither of the East nor of the West, whose oil would almost glow forth (of itself) though no fire touched it. Light upon light, Allah guideth unto His light whom He will. And Allah speaketh to mankind in allegories, for Allah is Knower of all things. (24:35)

Here we see that divine light is a function of divine knowledge, and vice versa. Allah is the Light of the heavens and the earth, because Allah is Knower of all things. Conversely, a Muslim reflecting on the omniscience of Allah could easily realize that Allah knows everything because his essential being is light: clarity, understanding, illumination. Light is so central to our experience of understanding, grasping meaning, that we are bound to apply it to the Understanding that grounds the world. To think about the intelligibility of the world is soon to ask whether light pervades it from the source. To attend to the experience of insight is to think that complete human fulfillment must include dazzling vision, thorough comprehension. That is why the medieval Christian theologians spoke of heaven as a "beatific vision." That is why many Muslim philosophers loved to ponder the mind of God.

The place of light in Confucian spirituality is less obvious, needs more to be inferred. Confucius did not speculate widely. We find little concern with the nature of God, the foundations of the intelligibility of the world. We do find, though, much interest in moral health. We can be sure that Confucius would have read the Johannine materials about walking in the light with understanding and sympathy. Integrity, moral uprightness, was the watchword of Confucian ethics and political science. Only when leaders were virtuous, morally strong, could one expect peace and prosperity. It took a lifetime's worth of effort to become fully virtuous, able to do whatever one wished because one's will and the Way had joined. In this great labor, there had to have been an important place for the light of conscience.

If people did not learn to purify their consciences, and then follow them, they would come to ruin. No rich, ripe humanity would grow, and so they would be a social menace. Confucius thought that virtue was its own reward. On several occasions he considered the sacrifices that a "gentleman" (morally mature human being) ought to be willing to make to preserve his honor, his integrity. The light needed for a successful government was the insight that there are no shortcuts. Only when people are good, insist on doing what is right and just, will a community flourish. Deals done in darkness, shadings of the truth, denials of justice and the demands of conscience—all of these rain body blows against the common good.

The diligent Confucian applied himself (few women were accepted as disciples) to learning because he had to master the sources of moral intelligence, both textual and personal. He had to understand why the ancient heroes who had codified the Way thought as they did. He had also to understand why human beings, including himself in the first place, resisted the ancient wisdoms. Gradually, Confucius promised, the light would dawn. If disciples would accept the discipline of the Way, their lives would clarify, their moral vigor would mount. In various ways, then, Confucian spirituality is amenable to configuration as a pursuit of light. In various ways, the Master urged study, diligent quest for understanding, that would transform one's character, make one simply good—transparent.

What is the significance we attach to this consensus about the importance of spiritual light? Why does light figure so centrally? Because we are looking at spirituality as mental health, profound human fulfillment, discovery or reception of the powers necessary to make the human community what we know, in our best moments, it might be, even ought to be. "Light" is a metaphor for wisdom: deep understanding of reality, habitual insight that grounds people in virtue. The great religious founders were nothing if not wise. For centuries, billions of human beings have taken them as models of the way to maturity, fulfillment, peace, joy, and usefulness. Each of the founders we treat spoke words of eternal life. Their disciples clung to those words as means to salvation.

Thus, in the traditional Buddhist, Confucian, Christian, and Muslim spiritualities, wisdom, moral, and religious enlightenment commanded paramount attention. It is not hard to make the argument that in any spirituality viable in the twenty-first century "light" will command similar attention. Unless we know the Way, we cannot walk it well. Unless we have a vision of mental health, human fulfillment, we are unlikely to achieve it. People do not blunder their way to sanctity. They progress, bit by bit, through a process of knowing and unknowing, gaining light and then realizing the limits of their gains. So, gentle reader, be on the lookout for indications of enlightenment. Ponder the challenge of living in the light, developing a pure, lightsome conscience, taking to heart the proposition that God is light in whom there is no darkness at all. If you do, your studies of the great religious founders are bound to be profitable.[5]

Warmth

The easy correlation is light/head, warmth/heart. This correlation is more correct than incorrect. In the spiritualities of the great founders, both head and heart were important. One had to think correctly and love well. Thinking correctly without loving well, without practicing what one preached, made one ineffective, if not a hypocrite. Loving well without thinking correctly made one unreliable, a person whose virtue might be accidental. If we maintain a dualism of the head and the heart, then, light attaches to the head and warmth to the heart.

But the great founders did not maintain this dualism. The experience of God or ultimate reality at the center of their lives was both lightsome and warm, both a knowing and a loving. Sometimes their disciples would speak of the heart as an organ of knowledge. Often the enlightenment on their disciples' minds was a matter of knowing how to love, what to love, which emotions to favor. The great religious founders were holistic rather than dichotomous, people concerned for integrity who distrusted dualisms. One could not really know ultimate reality, experience enlightenment, and not love it passionately, with whole mind, heart, soul, and strength. One could not love well, profoundly, and not gain an intuitive, connatural knowledge of what one loved, who had stolen away one's heart. Knowledge and love both express the core, inner spirit of the human personality. Equally, both nourish that core, inner spirit. And, inasmuch as both are primal experiences, we cannot elucidate them by something more original. So even though we must speak of them as two, to provide for the ways that light and warmth differ, we have to add that knowing and loving, seeing light and feeling love, are also not two, are also quite alike.

The great virtue in the Buddhist catalogue of moral strengths is compassion. *Mahakaruna* (great compassion) is the hallmark of the buddhas and *bodhisattvas* (saints)—the exemplars of Buddhist wisdom. When Gautama gained enlightenment, he saw the core of human suffering clearly. But this was no academic vision. What he saw led him to want to alleviate human suffering. For the second half of his life, after his enlightenment at about age forty, he led the wandering life of a spiritual teacher, to hand on what he had learned, offer sick human beings the medicine he had received. He thought nothing could be more beneficial, a greater benefaction, than showing people how to drop their worries, frustrations, and pains, how to enter upon peace and joy. Nothing could justify a human life better than delivering people from mental illness, sadness, hatred, rage, and the other malfunctions that caused them, and the people they dealt with, great hardship. In the Buddha's decision to teach others what he had learned, we find the model of subsequent Buddhist compassion. We also find the coherence of warmth, care, and kindly concern with dazzling light.

Confucius is stuffier than the Buddha, but no less compassionate. The wisdom he gained from hard study of the traditions of the elders and much reform of his own character led him to become a teacher. He gathered disciples because he felt a duty to hand on what he had learned, the light he had garnered. Beyond concern for the individual students he instructed lay the welfare of society at large. Confucius was convinced that until rulers were wise and good, their people would continue to live in misery. Political and military power not linked to moral wisdom was causing suffering up and down the land. It was a mercy, a straightforward act of kindness and compassion, to become a teacher of the Way. It was the only thing a gentleman, a person privileged to have learned the Way and taken it to heart, could do in good conscience.

One would not call the Confucian texts "warm." They are unemotional to the point of dryness in many cases. And yet, if we look at their intent, we can intuit an underlying warmth. Confucius loved the Way. He loved what it said about nature, history, and the potential of human society. He loved what it did for people, when they let it form their souls. To attend well-ordered ceremonies gladdened the Master's heart. To observe students studying diligently gave him great satisfaction. When social relations were ordered rightly, so that elders commanded the respect of youth and leaders commanded the respect of subjects, something beautiful occurred. Confucius loved this beauty, this order, this rectitude. From such love, he spoke warmly of the life of moral learning. From such love, he made it plain that the light he wanted to impart was not cold or arid. It was a light, a knowledge, meant to gladden men and women, elders and children. It was a wisdom meant to be fertile—to generate joy and satisfaction, reconciling people to life's unavoidable hardships and stirring them to gratitude for life's so many graces.

Warmth is most to the fore in the spirituality of Jesus. Jesus was a figure of wisdom, but perhaps even more a prophet. Standing in the tradition of the Israelite prophets, he preached about what the good life, the ordered personality and society, would look like. When it came to distilling this preaching or teaching, he spoke of a twofold commandment. If people would love God without restriction, and love their neighbors as themselves, they would fulfill everything that Jewish tradition required of them. Love was the most passionate and comprehensive of human acts. To love intensely and well guaranteed salvation (healing, union with God).

The love of God that Jesus himself displayed was warm and confident. When Jesus prayed, he addressed God as his Father. The portrait of him in the gospels makes him intimate with God, full of trust. Even when he felt abandoned, on the way to crucifixion, his Father's name stayed on his lips. In loving God, Jesus apparently nourished the depths of his soul. He also found the power to dazzle the crowds with poetic stories and prodigies of healing. The power that went out from him was the power of loving God, becoming free of all earthly treasures and filled with something supernatural.

Confucius is famous for the negative golden rule: do not do unto others what you do not want them to do unto you. Jesus agreed with Confucius, but he put his sense of equality or fellow-feeling positively: love your neighbor as yourself, do unto others as you want them to do unto you. This second, neighborly focus of love, which we might call horizontal (in contrast to the vertical love of God), begot much warmth in Jesus' life. Thus, we find him weeping over Lazarus, being moved by any human suffering, loving individual disciples. We find the reputed author of *John* calling himself "the beloved disciple" and laying his head on Jesus' breast. Great warmth permeates the gospels, especially that of John. In scene after scene, Jesus is a man of full emotion, burning with passion. He hates injustice. He loves mercy, poor people left alone on the margins of social interest, little children, lilies of the field. Jesus does not protect his heart. He lets himself be vulnerable, lets the crowds of people who want things of him wear him down. He dies because of his love. He will not render to Caesar the things of his beloved, his Father. He cannot help proclaiming the Kingdom of God, the time when God wants to make all human affairs whole. On the cross, he teaches Western civilization the mysterious connection between love and suffering. On Easter morning, resurrected, he beguiles Western civilization with intuitions of a love stronger than death—a love so divine that it is deathless.

We shall discuss the modalities of warmth and coolness in love and compassion. There will be occasion to sort out how passion and detachment, commitment and dispassion, all claim their places in the traditional spiritualities. For the moment, though, let us honor the warmth, even the heat, of the prophetic religious founders. For the moment, let us say that Jesus and Muhammad both came away from their encounters with God burning with zeal, possessed of hearts filled to overflowing.

Saying this, we understand better the poetic character of both the speech of Jesus, especially his parables, and the speech of the Qur'an, the "recitals" given to Muhammad by Allah or one of His angels. Muhammad's eloquence was one of the early arguments for the validity of his message. Arab culture of his day laid great stress on eloquence, and nowhere had people heard a purer language, a more persuasive Arabic. Language like that of Muhammad tends to spring from a spirit immersed in fertile mysteries. The people with the most eloquent speech are those who have been rapt into the silence of ultimate reality, the darkness of God. When they emerge, everything in creation cries out for beautiful naming. Their bodies crave a rhythmic speech that will reset their balance. Their souls want sacraments: beautiful material containers for holy meaning. Their language therefore tends to spring forth as something fresh, newly minted. They hate hackneyed, tired language, yet they love traditional cadences, scriptural turns of phrase that they can turn again, to new account. All of this linguistic sensitivity is a work of passion. None of it escapes the fire and warmth of the love that has taken over their souls.

Similarly, the prophets' passion for justice, right worship, giving God sole primacy in human affairs stems from souls branded, recreated, wholly fulfilled yet still shot through with longing. Like the mystics, the prophets insist that the love of God is like no other experience. Once tasted, felt, undergone, it turns all earthly joys into straw. On the other hand, this same love, come to maturity, warms prophets and mystics to the task of teaching their brothers and sisters, healing the sick, succoring the needy, trying to right social injustices, to beautify both cities and countrysides. Come to maturity, religious love does not blaze out of control. However ecstatic the prayer of the great founders and saints, they stayed reasonable, remained astute about what human hearts could carry, how much reality humankind could bear.

Our thesis, then, is that warmth, like light, plays at the center of all great spiritualities. However different their personal or cultural weightings, all our spiritual heroes can be called great lovers, of both ultimate reality (the divine, the sacred) and their fellow human beings. However cool, detached, controlled their analysis of either human problems or the ultimate constitution of creation, they were all men of great passion—for liberation, enlightenment, justice, union with God, alleviating human suffering. The fire in their hearts made them warm and attractive. No one could accuse them of not caring, not suffering, not being so fully human that they manifested divinity singularly.[6]

This Book

We have indicated how we understand "the great religions," "the religious founders," and "spirituality." We have also indicated what we mean by "light" and "warmth," suggesting their relevance to the spiritualities of the great religious founders. It remains to preview how our study of the great religious founders will unfold.

The order in which we present the great religious founders is chronological. Gautama and Confucius both lived in the sixth-fifth century B.C. and were contemporaries. But the likely date for the birth of the Buddha (about 560) precedes that of Confucius (about 550), so we grant the Buddha seniority rights. Jesus comes along about 500 years after Confucius, and Muhammad follows more than 500 years after the death of Jesus (A.D. 570). The total temporal span of our subjects therefore stretches nearly 1200 years (about 560 B.C.–A.D. 632). While that span includes many "todays" in which people could hear God's voice, it is not long compared to the entire history of human awareness. Tens of thousands of years preceded Gautama, and more time has elapsed since the death of Muhammad than lay between that death and the birth of Gautama. In a relatively compact portion of human history, then, arose the four personalities who have imprinted more spirituality on the race than any others.

For each founder, we follow the same format. First, we sketch the religious culture into which he was born—the tradition that he inherited. None of our figures created a new pathway from nothingness. Each was indebted to many forebears. If we are to understand how a given founder was creative, we have to appreciate both what he had to work with and how he transformed it.

Second, we offer a brief biography. It is useful, indeed imperative, to know at least the bare bones of when the founder lived, what events most shaped his life, how his personal spirituality developed, and how he died. Third, we try to suggest what the "personality" of the founder was like. Here we depend on his biography but move below it, in search of what was most likely to make him smile, what he most loved and hated, the kinds of people he found most attractive, the enemies who most preoccupied him. This sort of analysis is speculative, because the sources on which we must depend are both spotty and shaped by doctrinaire piety, but engaging in it allows us to humanize the founders, sharpen their profiles in our mind's eye.

Our fourth, fifth, sixth, and seventh tasks in each chapter amount to a sketch of the founder's worldview—sense of reality, ways of applying his spirituality to the major dimensions of human existence. These dimensions are four: nature, society, the self, and divinity—holy ultimate reality. By investigating what the founders had to say about these four dimensions, we can solidify our sense of who they were, how they lived, how the world unfolded before them, what they most wanted their disciples to take to heart. Also, we can provide key materials for comparing the founders.

Following the sketch of the founder's worldview, we take up (as our eighth task in each chapter) the history that has transpired since the founder's death. Obviously, in the limited space available to us we can only hit the highlights. Nonetheless, the sections on Buddhism, Confucianism, Christianity, and Islam after their founder's death should remind us that no founder determined subsequent history. Founders launch new ventures, but their initial impetus can slacken, reformers can arise (who may or may not keep faith with the original vision), new circumstances can force wholesale "translations" of the founder's message. All this relativizes the founder, reminding us that everything human is limited in many ways, including the influence of even the masters who initiated our religious traditions.

After surveying the history of the tradition after the founder's death, we offer a summary section. Here we present the heart of the whole matter, what we think the founder's spirituality amounts to in brief course. Naturally, there is much more that we could say, as there is much more that we have said to that point. But students should appreciate this digest of the founder's legacy, and we recommend using it as the final analysis—the last set of impressions to file away.

We conclude each chapter with what we call "friendly criticisms." These are efforts to step back from the founder's achievement and estimate its limitations, drawbacks, potential dangers. Nothing human is without flaw. Even if Christians believe that Jesus was divine, and without sin, they have to admit that he was limited, on penalty of forfeiting his genuine humanity. The same for Muslims who consider

Muhammad the exemplar of Islam, or the perfection of human being, and for Buddhists and Confucians who feel similarly about their founders. Reverence for a founder, even worship of a founder, should not mean, does not require, the destruction of one's critical intelligence. If the founder and his message were historical—really entered space and time—they were limited, and so we have a moral responsibility to test what they bequeathed us, separating the wheat from the chaff. (It helps that in all four cases we know that we are dealing with teachings and depictions of the founder shaped by many disciples. Even if we are loathe to attribute any failings to the founder himself, we can sift his legacy with full confidence that his disciples were fallible.)

After the four chapters that comprise the heart of this text, we take up several issues necessary to round out our study. In chapter 6, we deal with what we call "Further Questions"—matters lying in the background or to the side of what we have treated. Although not strictly necessary for the core of our work, these further matters are worth pursuing, because they help set the core of our work in context and relate the achievements of the great founders to other aspects of the world religions. Specifically, we take up: the relation between Buddhism and India's other great religious tradition, Hinduism; how Buddhism changed when it emigrated to East Asia; the comparison of Confucius and Lao Tzu; the relations among Confucianism, Buddhism, and Shinto in Japan; how Jesus compares with Moses, the formative figure in his native Jewish tradition; the relation of Christianity to Judaism; the place of Western atheism in the history of Christianity; what Islam owes to biblical religion (both the Hebrew Bible and the New Testament); the significance of fundamentalism in present-day Islam and Christianity; and how prophets such as Jesus and Muhammad relate to sages such as Gautama and Confucius—what the two different families of spiritualities have in common, and what they hold separately.

Our final chapter proposes what we call "A Foundational Spirituality." This is a distillation of the wisdom and example of the four founders we have treated, set forth for present times. In presenting it, we follow the fourfold breakdown of the founders' worldviews that we used in the core chapters: nature, society, self, and ultimate reality. The names we use for these four concerns suggest what updating the founders' legacy for the twenty-first century might entail: ecological sensitivity, social justice, personal integrity, and transcendence (dealing with God or ultimate reality). Our final section considers how light and warmth might translate into freedom and love. Throughout, we assume that we are addressing readers formed by Western categories. Other categories would be more suitable for students from non-Western cultures. We have done our best not to distort non-Western tradition, but readers certainly will benefit from listening to non-Western sources on their own terms.

NOTES

1. See Daphne Daume, ed., *1991 Britannica Book of the Year* (Chicago: Encyclopedia Britannica, 1991), p. 299.
2. See ibid.
3. Gordon S. Wakefield, ed., *The Westminster Dictionary of Christian Spirituality* (Philadelphia: Westminster, 1983), p. *v.*
4. Ewert Cousins, "Preface," in *Islamic Spirituality: Foundations*, ed. Seyyed Hossein Nasr (New York: Crossroad, 1987), pp. *xiii-xiv.*
5. See R. J. Zwi Werblowsky, "Light and Darkness," in *The Encyclopedia of Religion*, ed. Mircea Eliade (New York: Macmillan, 1987), vol. 8, pp. 547–550.
6. See J. Bruce Long, "Love," in ibid., vol. 9, pp. 31–40.

CHAPTER 2

THE BUDDHA

Indian Religion Before Gautama

Gautama (560–480 B.C.) lived in a time of cultural change. The Indian religious ways that had become traditional were under attack, and so he was not the only reformer who wanted a fresh start. What we call "Hinduism" began deep in prehistoric times, inasmuch as the natives of the subcontinent developed systems of myths and rituals focused on sources of fertility. Around 2,000 B.C. nomadic peoples invading from the northwest began to put a new overlay on such systems. These peoples, who referred to themselves as Aryans ("nobles"), celebrated the phenomena of the heavens—the sun, wind, storm, stars, rain, moon. In contrast, the greater interest of the native Indians had been earthly phenomena: vegetation, animal life, rivers, and mountains. Naturally, each group made a place for the phenomena that the other stressed, but their instinctive orientations differed. "Hinduism" is the amalgamation of these two quite ancient outlooks. Since the time when the Aryans came to have cultural influence, India has housed a great variety of religious emphases, supporting an amazingly catholic culture. The Indian way has been to incorporate rather than reject, add on rather than lop off.

The Vedas, Hinduism's most revered scriptures, reflect the dominance of the Aryans. The gods most important in the Vedas dwell in the heavens. Certainly, the earth also gets its due, but *Agni* (sun, fire), *Varuna* (sky, cosmic order), and *Indra* (storm) stand out as especially revered. Also established well before Gautama's day was the Indian social structure that divided people into four basic classes ("castes"). There were priests, warriors/rulers, farmers and merchants, and ordi-

22

nary laborers. Each had a different role in society, and each had a different religious standing. The priests represented the head: brains, vision, dealings with the gods, the topmost realities. The laborers represented the feet. The warriors, farmers, and merchants provided the trunk of society, its political and economic order. Developing their high religious status, the priests had elaborated many rituals for honoring the Vedic gods, placating them, getting them on human beings' side. Thus, by the time that Gautama began searching for a viable spirituality, what is called "Brahmanism" (the dominance of the brahmans [priests]) was in full sway.

In fact, Brahmanism tended toward a magical reliance on words. Many priests believed that if they performed the traditional, often complicated rituals perfectly, the intended results were sure to follow. But this led to a concern for externals that left deeper seekers uneasy, dissatisfied, ready to revolt. Contemporary with the Buddha were some of the authors of the Upanishads—speculative, interior writings that we now find at the end of the collection of Vedic texts. The Upanishads are poetic and philosophical, reflecting a search for unity and stability beneath the plethora of Brahmanic rituals, the great variety of Vedic gods. The Upanishadic seers glimpsed a direct communion with the ground of reality, the ultimate being on which all phenomena, including all the gods, depended. In a famous spiritual movement, they equated the center of the individual human self with the center of the cosmos. The individual center or soul, the atman, had to be of the same "stuff" as the Brahman, the world-soul. Otherwise, there would be no foundation for the self, as for no other existing things. Permeating all beings was being. Undergirding all phenomena—plants and animals, rocks and human beings, stars and clouds—had to be something self-sufficient, independent, to serve as the source, to escape the chain of derivation. In a word, Brahman became the first cause of the cosmos, while atman, the first cause of the conscious, reflective human self, became an aspect of Brahman, something whose inmost reality was identical with Brahman.

The psychological parallel to this philosophical reasoning was the practice of yogic meditation. The roots of yoga lie deep in prehistory, at the point where human beings began to contemplate their own interiority. When people realized that a light within them was responsible for their awareness, their knowledge of both the external world and their own thoughts and feelings, it was only a matter of time before some people began to study this light. Since such study could bring a considerable peace, it seemed worth the withdrawal from sensation and activity that it required. To turn one's senses inward, quiet one's mind and will, and eventually remain in an untroubled state, below words and images, letting the core of one's identity, one's soul (*atman*) express itself, could seem the best way to handle the endless spate of information and challenge that the external world kept forcing one to deal with. It could seem to offer an Archimedian lever with which to move the world, so that the world would become much less troubling.

Related to the appeal (to the spiritually gifted) of yoga was an Indian notion whose roots, like those of yoga, lie in prehistoric times. This was the notion of karma. Karma means a spiritual law of cause and effect. What we do today shapes our selves, and so tomorrow. What we are today is the result, the product, of our past experience—the acts of our yesterdays. Because Indians have long believed in transmigration—the passing of an atman from one body to another, and so a succession of lives—karma becomes the key to one's place in cosmic history. If one is a priest, living in a desirable place in the social order, one can assume that a good karma developed through one's previous lives. If one is a laborer, or a woman, one has to assume that a bad karma developed through one's previous lives.

The final dimension of this sense of cosmic time concerned the traditional Hindu analysis of both suffering and release from suffering. Living through life after life, always battling for good karma, having to die and be reborn, having to endure all the sufferings, physical and spiritual, that existence can impose—all this was terribly painful, a state more like a prison than a palace. It cried out for a solution, a way out. Hindus thought that if they could escape from karma, step outside the whole system of spiritual cause and effect, they would gain "release" (*moksha*). They would enter a new state, one of fulfillment, in which there was no more dying and being reborn, no more physical or spiritual suffering. The way to release was detachment, giving karma nothing by which to grasp one's soul. Inasmuch as yogic exercises seemed to develop detachment, they became the key to striving for release.

Gautama, the future Buddha, inherited all this Indian religious history. The rituals, the Vedic gods, the role of the priests, the division of Indian society into four major classes, and the convictions about yoga, karma, transmigration, and release all seemed natural to him. A generation before him, the holy man known as the Mahavira, the great man, had challenged the brahmanic system, stressing an extreme asceticism. The pathway of the Mahavira, which has come to be known as Jainism, depended on distancing oneself from karma. Jains thought of karma quite physically, as though it were a pitch sticking to one's soul. They therefore stressed cleanliness and detachment, which they expressed physically by going naked and spiritually by fostering nonviolence. The less injury they could inflict on any living creature, the more likely they were to get free of karma and so gain *moksha*, release and complete fulfillment. The rituals and gods of the Vedas were useless, compared to this program of nakedness and nonviolence. The Buddha also inherited the gains of the Mahavira. Thus, as we shall see, nonviolence became part of his "Middle Way."

The Life of the Buddha

Gautama was born into the second tier of Indian society, his family being rulers. Tradition says that he was born in the foothills of Nepal, the son of a petty ruler. Buddhist mythology records that his father received a vision or supernatural communication to the effect that the boy could become a savior of the world. Such a vocation, however, would require his leaving the family circle, venturing out into a wider world. This the father did not want, so he arranged everything to protect his son and promote his happiness. In this way, he hoped to have his son become a great worldly success, a king among kings. The birth of the child was miraculous, his mother delivering him painlessly from her side. Newly born, Gautama raised himself, took seven steps, and declared that this would be his final birth. In this lifetime, he would acquire release from the karmic circle, the endless round of births, deaths, and rebirths.

The boy grew up in the lap of luxury, was married to a lovely maiden, and with her begot a son. All seemed to be moving along swimmingly, but seeds of discontent began to grow. On the few occasions that he traveled outside the palace compound, Gautama was brought up short. One day he perceived a dead man being carried to his cremation. This gave the prince pause: what could life mean, be worth, if the certain end was death? Another day he saw a sick man, apparently on the road to death. This also shocked him: how fragile human existence must be, if disease can strike at any time. On a third visit outside the palace, Gautama saw an old person, wrinkled and gray, obviously on the far side of physical perfection, plummeting down the incline to death. This forced him to think long and hard about his situation. How could anyone enjoy levity, go about as though there were no disaster hanging over his head? Was it not the clear, obvious task of any person of substance to attack the problem of death, disease, and aging—to find a solution to the suffering that seemed encoded in people's bones?

Gautama thought that he had to wrestle with these problems, on pain of never enjoying any peace. So, aged thirty or so, he crept out of the palace at night, having bade his lovely queen and little son goodbye. If he were to keep faith with the deepest longings of his own spirit, he had to contend with human mortality, human misery. First he apprenticed himself to some teachers of meditation, learning from them the standard yogic proficiencies. These calmed his mind, but they did not solve his problem, lay bare the cure for suffering. Then he lived with some ascetics, following their program of harsh treatment of the body, fasting (legend says) so severely that when he touched his navel he felt his backbone. But this regime also failed to deliver what he sought, to bring him full release.

Finally, not knowing what else to do, Gautama resolved to sit under a pipal tree he found attractive and not leave until he had accomplished his mission. According to the most celebrated account of Gautama's life, the ritualized biography by Ashvaghosa, enlightenment, the successful accomplishment of his mission, occurred as follows:

> Having mastered perfectly all the methods of trance, the prince recalled, in the first watch of the night, the sequence of his former births. . . . The Rightly-Illumined One perceived all of these things and thus was de-

cisively awakened: when birth is destroyed, old age and death ceases; when "becoming" is destroyed, old age and death ceases; when "becoming" is destroyed, then birth ceases. When attachment is destroyed, "becoming" ceases; when craving is destroyed, attachment ceases; when sensations are destroyed, craving ceases. When contact is destroyed, sensation ceases; when the six sense organs are destroyed, contact ceases; when the physical form is destroyed, the six sense organs cease. When consciousness is destroyed, physical form ceases; when psychic constructions are destroyed, consciousness ceases; when ignorance is destroyed, psychic constructions cease. Reflecting his right understanding, the great hermit arose before the world as the Buddha, the Enlightened One. He found self (*atman*) nowhere, as the fire whose fuel has been exhausted. . . . For seven days, the Buddha with serene mind contemplated [the Truth that he had attained] and gazed at the Bodhi tree without blinking: "Here on this spot I have fulfilled my cherished goal; I now rest at ease in the dharma of selflessness."[1]

The account is stylized, made to fit Buddhist teaching about the twelve links on the chain of "conditioned coproduction." This is the Buddhist imagery for how the various forces in the world of karma interrelate and keep people in bondage. The progress of Gautama to enlightenment and so to release from karma involved destroying these links. At the end, he was selfless, completely emptied of desire. The account also reflects the conviction of Buddhist monks that meditation is the most important human activity—the way to attain enlightenment. When Gautama experienced the fire whose fuel had gone out (nirvana), he stood free of karma and all other worldly fetters. He could simply be, anticipating that at death he would never return to the world of suffering and illusion.

The next decision facing Gautama was what he ought to do with his illumination. Was it for himself alone, or had he the obligation to teach others? After some debate with himself, he opted to become a teacher of the Dharma. The most basic formulation of his insight was the Four Noble Truths: All life is suffering. The cause of suffering is desire. Removing desire removes suffering. The way to remove desire is to follow the noble Eightfold Path: right views, right intention, right speech, right action, right livelihood, right effort, right mindfulness, right concentration.

Buddhism has always revered the Four Noble Truths. It has used the Eightfold Path as a stimulus to develop a rounded, complete religious regime focused on three major concerns: wisdom, morality, and meditation. Clearly, the narrative of the Buddha's enlightenment reflects established Buddhist usage. Ashvaghosa's account is pious rather than scholarly, shaped by tradition rather than rendered afresh from empirical data. Nonetheless, few Buddhists have questioned the picture of Gautama sitting under the pipal (*Bodhi* = enlightenment) tree and vowing not to leave until he had reached his goal, solved the problem of old age, disease, and death. Similarly, few Buddhists have opposed the notion that the gist of what the Buddha experienced in enlightenment was the Four Noble Truths. Whatever the historical experience of Enlightenment, then, it shaped all the memories of the Buddha's life and teaching. Enlightenment was what made Gautama a buddha, what sowed the seeds of Buddhism. The parallel to the resurrection of Jesus is exact: without the resurrection, there would have been no Christianity. Without the Enlightenment, there would have been no Buddhism.

The Buddha spent the last half of his life promulgating what he had learned. His motive was the great compassion for all living things that illumination had given him. Compared to the light that had flooded him, bringing a rich measure of peace into his soul, nothing worldly had any appeal. Indeed, we may read the description of his stripping away all desire, all attachment, as the negative effect of the positive pull that nirvana now exerted in his soul. So he wandered serenely, begging his food, teaching any who wished to hear about his solution to the problem of human existence. By and large, Indians accepted the proposition that all life is suffering. They accepted the related propositions that the cause of suffering is desire and that casting out desire will cast out suffering. These were staples of Hindu spirituality. What was new, unique, was the elaboration of the fourth noble truth, the Eightfold Path.

As the Buddha elaborated the details of this path, it became the "Middle Way" between asceticism and indulgence. More important than bodily austerities was getting one's mind straight and one's body under a relaxed discipline. The development of Buddhist wisdom (deep and wide examination of how the world is actually constituted), morality, and meditation gave disciples much to learn, much to aim at assimilating. In themselves, however, these three pillars of Buddhist life were quite plain. One had to understand what one was doing in pursuing nirvana—how the world was a prison, why nirvana was the only truly fulfilling goal. One had to practice Buddhist ideals, live out the Buddhist sense of right and wrong, helpful and hurtful kinds of behavior. And one had to meditate: try to replicate Gautama's experience under the Bodhi tree, learn for oneself how karma entraps the spirit but right concentration can set it free.

Typical of the Buddha's early preaching, we are told, was his famous "Fire Sermon":

> O priests [monks], all things are on fire. The eye is on fire, as are the forms the eye receives, the consciousness the eye raises, the impressions the eye transmits, the sensations—pleasant, unpleasant, or indifferent—that the eye's impressions produce. All that has to do with our seeing is on fire. And in what does this fire consist? It consists in the flame of passion, the burning of hate, the heat of infatuation. Birth, old age, death, sorrow, lamentation, misery, grief, and despair are all expressions of the fire that comes into us through our eyes.[2]

The Buddha describes the other senses similarly, showing how our whole body is wrapped in desire, kept captive to a fire that threatens to burn us up. Only when we quench desire, cool our passions, let go of our bodies and even our selves will we enter into peace. Desire is the great enemy, the great source of our sufferings. The key to ending suffering is stopping desire. The entire Buddhist program evolved from this effort.

For the rest of his life, the Buddha elaborated his primary experiences, first formulations of the Teaching, and initial convictions about the way to liberation. He would wander to a town, beg his food, and establish a routine of teaching, resting, seeing people who wanted advice. The pious sources also picture him instructing the gods. Gradually he developed an extensive following, the most dedicated of whom took up his wandering life and became monks. Legend says that he finally yielded, reluctantly, to the entreaties of his aunt and allowed women to join his community (*sangha*). At the time of his death he had numerous disciples, well-trained and ready to continue his work. When he asked them if they had any further questions, no one said a word, so he knew that his work was done. He died peacefully, the earth quaking in honor and the heavens raining down flower petals. He had passed out of the karmic realm, the zone of suffering, into the endless bliss of nirvana. He had done all that a human being could do.

The Personality of the Buddha

By the time that he had assembled a significant community of monks, Gautama was fully comfortable in his role as teacher of the Dharma, founder of the Order, and model of the blessed life. If light was the central symbolism in the interior experiences that made him a Buddha, peace seems to have dominated his exterior appearance. He was kindly, but exact, even severe, when it came to religious truths. He was detached, unconcerned about himself or anything worldly, yet determined to preach the truth, do all that he could to help suffering creatures. Certainly the accounts we have of his teaching are at pains to make him seem perfect, but the main impression they leave is that he had found the center of his existence, a rock from which he could not be moved. Deeply at peace, he could not be disturbed by any human situation. There was nothing he desired. He had nothing to lose. Even his commitment to offer medicine to suffering souls was conditioned by what was possible. People could refuse to hear him. The time and place, the karmic situation, might not be ideal. So he would content himself with doing what he could, leaving the rest to fate. For the long run, he was confident that his Way would prevail.

That did not mean, however, that he took no pains to ensure that his followers understood the conditions that would have to be met, if the Way were to prevail. For example, once he addressed the brethren as follows:

> I will teach you, O mendicants [beggars], seven conditions of the welfare of a community. Listen well and attend, and I will speak. . . . So long, O mendicants, as the brethren meet together in full and frequent

assemblies—so long as they meet together in concord, and rise in concord, and carry out in concord the duties of the order—so long as the
brethren shall establish nothing that has not been already prescribed, and
abrogate nothing that has been already established, and act in accordance
with the rules of the order as now laid down—so long as the brethren
honour and esteem and revere and support the elders of experience and
long standing, the fathers and leaders of the order, and hold it a point of
duty to hearken to their words—so long as the brethren fall not under the
influence of that craving which, springing up within them, would give
rise to renewed existence—so long as the brethren delight in a life of
solitude—so long as the brethren so train their minds that good and holy
men shall come to them, and those who have come shall dwell at ease—so
long may the brethren be expected, not to decline, but to prosper. So long
as these seven conditions shall continue to exist among the brethren, so
long as they are well-instructed in these conditions, so long may the
brethren be expected not to decline but to prosper.[3]

The conservatism of this text probably reflects the views of editors
working some generations after the establishment of the monastic
order, when it was clear that concord was the key to survival and
prosperity. Gautama may well have intuited the importance of concord, from his enlightened understanding of human nature, but this
text suggests that some painful experiences had clarified the matter for
the disciples. It is noteworthy that Gautama thought of his group as a
democracy, in the sense that he wanted them to assemble frequently,
presumably to conduct the business necessary to sustain the order. It is
also noteworthy that he spoke of a way of life, a rule of established
conventions and proscriptions, that all would have to follow, if the
order were to prosper. We know that monastic legislation arose relatively early in Buddhist history, apparently in response to an obvious
need to codify what was and was not compatible with the monastic life.
This text assumes such legislation, as well as the living tradition of
elders. In urging his monks to honor the elders, the Buddha was doing
more than praising longevity. He was gambling that the elders, having
long tried to take the monastic way of life to heart, would be living
models of the Way, living texts that younger monks could read for
instruction.

The point about not falling under the influence of craving is simply a restatement, in a monastic context, of the fundamental teaching about uprooting desire. Desire, craving, is the cause of rebirth. Monks have set out to gain release from rebirth, the realm of karmic attachments. The worst thing they could do would be to feed the flames of desire. Even in the monastery, people could covet honors or comforts, concessions small or great that let them think themselves special. They would be well advised to prefer solitude to any distinction associated with craving. They would prosper in the measure that they sought only nirvana, supported only the solid, traditional monastic practices that maintained a clear focus on this goal. If they did that, they would be sure to attract new disciples. If their focus were correct, the outside world would not fail to see their sincerity, the genuine power of their genuine way of life. The result would be generous support. New candidates would apply for membership. The laity would offer financial help. The key to the future, then, was nothing gimmicky. The key was keeping faith with the venerable traditions, being in fact what one professed in appearance. The Buddha, it seems, was a great lover of truth and a great hater of sham. Integrity marks his sermons. He never allows short cuts.

Even though it is difficult, if not impossible, to reach behind the texts purporting to come from the Buddha and lay bare the full historical figure, the fully human personality, we may be confident that that personality was attractive. With all the founders we treat, there comes a point where one has to assume that personal charm, solid appeal, was what finally won the day. Certainly, one can admire clear teaching, profound insight, marvelous turns of phrase or figures of speech. One can also admire powerful deeds, acts of healing, the ability to lead men and women forward toward demanding, exhilarating goals. But probably more central is the trust that the great founders won. Probably in the final analysis most people who accepted the founder's way were persuaded by what they saw in his eyes, what they heard in his voice, what they perceived in his carriage, his response to opposition, his dealings with subordinates, his dealings with lowly people who came to him for help. The serenity that we find in Gautama, and the conservative rectitude that rings in many sermons, are best understood as expressions of his inner balance. That balance made his claims to possess saving wisdom persuasive. In all likelihood, his human personality was his most important argument, the proof that won most bystanders over.

The Buddha's Teaching about Nature

We have described the four noble truths in which the Buddha summarized his enlightenment. Closely related to the first noble truth are the three "marks" of all reality. Buddhists trace this further teaching back to Gautama. The three marks elaborate the first noble truth, "All life is suffering." When we reflect on the implications of this truth, we realize that the three marks characterize a cosmos that no sane person would want to desire. So, let us first explain the three marks of reality and then show the consequences for the Buddha's cosmology.

The three marks are universal characteristics. They apply to all beings, all existent things. The first mark is "painful" (*dukkha*). The second mark is "impermanent" (*anicca*). The third mark is "selfless" (*anatta*). Everything that one encounters, including one's own being, is stamped with these marks. Nothing that comes into human experience escapes their influence. The painfulness of all living things is clearest from their being born and their dying. They suffer coming into existence and they suffer leaving existence. Between these two terminal points, they also suffer. Constantly, they want things that they do not, perhaps cannot, attain. Frequently they suffer bodily pains. Their emotions go up and down, and this roller coaster ride is painful. They know they are going to die, so they have fits of anxiety, dread, wondering whether anything makes sense or is worth pursuing. Viewed with a dispassionate eye, seen for what it really is, existence turns out to be hellish. Constantly, living things are tormented. Seldom if ever do we find them at rest, enjoying peace.

Related to this suffering is the impermanence of all beings. Nothing is stable, let alone static. Nothing is secure against change, most of which is painful. Even rocks are worn away, even ancient trees are blighted or uprooted. Even the strongest of human beings ages, sickens, finally dies. The Buddha perceived this on his fateful trips outside the palace, when he was a young man trying to learn about the world. Life is fleeting. Everything is in flux. To attach oneself to anything is to increase one's pains. There is no constancy in nature, or in human affairs. There is no bank in which one can secure one's emotional investments, safeguard them against loss or pain. If we look outside, we find the changes of the seasons, the births and deaths of the animals, the shifting of the clouds and the waves. Sometimes such variety may please us, but its deeper message is that nothing lasts. There is no refuge in the world of sensory experience. Everything is subject to karmic influences, movements up or down the ladder of readiness for liberation, deliverance, release into nirvana.

A similar lesson arises if we look inside, study the course of our own thoughts. Doing that, we find that flux is the steady message. We are always changing what we perceive, imagine, think, judge, want, and feel. We are always getting tired, resting, feeling reinvigorated, and getting tired again. Our psychic balance, like our metabolic balance, is precarious. So always we have to take notice, be on guard, expend energy to achieve a temporary homeostasis. Always we have to worry that what we treasure will corrode, be stolen away, leave us poor and empty.

This interior experience is one of the best arguments for the third mark of all existence, that it is selfless. We do not even have a stable personal identity. Contrary to what the Hindus teach, there is no *atman* linked to Brahman, no solid self identical with the Self of the world. The psychic stream is as influential as the streams carrying water from the mountains to the sea. The mental horizon changes as surely as the physical horizon, what we see at sunrise or sunset. We age, and in the process change our strongest convictions. What we most want at twenty can seem worthless at seventy. Conversely, what seventy-year-olds prize can seem foolish to twenty-year-olds. In part this is a function of bodily changes, shifts in what we want to eat, how we feel about learning, our sexual appetites, our concerns about money, our interest in sickness and death, our inclination to fight. But another part of it lies deeper. The name that we carry marks a different person, decade by decade. We have the same parents and birthplace, but their psychic reality, the way they shape who we are, is different. With time, we forgive our parents many transgressions, and perhaps we accuse ourselves more harshly. Or, we may forgive ourselves early indiscretions, even early cruelties, because we know more about human depravity, have a broader view of the difficulties of acquiring virtue. In a word, then, we come to realize that not even our self is stable. Even who we think we are changes, slips from our control, taunts us as an illusion.[4]

These are only the barest indications of the implications that Buddhists have found in Gautama's teaching about the three marks of existence, the bedrock painfulness of being, but they should suffice to orient our inquiry into the naturalistic aspects of the Buddha's spirituality. He thought that existence was a stream, constantly flowing onwards. He was convinced that the only way to negotiate such an existence was to move lightly, be detached, desire nothing, accommodate oneself to the flux. More profoundly, he thought that one had to traverse this stream. True peace and security lay on the far side of physical existence, on a plane far different from that of dying and being born, living in the body, constantly suffering. "Nirvana" was a crucial yet empty symbol for this beyond, this far side. It was the state of the candle when the flame was blown out. It was existence without the fire of desire. It was not arid, sterile, empty in a negative sense. It was unconditioned being, existence without any lets and hindrances, any of the imperfections that mottled life in the body, life carried out under the illusion that we have selves or can find safe havens. The only safe haven lay beyond ordinary understandings of existence. The only worthy goal was defeating painful karmic existence by detaching oneself and moving beyond, being taken into nirvana by enlightenment.

With significant, yet in some ways only minor, differences from what Buddhism came to think, the traditional Indian culture that Gautama inherited thought of the natural world, the physical cosmos, as illusory. One could, indeed, had to operate in it, but it was not a full or lasting truth. Rather, it was a play of the gods, a sport, a dance, with overtones of both indulgence and cruelty. In the most optimistic scenario, Hindu theologians thought that the gods would spare human beings the ultimate consequences of enduring a world that was impermanent, had no final significance. In more sober scenarios, the gods themselves were good and evil, liberators from pain yet also forces that inflicted pain.

The Buddha accepted most of this traditional Indian mentality. His followers also came to think of the natural world as illusory, but only

inasmuch as it blinded people to the four noble truths and the significance of nirvana. The "middleness" of the Buddha's Way shows that he
respected the body. His agreement with the Jains about the desirability
of nonviolence can be read as an endorsement of all creatures' rights to
kindly treatment. True, the Buddha most wanted his followers to
detach themselves from the cravings, the desires for gain or revenge,
that lie behind most violence. But it seems that, after enlightenment, he
also found the natural world congenial. It remained a place of pain, but
enlightenment had detached him from most pain, so he could appreciate the beauty of birds, the power of storms, the lessons in the ways of
animals, the usefulness of symbols like the stream of life.

One of the most characteristic Buddhist symbols, that of a lotus
floating atop the muck of a pond, suggests Gautama's sense of nature—
how nature functioned in his own spirituality. The lotus was beautiful,
even magical. It floated serenely above its lowly antecedents, redeem-
ing them. The lesson was that even in a painful, dirty world, human
beings could live graceful, beautiful lives. The lesson was that when
one was free of desire and enjoyed enlightenment, lovely things like
lotuses did not stir one's cupidity, could be looked upon, even handled,
with no craving to possess them, no urge to profit from them. The
natural world was there, a string of objective facts. Enlightenment
made people supremely realistic, in the sense of becoming able to deal
with objective, factual realities simply and directly, of wanting to live
with things as they truly were, not as one might like them to be.

The "suchness" praised in the Buddha, made one of his titles after his
humanity had fallen into the background and his supernatural status
had come to dominate, captures much of this realism. There was no
need for him to shield himself from nature. It was such as it was.
Neither its beauties nor its cruelties could disturb his peace, sway him
from serenity. He could be compassionate toward all living things,
provide a foundation for later shifts in the Buddhist ideal of sanctity,
according to which the *bodhisattva* (saint) would postpone entry into
nirvana, in order to labor for the release of all other suffering creatures.
But there was nothing grasping or excessive in this compassion. Nature
did not cry out for protection any more than for dominance or vengeance. The physical world was simply there, as good or evil, as
helpful or harmful, as what one made of it. If nature helped people keep

perspective, nourished their sense of the true proportions of existence, reminded them how small their own egocentric fantasies were in the total scheme of things, all to the good. If it entrapped them, lured them to crave land or to produce, its influence was unfortunate. The spiritual trick was balance, detachment, clear-sightedness, emotional freedom. The spiritual trick was to let the world be and learn from its being, take lessons that would advance one toward nirvana.

The Buddha's Teaching about Society

It is hard to find a Buddhist social ethics. The only way is to consider a social ethics implicit in Gautama's teaching about such principles as nonviolence, the three marks, the denial of craving, and the paramount status of the quest for nirvana. Together, they relativize all social, political, economic, military, and cultural activity. The Buddha was realistic enough to understand that society is a fact, and that lay Buddhists would have to be a leaven in society, making it more amenable to the truth of the Dharma. But he felt no passion to provide a social teaching that would undergird ordinary social existence— business, family life, or politics as usual. His entire desire was to help people detach themselves from the world, extinguish the burning that characterized the world. He was much more interested in the life of the Sangha, the community of his disciples, than in what we might call secular society. In the case of outsiders, those who had not yet embraced his teaching, his main interest was their conversion.

The Sangha, we have seen, would prosper only if it was a community of concord—peace—rooted in a common observance of the monastic disciplines, a common conviction that the Way of the Enlightened One was the path to nirvana and precious beyond compare. The first charge of monks was to be what they seemed, practice what they professed. If they were, the Sangha would become a place of refuge, a school in which one could learn the perfections necessary to quit this wretched world and find peace.

Indian society of Gautama's time was structured into four main social classes, as we have seen. It assumed that each class had its proper place, created by karmic realities, and that there were four legitimate goals that people could pursue during their earthly lives. These four goals were, in ascending order of importance, pleasure, wealth, duty, and release from karmic bondage. Indian society was not puritanical. It thought that good food, good sex, beautiful art, beautiful gardens, friendship, enjoying children, and all the other decent pleasures one could imagine had their valid place, need not cause one to blush. Similarly, it thought that business, trade, the occupations of teaching and healing, ruling and farming, were legitimate and necessary. The "householder," as both Hinduism and Buddhism tended to refer to the layperson who lived in the world, managed a family and way of making a living, and contributed to the continuance of civil society, was a respectable figure, even though the monk or holy man had a higher status. The wealth that a person could accumulate through hard work helped to keep society going. It was tied into a large system of jobs, skills, needs, and the fulfillment of needs, that provided food, clothing, schooling, a dozen other services. So it was not to be despised. It was only to be handled carefully, with full awareness that it could be a trap, because there were higher goals than wealth.

Duty, the fulfillment of one's responsibilities as a priest or ruler, farmer or worker, stood higher than pleasure or wealth, because duty came from the divine forces that had ordered society into its fourfold design. When priests fulfilled their religious duties, rulers kept the peace, farmers and merchants were productive, and workers were diligent, everyone prospered. Life on earth was a miniature, blessed reflection of life in heaven. Thus when Arjuna, the hero of the Hindu work called the *Bhagavad Gita*, wants to lay down his arms and not go to war (against his cousins), Krishna, the incarnation of divinity, tells him he is making a great mistake. Arjuna is a warrior. His duty is to fight, whenever a just cause requires it. Better the fulfillment of this duty than the avoidance of it in the name of some supposedly higher calling. What might be permitted, even desired, in a priest is not fitting in a warrior. Society depends on people carrying out their allotted tasks. Duty is the way that people answer the call that the gods have placed in their beings, when the gods made them priests or warriors, farmers or laborers.

The fourth legitimate goal, striving for release from the karmic condition afflicting human beings, gained the highest honors in Hindu society. One who declared himself called to pursue deliverance (*moksha*, the Hindu equivalent of nirvana) stood free of many social obligations. He could leave wife and children, job and civic obligations. Gautama relied on this convention when he left the palace, his wife and son, and set forth to solve the problem of suffering.

The Buddha worked within this Hindu social framework, but he undermined it radically. He tolerated the breakdown of society into four main classes, but it had little hold on him. He would accept people of any class, as long as they were serious about pursuing nirvana. He might use the accustomed language that gave pride of place to brahmans, but his real concern was the holy, truly priestly soul, which might be best found in a laborer or merchant. The main intuition we have to take away, if we are to understand Gautama's sense of social life, is that the only imperative was pursuing enlightenment. Inasmuch as they could help in this pursuit, business or family life, traditional religious practices or the decrees of rulers, could be judged good. Inasmuch as, more frequently, they impeded the forthright, clearsighted pursuit of enlightenment, they were a nuisance, a hindrance, something to be avoided, escaped by an end run, or, in the final showdown, attacked as merely provisional, not ultimately serious or able to command a wise person's full allegiance.

When Buddhism moved to East Asia, having lost the battle with Hinduism for India's soul, it had to modify this other worldliness. Thus, Mahayana Buddhism, the family of sects that did best in China and Japan, Korea and Vietnam, accommodated to the this-worldliness of East Asian cultures. That meant some upgrading of the religious status of the householder, and some translation of enlightenment into terms that blessed this-worldly occupations and argued that the fullness of enlightenment made one feel at home in the world—reconciled, amused, even delighted with the dirt of the marketplace; full of compassion for ordinary, suffering human beings. This shift in emphasis could draw on the peace and gracefulness of the Buddha's own bearing, but it had an uphill battle when it came to finding in the founder a positive, in any way articulate social ethics.

One of the most intimate challenges that social life faces is creating just relations between men and women. Sexual justice is much on the minds of late twentieth-century Westerners, and even though we have to be careful not to become anachronistic, asking people who lived 2,500 years ago to have modern insights and sensibilities, it remains instructive to consider the place of women in the Sangha. As noted, the legends say that the Buddha acceded to the requests of his aunt, Pajapati, only reluctantly. Nonetheless, he did agree to her request, after many entreaties, and allowed women to become nuns—followers who would live monastic lives, giving up domestic responsibilities and delights to follow the Lord Buddha and dedicate themselves to the pursuit of nirvana.

Let us consider the conditions that Gautama is reputed to have set for the entrance of Pajapati and others into the monastic order. The Buddha is finally agreeing to the request of his favorite disciple, Ananda, and allowing his community to admit women, support nuns:

> If, Ananda, the Gotamid, Pajapati the Great [these titles admit his aunt's holiness] accepts these eight important rules, that may be ordination [acceptance into the monastic order] for her: A nun who has been ordained even for a century must greet respectfully, rise up from her seat, salute with joined palms and do proper homage to a monk ordained but that very day. A Nun must not spend the rains in a residence where there is no monk. Every half month a nun should require two things from the Order of monks: the date of the Observance day, and the coming for the exhortation. After the rains a nun must 'invite' both Orders [monks and nuns] in respect of three matters: what has been seen, heard, and suspected [to be an offense]. A nun, offending against an important rule, must undergo . . . discipline before both Orders. When, as a probationer, she has trained in the six rules for two years, she should seek ordination from both Orders. A monk must not be abused or reviled in any way by a nun. From today admonition of monks by nuns is forbidden, admonition of nuns by monks is not forbidden. Each of these rules is to be honored, respected, revered, venerated, and is never to be transgressed by a nun during her life. If, Ananda, Pajapati accepts these eight important rules, that shall be ordination for her.[5]

Needless to say, Pajapati accepted, and the Order accepted women as nuns. What we should make of the clear subjugation of women to men through these eight rules is both simple and complicated. Simply put, the rules show the patriarchy of traditional Indian culture, as of most traditional cultures, according to which women were second class citizens. More complicatedly, we have to deal with such issues as when this text arose, how much it owes to the historical Buddha and how much it derives from a later, more chauvinistic time, and whether the basic equality introduced by Buddhism (the enormous notion that women could attain nirvana, which Hinduism in effect denied) compensates for its retention of the patriarchal attitudes of its time. These are all matters of outlook as well as scholarship. They depend on the judge's own values as much as on any objective data that detached studies can uncover. At the least, though, they show the vulnerability of the Buddha to charges that his enlightenment did not benefit women equally with men, and so, perhaps, that his saviorhood was markedly limited.

The Buddha's Teaching about Self

In the Buddha's defense, we could bring forward his teaching about the self. The core of this teaching, as we have suggested, is that there is no solid, substantial self—no identity that does not change, no "I" to which a wise person would cling. This teaching applied to women as much as men. Therefore, the liberation that the Buddha offered targeted women as much as men. If Indian Buddhists nearly inevitably retained some of the misogynism of Hindu culture, which held that being born female was a sign of bad karma and that the best that women could accomplish through spiritual striving was to be born next time as men, they did develop a rationale for honoring the female "self" as a potential Buddha. Indeed, before long feminine saints and personifications of Holy Wisdom came on the Buddhist scene, putting a lovely grace in the middle of ultimate reality.

Another angle into the Buddha's teaching about the self comes from the basic ethical code that developed. This code (*sila*) applied to all Buddhists: monks and laypeople, men and women. It captures the spirit, if not the exact words, of Gautama himself. The five precepts of *sila* are simple and negative: not to kill, not to steal, not to lie, not to commit unchastity, and not to take intoxicants. By reflecting on the way that these precepts structured the personal lives of devout Buddhists, we get a good idea of how the Buddha wanted his people to develop—what traits of character he sought to inculcate.

We have mentioned the Jain teaching about nonviolence. Buddhist *sila* stands in this tradition. One is not to kill any living thing, if one can possibly avoid it. The implications of this commandment are vast. For example, it casts war in a negative light, putting the great burden of proof on those proposing to take up arms against their enemies. In the Buddhist view, war is always a defeat—a sign that virtue has lagged and imagination failed to do its job. People ought to be able to work out their differences. Certainly, they ought to be able to avoid killing one another because they disagree. The king Ashoka (ruled 273–232 B.C.) was converted to Buddhist ideals after gaining his crown through warfare. Repenting, he tried to build a political regime that would honor Buddhist moral principles, including the avoiding of bloodshed. The first precept of *sila* also forbade abortion, infanticide (long a problem in India, up to the present day, in the case of female infants), and killing animals. The further implication was that Buddhists should be vegetarians, not requiring any animals to give up their lives so that human beings might eat or take pleasure.

The second precept, not to steal, laid the foundations for social justice. If people did not take what belonged to others, much conflict would diminish. Beneath this precept lay the Buddha's teaching about desire. The way to stop stealing was to stop lusting for others' goods, stop thinking that possessing things could bring happiness. The implications for business, banking, and other exchanges of goods or money were enormous. Ideally, laws would restrain the greed to possess material things, discourage any sanctioned stealing (such as sharp business practices or shrewd manipulation of codes by lawyers themselves). In the monastery, the precept against stealing meant that claiming spiritual attainments of others was a serious offense. Monks ought to be content with the spiritual progress, the virtue or wisdom, that they themselves had earned. They ought not to pretend that something they had read or seen in the example of a holy elder had become their own, simply because they knew about it.

The precept against lying was another call for self-examination, another challenge to become more and more deeply honest. A person who did not report what was so probably did not love what was so, perhaps even could not determine what was so. Buddhist realism demanded that disciples become lovers of what was so. The social implications of this demand were again significant. If people told the truth, most of the lawsuits would vanish, much of the distrust that ruined so many families and places of work would go. Lying destroyed the social fabric as well as the individual's integrity. Lying was incompatible with buddhahood, because buddhahood meant full commitment to the light.

The fourth precept, not to commit unchastity, could be interpreted on many different levels. Adultery and fornication were the obvious acts to avoid, but the whole matter of interior chastity, purity of mind and intention, invited disciples to deep discipline. The monastic requirement of celibacy colored the precept about unchastity, as the celibacy of Christian monks colored Christian sexual morality. At times a monkish fear of women abetted Indian misogynism. The ideal for the monk (or the nun, with due changes) was to stand apart from sexual desire. How to translate this for laypeople was a considerable problem. Inasmuch as monks and nuns became spiritual advisors to laypeople, they could cause difficulties, as well as provide good counsel. The best counsel, from the Buddha's perspective, was that lust was a burning that kept people in karmic bondage. To love others without the distortions of lust was splendid, though difficult. If people could interact warmly but without the kinds of desire that created attachments, they could do one another much good. These general principles applied to homosexual attractions as much as heterosexual. Always the demand was to root out wrongful desire.

The final precept, to avoid intoxicants, applied to liquor in the first place, but by extension could apply to anything that threatened to distort consciousness—drugs, for example. Again the monastic influence was strong: people who meditated regularly became sensitive to the distortions of consciousness. They sought to purify their awareness, both interiorly and exteriorly. They could notice that what they ate and drank shaped how they thought and felt. Vegetarianism and teetotalism could seem to help people make spiritual progress. Heavy eating and drinking alcoholic beverages could seem to hold them back, entrap them in grosser habits. Indian spirituality has always been sensitive to the intimate, reciprocal relations between body and mind. Regularly it has included a physical detachment, asceticism, and purity as staples of its campaigns to free the person's core being from illusion and desire.

The five precepts of *sila* sketch the self that would please the Buddha. It would be restrained, gentle, self-controlled, captivated by nothing worldly, devoted to spiritual things rather than things of the flesh, and deeply honest. Although these precepts are expressed negatively, it is not hard to imagine their positive counterparts: kindly, protective feelings toward all living beings; poverty of spirit, so that one wanted nothing unnecessary; a profound commitment to living in the light; purity of heart and freedom from untoward desires; sobriety and self-control. The ideal Buddhist self was not dour. Its self-restraint did not make it gloomy or repressed. Rather, it was filled with the joy of living in the spiritual light, making progress toward nirvana, and so it radiated peace and attractiveness.

The Buddha's Teaching about Divinity

Sometimes analysts try to build a case that Buddhism is atheistic. Usually the basis for this case is the Buddha's relative disregard of the deities of the Indian culture contemporary to him, along with his stress on self-reliance. The gods of the Hinduism of his time did not give Gautama what he sought. They were not the source of his enlightenment and liberation. He achieved the blinding insight that made him a Buddha through his own efforts. No matter how rightly one might speak of good fortune or grace being at work in his achievement, the main source of his success was his own and so peace came from within.

When Gautama had clarified the nature and realms of reality, in light of his transformation into a Buddha, he located the gods and demons in heavenly and hellish realms which, in the final analysis, were not decisive for human destiny. In making this location of the traditional spiritual powers, he was following Hindu tradition. Apparently, he saw no surpassing reason to take up arms against the prevailing Hindu theology. Rather, he preferred to undercut it. The gods might be helpful, and the demons might be harmful, but only if one believed in their significance. His own experience told him that they were not decisive. What was decisive was stopping desire, finding the way to put out the fire that caused human suffering. The gods remained within the realm of karma. They needed release from the cycle of rebirths as much as human beings did. In fact, both Hinduism and Buddhism have taught that human existence is the only station from which one may gain release from karmic bondage. Thus, there is a significant sense in which it is better to be a human being than a divinity.

On the other hand, despite this gentle disparagement of the traditional Indian divinities, Gautama clearly had encountered the sacred. What he came to understand through the experience of enlightenment transcended ordinary human perception. He was taken to a realm beyond what we think of as the human realm. In entering into nirvana as much as a living person could (only at death could he enter fully), he came in contact with the transcendent (here in the form of the liberating dimension of human experience). Even though he was loathe to talk about nirvana, thinking that such talk distracted most people from the only pressing task, the practical one of solving the problem of suffering, he clearly felt that what he had glimpsed justified his whole way of life. He lived the poor, wandering life of a monk because the freedom of this life allowed him to concentrate on the one thing necessary: the realm of liberation. Even though he labored for the salvation of all living things, teaching them as best he could the way to liberation, the more central treasure of his life was communing with the ultimate, being in the state of fulfillment. Inasmuch as the ultimate, the state of fulfillment, is what many religious traditions mean by "heaven" (and tie to union with God), we have to modify our characterization of Buddhism as atheistic. The divinity that the Buddha rejected probably was not the living God spoken of by many religious traditions. In all likelihood, the Blessed One would have listened appreciatively to the high theologies of the major world religions, where the saints make it clear that "God" is not captured in any formulas or images, and that "seeing" God is the defeat of everything negative in human experience.

This is not to say that Gautama shows signs of having admitted, let alone worshiped, a personal God. When we try to align nirvana with divinity, we have to admit that the Buddhist ultimate is impersonal—a state of freedom rather than a personal savior. Indian culture did not personalize the ultimate. The many personal gods, such as Krishna and Shiva, could be foci of the ultimate, but when one spoke of Brahman or the foundations of existence, no definite face or singular "I" came to mind. The holy, the divine, was a transcendent realm of being. It was the perfection that occurred when desire was no more and what was simply existed, could be itself in full revelation and splendor. The Buddhist instinct has been to locate this transcendent realm of being in the midst of ordinary human experience—to say that the beyond is here, can be felt now.

Needless to say, Gautama did not claim divinity for himself. The earliest Buddhist traditions honor him as the height of human self-realization, but they do not argue that he was divine: the embodiment of the holy force responsible for creation. Certainly, later tradition venerates the Buddha as divine. Indeed, it multiplies Buddhas, making Gautama only one of many knowledge-beings in whom the ultimate light has shone forth. It follows that we have to distinguish between Gautama's apparent sense of divinity and that of many of his later followers.

The three "bodies" of the Buddha venerated in later Buddhism suggest the seminal beginnings of Buddhist theology. The physical body of Gautama serves as the historical anchor of enlightenment. Because Gautama entered into blissful light twenty-five years or so before 500 B.C., Buddhists could feel that enlightenment was not merely mythological or hypothetical. A real man, composed of flesh and blood, had gained perfection. In gaining perfection, however, he had contacted another Buddha-body, that of the Teaching that constituted the foundations of the world. The Teaching-body of the Buddha was somewhat like the divine Word later hymned in Christian culture. It was a symbol of the intelligibility of everything in existence, both individual entities and their connection into the patterns comprising evolution and history (we might now say). The third body of the Buddha was the form in which he existed blissfully in heaven. Devotional Buddhism loved to speculate about the beauty of this body, and such speculation flowed into desire to be reborn in "the Western Paradise," a place of complete fulfillment where one would be with the blissful Buddha.

The connection of these various bodies and modes of buddhahood with Gautama has been complex, but we may say that reflection, speculation, and piety in the centuries after the death of Gautama seemed many times to make him a divinity. Everything essential reposed in him. People prayed to him as their final refuge, their last and best hope. He shone with the splendor of sacred, ultimate reality. He was intimately related with the Reason that gave the world its order. Yet, for many Buddhist schools, this did not make him or his nirvana entirely separate from the world that human beings knew, the world of space and time. For Mahayana Buddhists, nirvana was the same as *samsara* (the karmic realm). One could find buddhahood, intrinsic lightsomeness, in the midst of the world, at the foundations of everything that was or acted.

This intuition and teaching probably advances beyond what Gautama himself thought and taught about divinity, holy ultimate reality. There is no indication that he wanted monks or laity to settle down in the world. He was calm and peaceful, not moved to distress by anything worldly. But he thought that the world was on fire with desire. He hoped that those who heard him would realize their danger, their sickness, and move their minds and hearts away from worldliness. In this regard, the Buddha seems best described as a sage with a prophetic mission. The strength of his message lay in his personal experience of passing from a suffering existence to one free of suffering. He did not ask people to worship him so much as urge them to take his message to heart—test it for themselves, follow him in *realizing* that all life is suffering, the cause of suffering is desire, if one stops desire one stops suffering, and one can stop desire by following the noble Eightfold Path, the program of wisdom, morality, and meditation that he had developed.

Buddhism after Gautama

After the death of Gautama, his disciples worked to consolidate his achievement. He had left them his own example, his teaching, and the community that they constituted. They had a wealth of memories of how he had looked, sounded, smiled, walked, sat in the repose of meditation. Equally, they had an oral tradition of what he had taught— both his main lessons, and his most striking examples. Finally, they had the common way of life that he had instituted for those who wanted to embrace his program, his vision wholeheartedly. These three legacies—the Buddha, the Dharma, and the Sangha—became the "jewels" of Buddhist life. Taking refuge in them was the formal way to become a Buddhist. Letting them shape one's deepest convictions and identity was the way to make progress toward nirvana.

During the first hundred years or so after the death of Gautama, loyal disciples labored to codify his legacy. In the area of meditation, many devout practitioners began to assemble reports of their experience, for the sake of helping others. In the area of monastic life, experience showed the need for clear rules about various subjects, both personal and communal. In the area of teaching, gifted minds began the process of elaborating the implications of Gautama's ideas. Where he had been practical, some of his followers were speculative, trying to reason through the things he had said about the three marks of reality, or the nature of nirvana, to make as coherent a statement as possible. On the whole, we cannot say what Gautama himself actually preached or taught about most topics. By the time that we get written texts, many people have worked over his legacy, adding their own expansions or clarifications. But we can be reasonably sure that the central emphases in early Buddhism derive from the example and teaching of Gautama. Thus, such linchpins as the Four Noble Truths, the Eightfold Path (condensed into a concern for wisdom, morality, and meditation), and the three jewels seem to be valid crystalizations of the Founder's work.

The monastic community quickly became the center of Buddhist life, taking responsibility for preserving Gautama's legacy and trans- mitting it far and wide. About a century after the Founder's death, we find in the Sangha the beginnings of the most basic split in Buddhist history, that between the Hinayanists and the Mahayanists. These names, coined by the Mahayanists, imply that the Hinayanists (small rafters) told disciples to concentrate on their own advancement toward nirvana, while the Mahayanists (large rafters) urged a concern for the liberation of all living things. In addition, the Hinayanists tended to be conservative in doctrine and interested mainly in the needs of monks and nuns. The Mahayanists were more expansive in doctrine and more concerned about the needs of lay people. Specifically, the Hinayanists tended to treat Gautama as merely a saintly human being, while the Mahayanists began to stress his supernatural qualities. The Hinayanists were sober in their prescriptions for Buddhist spirituality: wisdom, meditation, and morality were the game plan for all serious seekers. Mahayanists did not deny this, but they added devotional twists, such as prayers, pilgrimages, and veneration of relics, designed to attract lay interest. Both groups sought lay support for monastic life and positioned monks as the spiritual counselors of lay people.

These two orientations coexisted in India for nearly a thousand years. After the seventh century A.D., Buddhism declined in India, and both traditions found themselves relocated. Both had spawned various subgroups or sects. The Theravadins, the leading Hinayana sect that survived, dominated Ceylon (Sri Lanka) and such countries to the proximate east of India as Burma and Thailand. Mahayana sects became most influential in countries farther east, such as China, Japan, Korea, and Vietnam. A third branch of Buddhist tradition, known as Vajrayana ("The Thunderbolt Raft"), became the dominant Buddhist influence in Tibet. Vajrayana was a Buddhist version of the esoteric emphases that developed in both Indian Hinduism and Indian Buddhism. These emphases, sometimes collected in the name "tantrism," amounted to an attempt to engage the imagination, sexual energies, and emotions in the pursuit of enlightenment and nirvana. Teachers developed *mantras* (sounds thought potent), *mandalas* (visual figures thought potent), and such iconoclastic exercises as taking forbidden foods (for example, meat and alcohol) and engaging in forbidden sexual activities. The point was to help disciples get beneath the letter of the traditional laws, to penetrate their spirit, and also to help them realize the emptiness of all data of experience—how none, not even holy prohibitions, are things that one can lean upon. One can only lean upon nirvana, the extinction of desire.

For the past 1,500 years, Buddhists have continued to develop their legacy. The canon of Buddhist scriptures now numbers thousands of pages, as scribes have recorded what have purported to be oral accounts of the Buddha's teaching. The devotional lives of the laity have been enriched by many saints, to whom they could pray, many festivals that they could celebrate, and many images in which they could concentrate their faith. For example, the saintly figure Kuan-yin, a motherly *bodhisattva* (saint), has been paramount in East Asian Buddhist piety. The *bodhisattva* Tara has been equivalent to Kuan-yin in Tibet.

Buddhists have had considerable political influence in some periods of Chinese or Japanese, Ceylonese, or Thai history, while at other periods they have suffered persecution. Schools such as Zen have captured the imagination and loyalty of certain social classes, such as the samurai (warrior) class in Japan. Zen is also a good example of a Buddhist sect much involved with important cultural developments (for example, the tea ceremony, floral arrangement, and the martial arts).

Buddhist sects have shaped the indigenous religious practices and doctrines of the foreign countries to which they emigrated, and they have received influence from such indigenous practices. For example, in Tibet Buddhism interacted with native shamanistic traditions (the *Bon* practices). In Japan, Buddhist *bodhisattvas* could become interchangeable with Shinto *kami* (gods). In China, Taoism was a huge influence on Buddhism, while Buddhism forced Confucianism to develop a metaphysics. Nowadays, many Buddhist masters are translating traditional doctrines and practices for Western audiences, in the process entering into dialogue with Christianity, Judaism, and Western secularism.

On the whole, Buddhism after Gautama did what one would expect: unfolded his legacy, adapted it to new times and cultural circumstances. In the process, sometimes it seemed to leave its historical founder behind, paying more attention to given *bodhisattvas*, or stressing a meditation that might have to "slay the Buddha" to gain complete freedom, or pushing traditional Buddhist doctrine in the direction of atheism, humanism, or psychology. Because Buddhism has had no central authority, other than the collective influence of the leading components of the Sangha (and a few Councils through the centuries that met to restate or reform doctrine and practice), there has been a great proliferation of ideas, practices, and sects. Still, the vast majority of Buddhists have been responsible enough to try to justify their practices by reference to the Buddha. The vast majority have wanted to tie themselves to his enlightenment and taken great pride in calling him their Founder.

Buddhist Spirituality

Buddhist spirituality is cool. The hallmark of the Buddhas, as one meets them in lovely works of art, is a detached smile. The smile is not superior, condescending, or careless. Neither is it involved, engaged, concerned. The smile is full of joy and peace, light and lightness. The humor is mild, slight, not so much amusement as tolerance. The Buddha is the man who has understood—the pain of life, the folly of most human striving, the blessedness of enlightenment, the delicious taste of peace. Buddhist spirituality is not agonized, twisted with worry or effort. It is serene, detached, wise. People who have experienced enlightenment, or have made the profile of the buddhas their own, take human experience with a grain of salt. They hope to help their suffering brothers and sisters, but they are reconciled to the fact that most people will need more lifetimes before they grasp the essence of nirvana.

Central to the spirituality, the existential religion, that Gautama founded was the realization that nirvana, complete success, is the negation of *samsara*, painful ordinary existence. Nirvana lives within *samsara*, like the marrow of its bones. Thus Roger Corless, at the end of an admirable treatment of Buddhism, speaks of nirvana and *samsara* as follows:

> We can . . . characterize our reality, that is, samsara, and then indicate (rather than describe) nirvana as the unimaginable or incomprehensible . . . negation of our reality. Then . . . we can introduce positive analogies of the nirvanic state, but, as the modern linguistic theorists say, "write them under erasure." For instance, we can say that nirvana is joy, but we do not mean samsaric joy, for it is not a joy that is the opposite face of sadness and so it does not pall, that is, it does not decay into sadness. We can call it joy, not having a more appropriate word, but since it is the wrong word we cross it out . . . Samsara is repetition. We get out of bed, go to work, come home, sleep, get up, go to work again. We eat, get hungry, and eat again. We wash, get dirty, and wash again. Samsara literally means "constantly moving." Like laundry, it can be more of a problem or less of a problem, but it is always a problem, and it is never finished. In samsara we think ahead and try to meet new circumstances.

Nirvana, on the other hand, is continual freshness [written under erasure]. Zen calls it *shoshin*, "beginner's mind," like a child on Christmas morning. In nirvanic mode, the mind does not plan or work. It marries each moment flawlessly. It is spontaneous, it plays, it does not have an end in view nor a sense of time passing or space being passed through so as to get from here to there. Samsara is limitation. Nirvana is complete freedom of body, speech, and mind in the perfection of wisdom, of love, and of energy [all written under erasure].[6]

We may say, then, that Buddhist spirituality arises from an intuition of what an unconditioned, unimpeded human existence would be like. From time to time, we move with the flow rather than against it. We work spontaneously, freely, rather than laboriously. We love others and with them make a charmed circle in which everything is graced, instead of interacting with suspicion, torpor, lack of grace. The difference between the Buddha and other refined, favored people of his day was the depth of his intuition of what human beings can be, at their best, and his wisdom about the possibility that he intuited. Enlightenment gave him a sure sense of why we are so often impeded, pained, unable to be our best. Enlightenment also gave him great skill in expressing what he had experienced. He could describe what an existence without the pains consequent on desire would be like, and he could enumerate the practical ways to approach such an existence. He knew, simply knew, from having experienced it personally, that the extinction of desire was the onset of freedom. He could explain with example after example, metaphor after metaphor, what people had to do to gain freedom, because always he was aware of where he was trying to lead them, what they had to do if they were to throw off their chains and move lightly, follow the light of the wisdom that had gone beyond conditions and desires, chains, and conflicts.

The peace of the Buddha is the peace that flows from understanding. It is not a peace that surpasses understanding, except in the sense that its understanding is ineffable—cannot be articulated. The only way to understand the Buddha's peace is to experience it, and the only way to experience it is to come to enlightenment. When the light floods one's being, peace and joy flow as inevitable consequents. There is no enlightenment without light, joy, and peace. There is no radical joy and peace, light and fulfillment, without enlightenment. Some people, not having experienced enlightenment, question the possibility of profound joy and peace. Standing in the midst of human suffering, they cannot conceive a state without pain. Not to suffer would be inhuman, they think, for they have made suffering essential to having a body and a spirit, being an animal with reason. Buddhist spirituality says "not so." The essence of being human is not suffering. The essence of being human is being full of light, realizing the potential aglow deep in one's being.

Nirvana, the far side of human existence where the flame of desire and so the pain of death and rebirth are blown out, is both the cause and the goal of Buddhist spirituality. Because Gautama had passed across the stream of suffering, gaining the far side, he lived in a nirvanic state. Because he knew how wonderful it was to escape from suffering, enter into the peace and joy of unconditionedness, he set nirvana before his followers as their own goal. If they could gain enlightenment in his footsteps, according to his model, they too could be buddhas— enlightenment-beings, people aware that their inmost nature was light.

A spirituality of light encounters difficulties in a world full of darkness. People who hate the light, because their deeds are evil, oppose it with might and main. Empiricists, convinced that experience is tied to the senses and matter, do not know what to make of a spirituality that stresses the immaterial, free side of human nature. It is beyond their ken and hope, so they tend to disparage it. Modern Western culture is empiricist, so modern Western culture more mocks Buddhist spirituality than gives it a serious hearing.

Idealists, thinking that matter is finally an illusion, also miss the Buddhist mark. The Buddha's Middle Way did not disparage the body or the material world. They are part of what is so, so any realistic, truly enlightened spirituality takes them for granted and tries to make them beautiful. That is the reason that Buddhist art, Buddhist grace in ritual, Buddhist affinity for swordsmanship, tea ceremonies, and floral arrangements arise generation after generation. That is the reason that masters of meditation urge people to concentrate on their breathing, keep their spinal column erect, try to perform each task perfectly. Buddhist spirituality does not try to move people out of their humanity. Nirvana is not outside the mind-body complex. Nirvana transcends the mind-body complex, in the sense that usually this complex does not function in a nirvanic mode. But when desire is blown out, both the mind and the body prosper. When enlightenment dawns, the brain and the hands rejoice as much as the spirit. Buddhist spirituality is holistic. At its best, it makes every part of a human being and his or her experience glow with light.

Friendly Criticisms

What are the problems that an admirer of the Buddha is apt to find with his spirituality? Take a person persuaded that Gautama is a great spiritual hero; what is he or she apt to stumble over, in light of either the history subsequent to the Buddha or insights from other traditions of wisdom? Naturally, much in the answer to these questions is idiosyncratic—dependent on the answerer's own priorities. Still, it is useful to raise such questions, because they remind us that even the great religious founders were fully human and so limited.

Two major criticisms dog the footsteps of Buddhist spirituality. One is that it has lacked a strong social ethics. The other is that, compared to passionate love, its dispassionate, desire-free ideal is superficial or unattractive. Let us develop these criticisms, as a way of taking the Buddha seriously enough to challenge his program for human liberation.

The first criticism, that Buddhism has lacked a strong social ethics, has on its side the obvious focus of most Buddhist preaching. Gautama targeted individuals, and so have most of the Buddhist preachers and teachers who have succeeded him. He believed that individuals were the only ones who could liberate themselves. "Society" was an abstraction. Whatever changes might improve society, making it more just, compassionate, or efficient, were certainly desirable. The better that societies ran, the more likely people would be to realize that no society can solve the truly pressing problem: the suffering that afflicts all beings. This suffering is inextricable from *samsara*. Only by taking away samsaric desire could one root it out. Only by challenging the entire dynamic by which societies the world over run could one lay bare the real, existential issues.

The strength of this argument is apparent. Social engineering, of

whatever stripe, has never brought widespread peace and joy. Nonetheless, the analysts who reveal the significance of social influences—
the atmosphere in the home, the economic opportunities in the neighborhood, the quality of local schooling—force us to challenge Buddhist individualism. Even if we admit that no group can liberate a
given individual (that he or she has to hoist this work personally), we
can argue that environment, social milieu, is so influential that a
spiritual program ought not only to take it into account but also
should transform it.

Of course, some Buddhists have attempted to do this. Ashoka is the
most prominent, but many other Buddhists have labored to have the
Dharma shape politics, education, and the arts. In Buddhist countries
such as Thailand one feels the impress of the Enlightened One's peace.
Even when the politics in such countries is corrupt, or there is much
violence, or teenage prostitution argues that women get little respect,
the Dharma remains a helpful, ameliorating influence. Bad as any
specific Buddhist country might be, it might well be worse without the
historical influence of the Dharma. (Christians are familiar with this
argument, which is both vulnerable and suggestive. Bad as the Christian West could be in some periods, the glories of Western civilization
are unthinkable without the influence of the Church.)

The problem is that social questions did not capture Gautama's
interest and received relatively little articulation in Buddhist history.
One can admit that the seeds of a marvelous social ethics lie ready to
hand in the Buddhist doctrine of nonviolence, but the fact remains that
Buddhists have not developed anything like the full economic, political, military, or social implications of nonviolence necessary for it to
transform complete societies, especially complicated modern ones.

The second criticism, that Buddhist dispassion makes Buddhist
spirituality compare badly to its competition, tends to come from
Western critics shaped by biblical ideals. Working from the context of a
personal God covenanted to human beings, such Western critics tend to
think that marital relations furnish the best analogy for profound
interactions with ultimate reality. Not targeting a personal God, Buddhist spiritual masters have avoided this analogy (though there are
qualifications: a devotional Buddhism, on the model of that developed
by the Japanese saint Shinran, can so stress mercy and love that it

comes into the same emotional field as much Western personalist spirituality).

The question then becomes, what are the advantages and disadvan-
tages of the two spiritual profiles. Buddhism is cool and impersonal.
Western traditions such as Judaism, Christianity, and Islam have been
warm and personal. Do the Western traditions from the start default on
the matter of undercutting *samsara*? Is the Christian embrace of suffering (stress on the cross of Christ as the paramount sign of divine love) a
perverse sanctioning of the first noble truth: all life is suffering? Can
one better get to the heart of the human matter by detachment or
engagement, extinguishing desire or pushing desire to purify itself and
become ardent, selfless love?

Individuals have to answer these questions for themselves. Their
own experience is bound to shape if not determine where they stand,
how they line up. People who can say that they would never give up the
experience of a profound human passion (whether for a lover, or a child,
or a friend, or a personal God) are bound to think that Buddhist
spirituality tries to avoid the crux of what it means to be human. People
who think that desire is bound to bring ruinous pain are likely to think
that Gautama was wiser than Jesus. Were there time enough, knowledge enough, good will enough, the two founders, if not their followers, might be able to negotiate their apparent differences. Love
passionate enough to empty itself and suffer for the beloved may not be
much different from Buddhist *anatman* (no-self). The lessons of passionate love may include the stark realization that nothing human can
satisfy the human heart, only a God with many of the attributes of
nirvana.

At the extremes of human experience and insight, where wisdom
dances teasingly, many apparent contradictions begin to melt away.
The way up is the way down, and vice versa. Desire purified by love
can be so changed that it is hard to recognize as desire and seems to be
the dropping of desire. Buddhist compassion can so alter our initial
sense of Buddhist desirelessness that we can find Buddhist and Western
saints little different in their blend of labor to help suffering human
beings and abandonment of ambition to the will of God or the structures of nirvana. The beauty of dialogue between foundational spiritualities is that the full mysteriousness of the human venture after

perfection, into the obscurities of sacredness, comes into view. In the realm of transcendence, there may be many answers to a given question, many ways to the center. If only because doing so can move us toward this ultimate vantage point, we should criticize any founder's spirituality as honestly as we can. Inevitably, we will find that such a spirituality comes back to criticize *us*. Inevitably, the great masters of the spiritual life, the true classics, instruct us far more than we instruct them.

NOTES

1. William Theodore de Bary, ed., *The Buddhist Tradition* (New York: Vintage Books, 1972), pp. 68–69.
2. See Henry Clarke Warren, *Buddhism in Translations* (New York: Atheneum, 1973), pp. 351–353.
3. *Mahaparinibbana Sutta*, no. 6, in T. W. Rhys Davids, *Buddhist Suttas* (New York: Dover, 1969), pp. 6–7.
4. For a good discussion of the three marks, see Trevor Ling, *The Buddha* (New York: Penguin, 1973), pp. 134–135.
5. *Vinaya Pitaka*, 2:253 ff., in Edward Conze et al., *Buddhist Texts Through the Ages* (New York: Harper & Row, 1964), pp. 24–25.
6. Roger Corless, *The Vision of Buddhism* (New York: Paragon House, 1989), pp. 280–281. Other relevant studies include George Marshall, *Buddha: The Quest for Serenity* (Boston: Beacon Press, 1978); Michael Carrithers, *The Buddha* (New York: Oxford University Press, 1983); H. Saddhatissa, *The Life of the Buddha* (New York: Harper & Row, 1973); and Maurice Percheron, *Buddha and Buddhism* (Woodstock, NY: Overlook, 1982).

CHAPTER 3

CONFUCIUS

Chinese Religion Before Confucius

The traditional date for the birth of Confucius is about 550 B.C. For thousands of years before the Master, the people we now call the Chinese had been elaborating convictions about the construction of reality, the ideal shape of family life, how government ought to proceed, and what ultimately brought good fortune or bad, a blessed life or a life to be lamented. To the present day, the vast majority of China's huge population have been peasants (80 percent still live in rural areas). Living in intimate contact with nature, trying to scratch out their sustenance from the land, these people have done what their ancestors did: venerated the forces of fertility, prayed to the god of the river and spirit of the field. Their operative religion has been a mixture of fear and awe in face of the natural forces that controlled their lives. They have realized that sun, rain, and wind had more say about their survival than any human efforts. They have taken comfort from the knowledge that their ancestors had faced the same basic problems, and so they have venerated their ancestors.

Peasant wisdom is both estimable and easy to criticize. On the one hand, it is hard not to agree that nature is more significant than human beings, that survival and prosperity depend on unfathomable forces of fertility. What makes the crops grow, women fertile, men long-lived, the seasons regular—all this escapes human ken and control. The best that human beings can do is bow low in reverence before what they cannot understand yet know controls their destiny. Life and death are the great poles and questions shaping all peoples' existences. Why we come into being and where we go at death put huge brackets around our

significance. So we have to admire the forthrightness of Chinese peasants, or any other peasants, whose daily interactions with the natural
world made these questions paramount.

On the other hand, we have also to question the credulity of peasant
religion, its easy slipping into magic, its natural bent for astrology, its
spawning of diviners and shamans trying to discern the future, control
the gods, bend heaven to the will of human beings. The many differen-
tiations of consciousness that have occurred on the way to cultures
"higher" than those of peasants suggest that human reason ought to
stand against peasant submission to the forces of nature, peasant un-
willingness or inability to separate imagination from verified reality,
fantasy from judgment.

One way of looking at Confucius and the tradition he sponsored is as
a break with peasant mythology. In Confucius we find a sober, controlled reason. This master wants nothing to do with superstition,
uncriticized traditional ways, submission to imagination or magic
rather than prudence and virtue. We see him stepping out of the
cosmological myth that considers nature to be a living whole and
asserting the rights of the human mind. We see him arguing for an
anthropocentric vision: in the person of the sage, the man (in Confucius's eyes women could not be sages) who had appropriated the best
ancient traditions and molded his spirit to their dictates, lies the criterion for all political action, all estimates of how human beings collec-
tively ought to think about nature and their interactions with one
another.

Prior to Confucius, the line of sages that people like him respected
receded into a mythological past. Legends about past sages suggested
that they had had the power to make water flow upstream, fend off high
winds and droughts, govern their fellow human beings indirectly, by
their mere example. Where did this power come from? From their
familiarity with, immersion in, fidelity to the Way (*Tao*). Chinese
tradition bequeathed to Confucius the firm conviction that a pathway
through the apparent caprice of nature, human beings, and the individual self lay ready to hand. If one put forth study and self-discipline, one
could find it. This Way ran the natural world. One could call it the Way
of heaven, implying that the divine powers "above" the natural and
human worlds directed it. Or one could call it the Way of the ancients,

implying that it was the pattern discerned by the heroes of yore, the models that potential sages like Confucius revered. Either way, discovering the Way and keeping faith with it were prized long before Confucius. Even peasants in the fields wanted to harmonize their lives, their selves, with the Way that nature ran, the rhythms governing the turning of the seasons, the fertility of the animals, the passage of men and women from birth to death.

In their reflections on these matters, pre-Confucian Chinese thinkers devised several schemes. One was the scheme of yin-yang relations. Essentially, this was a dualistic outlook, according to which everything was a composite of opposite yet complementary forces. Yin was dark, feminine, wet, cold. Yang was light, masculine, dry, warm. While patriarchal China favored yang qualities over those it considered yin, at bottom all theorists acknowledged that the two forces were irreducible to one another and so equally necessary. Nature was a harmony of yin and yang forces. Human beings did well to try to harmonize the yin and yang aspects of their own personalities, diets, and activities. Living immersed in the rhythms of nature, which seemed more circular than linear; Chinese peasants and pre-Confucian intellectuals did not expect "progress." Indeed, their inclination was to look to the past for wisdom while suspecting the goodness of present or future times. So the great watchword was "harmony" or "balance." Indeed, today we might say that the ideal was homeostasis: all systems in phase, no system wandering off on its own or challenging the traditional patterns.

Pre-Confucian thought about nature also spoke of five basic elements or vital forces: water, fire, wood, metal, and earth. This scheme could exist alongside the scheme of yin-yang relations, because it was more analytical—more concerned to break entities down into their component parts than imagine their basic polarities. On the other hand, because these five elements interacted, and their proportions determined the character of any given entity, the scheme of the five elements was like the scheme of yin-yang relations in searching for combinations, ratios, insights into which way a given being leaned. Naturally, so simple a scheme had to become quite ingenious when it came to complex entities like the human being. Naturally, the five vital forces became as much metaphoric as literal. But Confucius could draw on a protoscientific tradition, when he sought to establish reason as the key to political philosophy. He could depend on the work of prior, more naturalistically oriented philosophers, when it came to justifying his efforts to understand past tradition and become quasi-scientific about it. Traditional China approved the idea of investigating nature. Its reverence for the forces of fertility, the powers of the heavens and the earth, did not forbid inquiring into how such forces operated. The Way of Heaven beckoned as a source of understanding. The fact that nature ran consistently, most of the time, invited people to study the tides, the phases of the moon, the movements of the stars.

Also pervading pre-Confucian Chinese thought was an ancient concern with spirits, both good and evil. Peasant religion was animistic, in the sense that it believed spirits were at work everywhere. The trees and the streams had their spirits, their sources of life and power. The wind was a spiritual force, and so was the source of human insight, skill, virility, or rage. Shamans were revered in ancient China, because they could deal with such spirits. Departed ancestors were feared as well as respected, because they could remain at the family homestead, causing much trouble if they were not placated. On occasion an evil spirit could possess a person and, by the time that the movement (reverence for the Way) known as Religious Taoism had become organized, priests were available to exorcize demons. The spirit of the hearth, god of the family dwelling, merited honor day and night— small sacrifices, gifts of grain or flowers.

Everywhere in traditional China, both prior to Confucius and continuing long after him (at least among the common people), religion was largely a matter of warding off bad spirits, agents of misfortune, and soliciting the aid of good spirits, agents of good luck. Everywhere, people were concerned to site their houses favorably, marry at times the astrologer considered fortunate, protect their children from the evil eye, avoid the wrath of hungry ghosts. Confucius stands as a landmark break with this peasant, animistic tradition, but he did not overcome it. Indeed, it shaped much of his own thought, in subtle ways, and it coexisted with the tradition that he founded on higher ground.[1]

The Life of Confucius

The traditional dates for Confucius are roughly 551–479 B.C. They make him the contemporary of the Buddha. There is no indication that the two men ever met or heard of one another. Still, both lived at times of upheaval, when the surrounding culture begged for radical change. In the case of the Buddha, the radical change was spiritual: a way out of the proliferation of rites and deities sapping brahmanical religion, a way through the problem of suffering. In the case of Confucius, the radical change was political: a new way to configure human relations, a new handle on power. A major difference between the two founders is that Gautama claimed to be an innovator, while Confucius claimed to be restoring ancient wisdoms. Gautama said that his experience of enlightenment had shown him the solution to the problem of human suffering. Confucius said that the sages of ancient times had found the way to live well, and thus a sage of present times had only to renovate their teaching.

We do not have the data necessary to write a complete biography of Master Kung, but tradition supplies the following outline of his life. His followers believed that Confucius came from a noble lineage in the state of Sung. Legend had it that his father had been a hero, responsible for the escape of some comrades from persecution. We know nothing about the Master's mother. Tradition says that Confucius was orphaned at an early age, and that he grew up in poverty. Still, from his youth he loved learning, and this became his distinguishing feature. He had to labor at menial tasks, but by age fifteen he had determined to become a scholar. As he progressed in mastery of traditional political thought, he began to look for an office in government. Failing to secure a significant post, he sought to become a counselor to local dukes and lords, but this ambition also came to naught. Toward the end of his life he reconciled himself to the fact that he was not likely to exert any direct influence on governmental policy. This led him to accept that his vocation would have to be teaching. He became a tutor to the sons of middle-class families wanting to prepare for government service. The *Analects*, which come closest to giving us Confucius's own words, are notes that his students took. They have the form of brief sayings or stories and provide no sustained development of the Master's ideas. Still, they have been provocative enough to generate nearly 2,500 years' worth of commentary.

One of the reasons for such influence is that the *Analects* show a man dedicated to learning in what the noble, socially useful life consists. No break separates the man Confucius from the Teacher bent on gaining the wisdom necessary to become fully human. The Master takes pride in this singlemindedness. It is a point of honor with him that he has pursued learning rather than wealth or empty praise. Through the painful lesson of having rulers more often reject his advice than take it, he has become convinced that the Way he venerates is not for the many. Most people do not care about full humanity. They will not suffer or sacrifice for wisdom. So he is engaged in an elitist work. Even though what he has to pass on could improve the lot of all people, from the lowliest peasant to the highest ruler, it will only attract a few people willing to give their lives. The Way is demanding. The Way is a matter of solid understanding and virtue—things that cannot be finessed. So, in his own eyes, Confucius became a prophetic figure, crying alone in the wilderness. He died without overwhelming influence, and only a series of historical accidents pushed him to the fore of later Chinese culture. The sobriety of his teachings, and their support for good order in government, became attractive to later rulers. In ways that might have surprised, or even appalled him, he became the Patron of Learning and source of the lore that dominated the examinations for entry into civil service. The aphorisms of the *Analects* even inspired sayings inserted into fortune cookies, and the Taoists (the main opponents of the Confucians) hung on him the image of a stuffed shirt.

Perhaps the most significant autobiographical reflection in the *Analects* describes the Master's life as follows:

The Master said, "At fifteen I set my heart on learning; at thirty I took my stand; at forty I came to be free from doubts; at fifty I understood the Decree of Heaven; at sixty my ear was attuned; at seventy I followed my heart's desire without overstepping the line."[2]

The translated text is obscure enough to invite considerable speculation. The end points—commitment to learning at age fifteen and freedom to follow his heart at age seventy—are relatively clear. In youth Confucius discovered that he was hungry to understand his situation. Perhaps being orphaned and poor stimulated this hunger. Assuming that he had a good mind, his early sufferings could have made him precocious: interested in big questions long before he could grasp their full significance. We do not know what sort of schooling Confucius received. Obviously he learned to read, probably he learned to write, and the *Analects* furnish many indications that he considered it incumbent on a "gentleman" to know the details of the public rituals. He was also interested in social etiquette, thinking it crucial for public order. So we may suspect that he focused his studies on the ancient texts dealing with ritual and government. His great veneration for the ancient masters suggests that he looked on these texts as holy books, sacred scriptures. In them he might find the key to how to live well— how to prosper spiritually and become a benefactor of his fellow human beings.

Tradition says that Confucius married and begot children (a heavy obligation in traditional China, where it was imperative to continue the family line and provide sacrifices for the dead), but neither his wife nor his children are prominent in the asides of the *Analects*. Perhaps his wanderings precluded deep involvement in domestic matters. By thirty, it seems, he was convinced that studying ancient tradition was to be his life's work. He no longer was casting about for a vocation. He had found what he wanted to do, how he planned to make his contribution. At forty, perhaps, he knew what he believed, how he interpreted ancient tradition—at least sufficiently well to be free of doubts about either what he had to offer or devoting his life to public affairs (showing how they should be ordered).

At fifty, he had accumulated enough experience to understand how the Way tended to work out in human affairs, and also what Heaven likely had in store for him. It was becoming clear that he would not get a ruler to put his ideas into practice. It was becoming obvious that the lovely wisdom of the ancients got besmirched when one handed it over to political practitioners. Yet all of this had to be providential. Heaven must have decreed that things were ever thus, virtue would always have less popular appeal than vice.

At sixty, Confucius felt that he heard all the overtones of the Way.

Few nuances escaped him. All the notes sounded, and he could let himself enjoy their harmonies, both subtle and great. He was no longer listening for any other voice, no longer submitting to any other authority. The Way had proven itself. It was the only music, the only song, about which he cared. So at seventy, he could say that the Way had fully taken over his heart. He wanted nothing that conflicted with the way. The center of his being reposed in what the Way commanded, held out as how to live. He was consummately free, because he had no untoward desires. Vice, or even disobedience to the Way in small matters, held no appeal. If, as another text suggests, he could hear the Way in the morning, he could die in the evening content. He had become a thorough contemplative. What the Torah has meant to pious Jews, or the Gospel has meant to pious Christians, or the *Qur'an* has meant to pious Muslims, or the Dharma has meant to pious Buddhists—this the Way of the ancients meant to Confucius. It was a lens through which ultimate wisdom, ultimate reality, what he held most sacred came into his mind and heart. It was the wellspring of his life, the source of his consistency and renowned wisdom.

The Personality of Confucius

If the *Analects* be our guide, the Master was a precise man, not fussy but aware of his dignity. The pride of his life was the virtue he had attained. He had not come by it easily, and he did not expect much of human nature. On the other hand, he was convinced that virtue is attractive. If the people saw a ruler who was good, they would want to be good in return. So the Master gave a mixed message. Virtue, full goodness (*jen*), does not come easily, yet it is so human, so much the fulfillment of what our minds and hearts seek, that we are drawn to it almost despite ourselves.

We have mentioned Confucius's scorning of wealth. *Analects* 4:5 says:

> The Master said, "Wealth and high station are what men desire but unless
> I got them in the right way I would not remain in them. Poverty and low

station are what men dislike, but even if I did not get them in the right way I would not try to escape from them. If the gentleman forsakes benevolence [*jen*], in what way can he make a name for himself? The gentleman never deserts benevolence, not even for as long as it takes to eat a meal. If he hurries and stumbles one may be sure that it is in benevolence that he does so."[3]

Confucius was the rare man free of the ambitions that drive most people. If he was ambitious, it was to achieve benevolence, attain the status of a true gentleman. He lived for what we are calling spirituality. His delight was to understand the Way of the ancients, see how it ordered human affairs. When he felt that he was progressing in this Way, he was happy. When he saw his pupils making progress, or was able to consort with other lovers of the Way, his heart took flight. Somehow living for the Way, in the Way, was its own reward. The consolations it brought meant more than any advantages he might have gained by forgetting the Way, or transgressing its precepts.

This did not mean that Confucius was a simple soul, desiring to be alone with the Alone, concerned only with the music of the spheres. The wisdom that he sought was, in its own fashion, practical, political, geared to changing how people lived. Confucius was a man of affairs. If he could not gain office, or the ear of a ruler, he could still examine how public affairs were proceeding, where they were going wrong. He was more interested in the golden age of the past than in recent happenings, but recent happenings were also his province. The image he projects is not that of a monk. He is content to be a teacher, but mainly because his students might grasp how the Way could change society. In his heart of hearts, he is a ruler, showing the people how to live.

We shall consider what Confucius thought about the major dimensions of reality, how to relate to the natural world, other people, one's self, and ultimate reality. Here we should note that his own thinking, his personal bias, was hierarchical. Confucius stood on his dignity as a master of ancient wisdom. With his pupils he made it clear who knew and who did not—had yet to learn. He extended this sense of status to politics at large. Rulers ought to rule and subjects ought to obey. Men ought to precede and women ought to follow. The great need in domestic life was for children to honor their parents. Younger siblings ought to obey older siblings. Each station had its place, and it was important to stick to one's own station.

China was not so rigidly structured as traditional India. It did not have an elaborate system of caste. But it was a society, a culture, in which people were well aware where they stood on the social ladder. It was a place where etiquette, social intelligence, was a subtle, complex affair. One did not speak to peasants as one spoke to middle-class equals, let alone as one spoke to superiors. Social intercourse required complicated rituals. For example, if a former pupil came into town, the Master expected to receive one of his first visits. In the circle of disciples, the brilliant had rights not granted the dull.

So the personality of the Master of traditional Chinese culture comes into focus as rather formal. He was not a man to whom one would say, "Yo. How 'bout a beer?" He would not like to be a buddy, an easy familiar. The benevolence he had attained was attractive, but it did not invite casual approaches. He was a serious man, a punctilious man, a man not often seen laughing. He delighted in ritual, both public and private. Public rituals were solemn affairs, ordained to gain the people harmony with nature and consolidate their sense of themselves—as the offspring of such and such ancestors, the subjects of such and such rulers, the pawns or blessed beneficiaries of such and such deities. Private rituals were the unguent that kept social frictions minimal. The bows and formulaic words, the approaches to intimacy and the withdrawals, unfolded like a ballet. Undergirding them lay the conviction that rituals form the inner spirit. Let people act in the prescribed patterns year after year and slowly they would become what they performed. Slowly they would more clearly, more actually, be ruler and subject, master and pupil, man and woman—as the rites assumed and promoted.

This suggests that the Master was also conservative. His heroes lay in the past. For current times he felt mainly suspicion and contempt. He wanted the traditional rites to be performed well. He loved the old virtues of reverence for elders, dedication to learning. He had little love for women, and nowadays we are bound to find him patriarchal, if not misogynistic. How thoughtful this prejudice was is not clear. In his day daughters had to be provided a dowry, were they to marry, and when they married they moved into their husband's household. It was easy to think of them as a burden or a labor soon lost. Why Confucius could not see how they could bring great benefits, both substantial and charming, is not clear. He worried that lust would distract his students from learning. His sense of the Way gave little place to romance. So in his scheme of things women were only important to keep the race and family going. Beyond that, the Master was not interested.

Much in how we evaluate the personality of Confucius will depend on how we think about social order. If we are sympathetic to his instinct that governing people well is the key to public peace and prosperity, we may consider him admirably detached, wise, instructive about the foundations of good rule, sober about there being no short cuts. If we chafe at rituals, distrust precepts and laws, think that social influences are far less significant than interior, personal experiences, we may find Confucius dull, superficial, or even dangerous. The survival of billions of Chinese through a cultural history indebted to Confucius more than any other historical figure suggests the perceptiveness of the Master's instinct that public order comes from articulating social relationships into rational, hierarchical patterns. The suppression of individuality throughout Chinese history argues that this instinct should not be the whole story. As we understand his personality, Confucius would smile at the prospect of rebutting such an argument.

Confucius's Teaching about Nature

Two verses from Book VIII of the *Analects*, both rendered in Ezra Pound's quirky translation, give us a glimpse of how Confucius thought about the physical world:

> He said: lofty as the spirits of the hills and the grain mother, Shun and Yu held the empire, as if not in a mortar with it. He said: How great was Yao's activity as ruler lofty as the spirits of the hills; only the heavens' working is great, and Yao alone on that pattern, spreading as grass, sunlight and shadow, the people could not find it a name. How marvelous the way he brought his energies to a focus. Brilliant-gleaming? the perfect expression of his statutes (VIII: 18-19).[4]

Shun, Yu, and Yao are legendary rulers, models from the past whom Confucius admired. The implication of these verses is that the power by which they ruled, their virtue, was tied up with the Way that runs the world. The Way runs the world through the spirits of the hills, the mother who provides the grain. Confucius accepts these peasant instincts about the vitality of nature, applying them to the heroes he wants to honor. He wants to honor them not as an exercise in nostalgia, but as a reminder of how an effective ruler would appear in contemporary times, the Master's own day. He would appear to rule as effortlessly, as much by natural right, as the spirits of the hills and the grain mother. They represent how things are, how the world runs, how the Way manifests itself. In another context, Confucius might question the adequacy of these animistic images, but here he does not pause. Human affairs are not separate from nature. The Way that runs nature is the same Way that human beings have to follow, if they are to prosper. The rites that rulers carry out seek fertility in the fields, protection against malign natural elements. Rulers are links between heaven and earth. Their power derives from the power of the cosmos, the power of creation. If they can make human affairs as harmonious as the affairs of nature, they will succeed admirably. If their power is outstanding, they will shine like natural spirits, divinities responsible for good order in the hills or fertility from the earth.

Not to be in a mortar with the empire was to be unconcerned—aloof from the hurly-burly, unmixed with the fractious elements. The legendary rulers had no more worry about how the empire would go than the spirits controlling the hills had about the hills' greening. How could this be so? Only if the legendary rulers were completely attuned to the Way. The Taoists spoke in this fashion more than the Confucians, but here Master Kung seems to share their mystical instinct. The order of nature sets the pattern and foundation for the order of human affairs. When human affairs run correctly, they are as unthinking, as straightforward, as the passage of the winds over the hills or the growth of the grain in the fields.

In *Analects* VIII:19 there is the pregnant line, "only the heavens' working is great." We discuss Confucius's theology in a later section, but here we must note that "the heavens" was a phrase with much import from earlier Chinese history. On a simple level, Chinese had long looked to the heavens as the realm of the gods, the source of cosmic order, the "above" that human affairs on earth, "below," ought to imitate. The emperor was the son of heaven. The power that he possessed came from heaven, as a mandate. When he fell out of favor with heaven, he lost that mandate, and others could lawfully overthrow him. The royal ideology was that the emperor ruled by divine right. He was heaven's man, heaven's legate. The prosperity of the entire realm, from flowers and grain to fertile wives and successful businesses, depended on his good connections.

Most of the rituals that the emperor celebrated acknowledged some special turn of the natural year. The beginning of the new year, the arrival of spring, the benevolent days of summer, the ripe days of fall harvest, the dying of the year in winter—all this had a great hold on the imperial as well as the popular psyche. Confucius helped China step out of the cosmological myth, move toward a more rational view of human affairs as things that human understanding ought to direct, but he never abandoned the cosmological context of human existence. The workings of the heavens were the final determinants of everything that happened on earth. The fate of all empires finally lay outside human control. One had to keep good relations with the heavens, through exact, beautiful execution of the traditional rites. One also had to possess rulers who loved the Way of heaven from the heart and had been formed by its precepts. The rule of Yao was so splendid that it reminded Confucius of the rule of the heavens in the natural world. It proceeded as uneventfully, yet marvelously, as the interaction of grass, sunlight, and shadow, as the seamless growth and change of the nonhuman world. So subtle, simple, elemental was the rule of Yao that the people could not even name it. It seemed part of the objective world order. It seemed a thing of nature, as right and unquestionable as the turn of the seasons, the growth of the grass.

And yet, in Confucius's view, the very ordinariness of this rule gave it splendor. Yao was so focused that he gleamed. The laws he enacted were brilliant, in the root sense of shedding light on everything they touched. The people walked in this light, but they were no more conscious of it than they were of sunshine. Yao's statutes were a medium for graceful, prosperous living, not an end in themselves. They enabled people to be human, without calling attention to themselves.

They enabled life to be as it ought to be: simple, orderly, well-structured. Naturally, this is an idealized view of Yao that Confucius is indulging. Naturally, there is no historical basis for thinking that Yao ever presided over a golden age in which human beings lived in a "state of nature," without the conflicts that reflection and disagreement introduce. Yao is a symbol more than a historical lesson or a practical model. What Confucius wants to draw from the legends about him is an orientation, not a pattern.

Good rule is like the Way of nature. Nature furnishes human beings many lessons. The more human beings appreciate the ways of nature, its beauties and fecundities, the more they will intuit how they themselves ought to live. Confucius never doubts the reality of the natural world. It is never a place of illusion, as Indian culture sometimes tempted people to think. Nature is more reliable than human culture. Human culture has some superiorities based on reason, but nature is more durable, less dubious. So to rule like a natural force was a high achievement. To be likened to the spirits of the hills or the spread of grass, sunlight, and shade, was high praise. The Master loved the beauties of song and nature. In his political science, they bore great significance.

Confucius's Teaching about Society

Although Confucius accepted nature as the given context of culture and found in the ways of nature many intimations of the Way, his forte was human affairs. He was interested in how to govern human beings, what virtues were required. His conviction was that if gentlemen, fully mature human beings, were in charge, human affairs might proceed smoothly. In this he was like Plato, who longed for a philosopher-king. Marry wisdom to power and you might create an ideal state. Wisdom without power was feckless, while power without wisdom was dangerous, a horror. So Confucius concentrated on the individual human being. Again and again we find him showing his pupils what would or would not be fitting for the gentleman, how the gentleman would or would not think, feel, or act.

We have noted the Master's own ideas about wealth. If wealth came virtuously, through no untoward means, it was fine, even a blessing. But honest poverty was better than ill-gotten wealth. The same for ill-gotten power. It was better for the gentleman to be impotent, in the eyes of the world, than for him to rule through bloodlust, machinations, any deals that would compromise his integrity. You could not have good government without integrity. That was the Master's bottom line. There were no shortcuts on the road to virtue and genuine power to rule. Until a people gained a ruler who actually was just, benevolent, and wise, they were bound to languish in misery. Until a king or duke commanded the allegiance of his people from the heart, because they loved the goodness that flowed out from him, human affairs would continue to be a shambles.

We have mentioned goodness, humaneness, benevolence—three translations of the premier Confucian virtue: *jen*. Now we must mention the complementary virtue *li*. *Li* denotes ritual, etiquette, an appropriated, truly personalized sense of how things should be done. If *jen* is what makes a person fully human, *li* is what puts that person into graceful relations with others. *Li* could be learned. The students who came to Confucius could go away with a finely tuned sense of what was fitting, decent, expected in a great variety of circumstances. Eventually *li* depended on the gentleman's instinct for what would enhance human relations, but on the way to the full flowering of such an instinct there were many exercises that could sharpen it.

When Confucius discoursed on the great rulers of yore, he was telling his students stories of how such models comported themselves, what virtue or union with the Way looked like in their lives. When he passed judgment on given attitudes, praising some and condemning others, he was driving home lessons in how the mature human being, the person apt for influence in human affairs, would react to given situations, what he would feel and what he would not. Feelings, as well as judgments, figure in the Master's teaching. Becoming a disciple of the Way was more than a notional business, called for more than clear and distinct ideas. *Jen* was a matter of the heart, even more than a matter of the head. What were the treasures upon which the gentleman set his heart? For what would he die, and for what would he live?

To know the answers to these questions, one had to sense why *li* was important, what it could and could not accomplish. Herbert Fingarette has written a marvelous little study of Confucius focused on what *li* could accomplish. The following lines suggest the gist of his study:

Confucius saw, and tried to call to our attention, that the truly, distinctively human powers have, characteristically, a magical quality. His task, therefore, required, in effect, that he reveal what is already so familiar and universal as to be unnoticed. What is necessary in such cases is that one come upon this "obvious" dimension of our existence in a new way, in the right way. Where can one find such a new path to this familiar area, one which provides a new and revealing perspective? Confucius found the path: we go by way of the notion of *li*.

One has to labor long and hard to learn *li*. The word in its root meaning is close to "holy ritual," "sacred ceremony." Characteristic of Confucius's teaching is the use of the language and imagery of *li* as a medium within which to talk about the entire body of the *mores*, or more precisely, of the authentic tradition and reasonable conventions of society. Confucius taught that the ability to act according to *li* and the will to submit to *li* are essential to that perfect and perfectly human virtue or power which can be man's [the human being's]. Confucius thus does two things here: he calls our attention to the entire body of tradition and convention, and he calls upon us to see all this by means of a metaphor, through the imagery of sacred ceremony, holy rite.[5]

Fingarette's thesis is that Confucius sacralized the secular. That is to say, Fingarette sees Confucius as having found the ordinary, the workaday, the this-worldly to have a magical, holy potential. When human beings were fully human, they seemed extraordinary. If they worked, conversed, cooperated with one another as they could at their best, they seemed more than human. Human beings were the peculiar species that could be less or more than what they were, if one estimated their being by how they usually appeared or performed. Biblical thought has worked in this area, on this problem, with the concept of sin, both original and personal. For biblical thought such as St. Paul's, the good that we would do we do not, and the evil that we would not do, don't want to do, we do. This raises profound questions about who and what we are, why we cannot command our own selves.

Confucius had no story of a fall from paradise, did not think in terms of original sin and heavenly salvation by grace. He thought that human beings could become truly human, could actualize their potential, if they submitted to the disciplines of *li*. Let men and women act as tradition counseled, forget and sacrifice themselves as the long-hallowed precepts proposed, and over time they would become more and more virtuous. One day, they might actually be human, no longer simulacra of humanity, animals able to laugh and talk, but truly rational people, men and women dominated by the Way, rooted by the Way in *jen*.

It is instructive to think about *li* as Fingarette proposes. It is stimulating to look at Confucius as a person who worked from the outside in, confident that if one submitted to discipline one's mind and heart would change. Apparently this was the Master's biographical experience. Apparently he only felt free, fully human, after a lifetime's submission to the disciplines of the Way. Some rabbis have thought similarly about Torah. To their mind, it is more important to do what the religious Law, the Word of God, commands than to understand it, or even to believe in it. Some Christian masters of prayer have spoken analogously: Bless yourself with holy water, genuflect, compose yourself in prayer. Be faithful to the ceremonies of the liturgical year: show up and act as the rubrics specify. Then you will start to understand. First you must believe, by submitting yourself to the tradition, the discipline. Second will come understanding, insight, the wonderful realization that the Way is not false, the ancients have not misled you.

Confucius was concerned with more than the letter of ritual instructions or conventions for social interactions. The accusation of his enemies was that he cared only for the outer shell, but this was a caricature. Inasmuch as he revered *li*, he gave its due to the great significance of social pressure, social milieu, what "they" are saying and doing. Most people follow the herd, are not strong enough to decide for themselves or live according to their own lights. It is crucial, therefore, to make the ways of the herd healthy, right, conducive to growth in genuine humanity. It is crucial to educate people in sound morals and mores. If people grow up in a healthy atmosphere; if the assumptions of the many, the crowd, are decent; then the majority will grow up straight and honest. If mores, accepted values and etiquette, are not healthy only the rare, extremely strong people will turn out well.

When the Master discoursed on goodness (*jen*), he gave the lie to all extrinsic interpretations that made him merely a formalist, a teacher content that his pupils observe the expected etiquette. Some sayings from Chapter Four of the *Analects* make his position plain:

> The Master said, It is Goodness that gives to a neighbourhood its beauty. One who is free to choose, yet does not prefer to dwell among the Good—how can he be accorded the name of wise. The Master said, Without Goodness a man cannot for long endure adversity, cannot for long enjoy prosperity. The Good Man rests content with Goodness; he that is merely wise pursues Goodness in the belief that it pays to do so. Of the adage "Only a Good Man knows how to like people, knows how to dislike them," the Master said, He whose heart is in the smallest degree set upon Goodness will dislike no one (IV:1-4).[6]

The inmost heart of good social bearing is a desire for goodness. Some translators even render *jen* as "love." *Li* without goodness or love would be sterile. *Jen* without *li* would have little social body, little way to animate relations among people and humanize them. The person set upon goodness dislikes no one because he or she perceives the humanity of other people. *Jen* is a fellow-feeling, a sympathy in the root sense of a "suffering with" other people. Confucius's greatest disciple, Mencius, gives the example of a child crawling toward a well. It is instinctive for human beings to look out for the child, rush to keep it from falling in. The child is not separate from any adult observer with even a grain of humanity or maturity. It does not matter that we do not know the child's name or to whom it belongs. For a moment it is our child, any and everyone's, because we are bound to it by a common flesh. Not to rush to save the child would be monstrous, shockingly inhuman. Mencius thought that political science ought to build on such fellow-feeling. In his view, the way to govern a state was to activate people's intuitive sense that they shared a common nature, a common destiny.

Confucian social theory, then, is well worth pondering. What do our daily rituals mean? When we shake hands, on meeting, what are we symbolizing? Does the physical contact express a spiritual accord, or are we merely fulfilling an empty form? Suppose we were to take the symbolism seriously, to think about the power of locked hands, bonded beings? Where would such thoughts lead us? How would we have to vary such thoughts if men preferred to kiss one another? How do our adults greet children? How do children greet one another? What do we say if we have no good rituals for children's greetings? What do the bows of other cultures suggest in this context? Social theory ought to rise from a close study of ordinary rituals. What is possible among human beings ought to become clear from our lived expressions of *li* and *jen*.

Confucius's Teaching about Self

It follows from this concern with ritual and goodness that Confucius thought of the individual human being as part of larger social entities. The individual was crucial, inasmuch as he or she was the building block of such larger units. But the larger units formed the individual. If the traditional wisdoms about proper order in the household, the state, between masters and pupils, between men and women did not guide the individual's upbringing, social chaos would result. Equally, individual human beings would be miserable. Confucius thought that traditional wisdom, the Way long handed down, was objective. One could not ignore it or violate it without causing great suffering.

When we consider some of the specific traditions into which the Master wanted parents to insert their children, we realize the limits of the Chinese system. For example, women were inferior to men. Not only were women supposed to follow the lead of men, obeying their fathers, husbands, and even (in old age) eldest sons, they were in the Master's eyes less human than men. The main function of women was to keep the race going. Certainly, it was good to find affection between men and women. Certainly, children were supposed to love their mothers as well as their fathers, obey their mothers as well as their fathers, grieve at their mother's funeral. But the natural order of things, as Confucius saw it, made females secondary to males. Along with this judgment went typically patriarchal opinions about the nature of women: emotional, irrational, unfit for higher learning and political rule. Chinese women were vulnerable to physical and emotional abuse by men. Confucius was no supporter of such abuse, but he thought that women came under the control and discipline of men, so he gave women no basic equality with men—no natural rights to treatment as men's equals.

Even more important than this male supremacism was the status that Confucius gave to the elderly. Elders were more important than juniors. The worst domestic sins were failures to obey and honor one's parents. The greatest offense was to bring shame upon those who had given one life. The assumption was that wisdom only came through experience. Those who had lived longest would be wisest. Of course, the Master had eyes in his head and could see that many people grew old without becoming wise. But he thought that reverence for the elderly was a good general rule. In the same way, he thought that the traditions handed down by the ancients were the best traditions, because they had best passed the tests of time.

The most revolutionary possibility that Confucius held out to the individual was that learning the tradition, becoming a master of the Way of the ancients, could gain one a special status. One could become a "gentleman," a fully mature human being. This was a rare achievement and status, but it carried its own reward. To know from the inside, from the core of one's own self, that the Way was beautiful and true was the best of rewards. Ideally society at large would recognize people who had gained such knowledge. Ideally, such people would become the most influential teachers and advisers, if not the actual rulers of the state. But even if society at large paid the gentleman little heed, he could be content. His wisdom and virtue were their own reward. The flourishing of his being was more important, and more satisfying, than any external honors.

Though Confucius did not elaborate all its implications, this radical option for a life of learning the ways of the Way had the potential to challenge the otherwise almost brutally hierarchical character of the Confucian worldview. Let a peasant gain great learning and he would be free of most of the burdens of class, wealth, status. The same for a woman. In principle, a woman learned in the traditions of the ancients would have considerable leverage against male chauvinism. In practice, few peasants or women got the opportunity to study. Confucius himself accepted no girls as pupils, and while he had no aversion to poor students, most of his pupils seem to have come from the middle classes. Nonetheless, by the very fact that he himself had never gained much political power (or even, during his lifetime, widespread recognition for his virtues), the Master was driven to make the real definition of human success independent of wealth, status, political power, or the other forms of recognition that society could bestow. He even had to make it independent of the judgments of one's parents and elders. Much as such judgments demanded attention and obedience, they could not substitute, in the core of the individual, for adherence to the Way.

So we find, in even the most formalistic aspects of Confucian teaching, what the student of religion finds wherever human beings intuit that something transcending human affairs is their only valid norm or judge. We find a blessed freedom from social conventions, even though the Master wanted *li* to be the great educator of the people at large. The mature individual does what he or she does because the Way requires it. What Western religionists might call the Word of God echoes in the Confucian reverence for the Way of the Ancients.

In the crunch, the gentleman has to follow his conscience. It would be better to die than to give up one's honor, prostitute one's soul. The Master did not follow through and deal with the rights this principle can bestow on children over against their parents, women over against men, subordinates over against superiors. But it lies at the center of his thought, at the heart of his psychology. The Way that he lays before an eager student of promise is a Way to freedom. When one has gained self-control, knowledge of the wisdom of the Ancients, a connatural understanding of what virtue requires in given situations and why *jen* and *li* are the great treasures of the mature personality, nothing external can tyrannize one's spirit. The end of Confucian wisdom is a liberation from even the authority of the figures that the Confucian system thought crucial for social order: elders and men. Certainly, the mature Confucian would balance any idiosyncratic tendencies that special insight into the Way might generate with the requirements of social order—the duties of being a good son or daughter, a good citizen or employee. But none of these duties could substitute for a personal appropriation of the Way, and with a personal appropriation of the Way came a blessed indifference to the judgments of other people, a blessed freedom to be oneself under the eye of a power more than merely human.

Confucius's Teaching about Divinity

Is it stretching the evidence to find in the *Analects* a power more than merely human? Many commentators, impressed by the humanism of Confucius, have interpreted his philosophy as naturalistic. Not for him, they have said, any dalliance with the supernatural. The proper business of the gentleman, in their view of his view, was human affairs. It was hard enough to conceive how human beings ought to treat one another and structure their social dealings. To dabble in how divinity ran the world would have been to go afield from human competence and so misstep tragically. It would have been a case of the best becoming the enemy of the better, or even an enemy of the good.

Many texts support this prejudice in Confucius. On the whole, he did not concern himself with what we might call theology. In good measure, that was because the "theologians" of his day were shamans, diviners, or priests concerned with public sacrifices. Their interpretation of long-standing Chinese tradition gave a view of divinity in which local spirits held pride of place. Confucius could appreciate the need many human beings felt to contact a local spirit and draw it to their side. He knew how helpless fate could make small men and women feel. But his own interest lay in the intersection of the Way of the ancients with the workings of the natural and human worlds. His own sense of divinity or God was muted by an appreciation of how little we can say about the nature or doings of what transcends human understanding, what is wise or good in transhuman ways.

Nonetheless, there is a singular text in which Confucius makes it clear that he was no secularist. He did not agree with those who thought that common sense required people to pay no heed to what "Heaven" supposedly thought or required and concentrate on practical affairs. The Master's appreciation of human existence went much deeper than what secularists or pragmatists usually perceive. Thus, in *Analects* 3:13 we find the following exchange:

Wang-sun Chia asked about the meaning of the saying, "Better pay court to the stove than pay court to the shrine." The Master said, It is not true.

He who puts himself in the wrong with Heaven has no means of expiation left.[7]

The stove is household affairs, practical matters, business as usual—what gives warmth to one's family, puts food on the table. The shrine is where people deal with the holy, the uncanny, the more-than-practical. The saying could have a benign form: attend to what you can control, and don't worry about what you cannot control. But the Master rejects this benign form, probably because he sensed a great danger in allowing any pupil to think that Heaven had no place in realistic thinking. If we neglect the shrine, pay no attention to what lies outside practical human affairs, we have no recourse, no higher viewpoint or greater power that might keep our lives from seeming absurd. The hidden premise in the exchange is that practical affairs always go awry. Every life is filled with pains, failures, irrational happenings, bad luck that we cannot explain in purely human terms. The best laid plans of mice and men can come to nought, and with them the easy optimism of the busy secularist. What can secular people do, when naked evil digs in its claws? How can they wail properly, when a child dies, if they have no access to more-than-human perspectives? These are the intuitions lying behind the Master's crisp rejection of the saying that Wang-sung Chia brought to him.

Let us attend, though, to the exact words that our translator puts in Confucius's mouth. The saying is not true. If we put ourselves in the wrong with Heaven, we have no means of expiation. Evidently, "the shrine" calls to the Master's mind the great Overlord of traditional Chinese culture. "Heaven" was the nearest thing to a sovereign God in the pre-Confucian era. On the whole, it was an impersonal force, but one could offer prayers and sacrifices to it. Indeed, the Emperor sacrificed to Heaven regularly, thinking that such sacrifice was the ultimate source of any prosperity that the realm enjoyed. Confucius seems to assume that paying court to the stove, rather than to the shrine, would put one in the wrong with Heaven. This makes it clear that, in his view, the saying was antireligious—not simply benign, but a push to make human affairs the measure of human significance.

Plato rejected this equation: the human cannot be the measure, without distorting all realism. Only the divine can be the measure. The human has to fit itself to the divine. For the human to ignore the divine, or try to fit the divine to itself, is a great perversion. Such an ignorance can be speculative or practical. Heavy thinkers can propose that there is no divine, or that the divine is only a projection of human needs and hopes, and so can conclude that there is nothing but the human (or, perhaps, the natural) to serve as the measure of reality. Ordinary people can get lost in their daily affairs and so become practical atheists: people who ignore the divine, for all intents and purposes.

Either way, to ignore the divine is madness, because (for Plato and Confucius) the divine is utterly real. We cannot have the world that we have without its sacred source. The sacred is as much a datum of experience as the bread that satisfies bodily hunger. The soul hungers for the sacred, the really real, the meaning that will not let it down. For the human being to deny the sacred, the divine, is to starve the soul, denature the self.

This is our unpacking of what Confucius says, and it is vulnerable. Plato is much more explicit about the limits of any human measures than Confucius is. But the logic of the Master's brief response seems to run to the conclusion that Plato reached. The logic seems to be that Heaven is a norm, a measure, a reality, a recourse that we ignore on peril of disfiguring our very selves, denying our actual situations. The further thought, that it is important to keep means of expiation, takes us in the direction of moral failures. We only need to expiate what we have done badly. We only have to do penance, make amends, when we have sinned. The profound possibility in Confucius's second sentence is that he realizes that paying (excessive) court to the stove is sinful— something that demands expiation. Alternatively, the Master may be saying that we human beings always have on our consciences things begging expiation, and that unless we pay court to the shrine we have no means of relieving our guilt. Either way, the intriguing thing is that Confucius will not let human affairs be the moral measure. Only Heaven can handle the resolution, the adjudication, of our moral failings. Only Heaven can grant us forgiveness.

This is a small yet telltale chink in the formalistic armor of Confucian thought. Generally, the Master implies that *li* is adequate to the task of smoothing human affairs, directing human actions and affections to the common good. Here we find the possibility that the depths of human need, both social and personal, fall outside the ministrations of *li*. For forgiveness, we need something more than traditional, something directly engaging the source of moral integrity. Certainly, human beings have to forgive one another, and social codes have to provide forms for forgiveness: apologies, and their gracious acceptance; expressions of regret, and the counter-expressions that spread the blame, acknowledging that most blowups are a two-way street. But below this level of forgiveness lies a deeper one.

In the depths of conscience, human beings can feel that they have offended something cosmic, or that they can never muster the honesty, the goodness, the purity that they wish they had—that they know would characterize them if they were fully human. At this deeper level, a Heaven or God has to offer forgiveness, encouragement, the chance for new beginnings. Something more than human has to whisper that it's inevitable that human beings fail, because they are not the measure, cannot be the ultimate in meaning or goodness. By paying court to the shrine, we give such feelings and needs fitting expression. We bow before what we do not understand, what we shall never be able to please, and ask that it be merciful as well as just, loving as well as honest and powerful.

In this text the Master is hinting that the gentleman, even more than the ordinary person, feels the need to worship what is his moral better. Asking for expiation is merely the first step on the road to venerating what never needs expiation, what is purely and simply holy. If we pay court to the shrine in the proper way, with the proper consistency, we can realize that Heaven is truly the guardian of our humanity. Without Heaven we would have no recourse when our humanity broke down, failed to perform, and so threatened to dump us into bogs of chaos, quicksands of absurdity.

Confucianism after Confucius

Confucius apparently was the most revered teacher of his own time, but it took generations before his teachings gained canonical, even scriptural status. The *Analects* already reflect considerable editing, so we may regard them as indicating the concerns that Master and pupils studied. The three major topics were *jen*, the character of the gentleman or sage (*chun-tzu*), and the keys to good government. What the Master thought most important, and what his students most wanted to learn, focused on these three topics. Next came questions of propriety in ritual and social affairs, as well as questions of filial piety. Texts from the second generation of students—those who did not know the Master in the flesh but studied with one or more of the seventy or so pupils he had considered talented—show the beginnings of a movement to standardize or codify the Master's teachings. For example, *The Great Learning*, originally part of *The Book of Rites*, organizes the Master's thought into eight steps: how to investigate a problem, extend one's knowledge, make the will sincere, rectify the mind, cultivate the full person, regulate the family, order the state, and bring peace to the world.[8]

Here the obvious bias is that reform starts with the individual. Let the individual of talent grow into right order, and he (or she) can reset relations in the family, the state, and perhaps the entire world. The beginning of personal development is learning how to learn: rousing curiosity and disciplining it. This will lead to the broadening of intellectual horizons. However, Confucianism is interested in more than factual or speculative knowledge. It aims at transforming the entire personality, so it includes training for the will. The result of intellectual and moral formation should be a "rectified" mind: one solidly planted in realism and virtue. With a rectified mind, the entire personality can expand, grow, be cultivated like a rich, well-cared for garden.

Another text that entered the canonical list of Confucian classics and eventually was attributed to the Master was the *Doctrine of the Mean*. In this text we find Confucius's moderation extended to include not just how human beings think and act but even how nature itself operates. Balance or harmony becomes the crucial virtue, and Confucians are urged to gain an equilibrium of mind, will, and appreciation of nature. The text suggests that superior people, well trained and well disciplined, can gain access to the secrets of nature and so live in harmony with it. The ultimate Way of nature exceeds any human being's understanding, but pursuing virtue and knowledge places people in a position to intuit what limited beings can of the ultimate patterns by which the world runs.

The two most influential disciples of Confucius, Mencius and Hsun-tzu, lived more than a century after the Master's death. In their work we find the tradition interpreted creatively. From their labors came the themes that ruled later Confucian thought: the singular status of the Master (eventually he was deified); the belief that all people have the capacity to become "gentlemen;" the centrality of humaneness and moral probity; the importance of education, right terminology (the "rectification of names," as a guide to clear thinking), and benign rule (light taxes and punishments, a distaste for war). They also agreed that society ran best when people observed distinctions between elders and juniors, men and women, higher and lower classes.

Mencius believed that human nature is good in its foundations. The reason that individuals, and groups, go wrong is that they refuse to cultivate their basic nature. Education is the main way to cultivate human nature, and learning is more than intellectual. People have to work hard to gain the knowledge of what they ought to think and do, but they have also to practice this knowledge. Thus, Mencius stressed what we might call the formation of character. The most important imprint of an education is the way that it forms people's morality, their values. Students can only learn values by absorbing the overall example of their virtuous teachers. Learning is an apprenticeship in maturity and wisdom. The student who only heard the master's words and never took to heart the master's example would emerge half-baked.

Hsun-tzu thought very differently about human nature. Although Mencius did not know of him, he (about eighty years younger) learned of Mencius's teachings and attacked them. For Hsun-tzu, human nature is initially, basically, corrupt. The desires that naturally come to mind are evil, and so they must be restrained. Lust and envy threaten to corrupt both the individual and the community. Restraint and disci-pline therefore become the watchwords for the individual, while strong laws become the recipe for good public order. The function of education is to produce disciplined individuals who will stay on top of their untoward desires. The function of the rites is to civilize the people at large—form them in the attitudes of reverence and obedience necessary for social coherence, good order, and peace.

Each interpreter could claim a solid footing in texts attributed to Confucius himself. The Master had not committed himself so decisively on the question of human nature that either interpretation was obvious. Mencius has gained more honors from idealistic Confucians, while Hsun-tzu has been more congenial to rulers seeking an ideology to govern their realms. The legalists, as the followers of Hsun-tzu are sometimes called, had more influence in government. Indeed, about a hundred years into the Han Dynasty (206 B.C.–A.D. 220) Confucianism of the legalistic sort became the official doctrine sanctioned by the state. From that time Confucianism had more influence at court than either Taoism or Buddhism, though the latter enjoyed periods of ascendancy. Confucius entered the list of deities for whom there was to be an official cult, and Confucian scholars gained an aura of almost magical potency.

During the Sung Dynasty (960–1279) a revival so transformed Confucianism that many commentators speak of Neo-Confucianism dominating the next thousand years of Chinese culture. The beginnings of this movement lay with teachers who insisted on going back to the classical texts and stressed the primacy of the ethical life. Their goal was the formation of character, as education had been in the time of Mencius and, they believed, the time of Confucius himself. Numerous other renovators followed suit, until Chu Hsi (1130–1200) produced what is usually considered the greatest synthesis of Neo-Confucian thought.

In Chu Hsi we find a response for the influence of Buddhism, which had introduced cosmological speculation, meditation for individual development, and special concern with death. He battled the Taoists, working out a view of the Great Ultimate that was different from their interpretation (which was largely negative: nonbeing, nothingness). In addition to his construction of an impressive Confucian metaphysics, Chu Hsi left the impression that Confucius himself was the great font at which Chinese culture ought constantly to renew itself.

In summing up the influence of Chu Hsi, Wing-Tsit Chan, one of the foremost modern interpreters of Chinese philosophy, has stated:

> Chu Hsi's impact on philosophy, education, and state ideology is unparalleled in Chinese history. Apart from the nine years he served as a local government official and his forty-six days as lecturer to the emperor on the classics, Chu Hsi spent virtually his entire life as a teacher. In 1190 he published the Analects, The Great Learning, the Doctrine of the Mean, and the Meng-tzu [Mencius] in a collection he termed the Four Books. From 1313 until 1912 the Four Books and Chu's own commentaries were used as the required texts for public education and as the basis for the questions on the civil service examinations. Chu Hsi compiled the Four Books and wrote the commentaries both to emphasize his concern with daily moral and social affairs and to build a new Confucian orthodoxy. He established an orthodox line of transmission . . . that began with the ancient sages, continued through Confucius and Meng-tzu, and then, after a lapse of several hundred years, resumed with the Sung Neo-Confucians. . . . More than once he hinted that he himself was in the direct line of transmissions, and indeed, the line of transmission from Confucius to Chu Hsi was accepted in China, Korea, and Japan.[9]

With the rise of Maoism in the twentieth century, Confucianism fell into disfavor. Confucius was associated with everything backward, unprogressive, feudal. However, despite their efforts to inculcate a new ideology, the recent rulers of China have not eradicated the basic cast of character imparted by centuries of Confucian influence. Indeed, they have played on this character, and exhibited it themselves, though how calculatedly has been a matter of debate. China remains a highly bureaucratized country, with great sensitivity to classes, ranks, procedures. Children remain greatly indebted to their parents and elder siblings. Even veneration of deceased ancestors continues. So deeply did Confucianism identify itself with the immemorial Chinese ways, and so successfully did its proponents present it as the most accurate and effective expression of native Chinese tendencies, that it remains crucial to understanding East Asian cultures to the present day.[10] For example, one of the best explanations for the high academic achievement of Asian-Americans is their Confucian concern to bring honor to their parents and improve their character (which can include their habits of study and dedication to learning).

Confucian Spirituality

Confucian spirituality is more humanistic than religious. The examination of Confucian attitudes toward the shrine showed us that the Master set definite limits to the adequacy of humanistic (in the sense of secular, this-worldly) judgments about the ultimate nature of existence, but the preponderance of statements by both the Master and his followers deals with human affairs. Heavenly, transcendent matters are peripheral to the greatest interests of mainstream Confucianism.

The spirituality created by this humanism can be seen in a recent essay by Tu Wei-ming, a leading contemporary Confucian scholar. Tu speaks of ultimate meaning in the following terms:

> The living person, in the Confucian order of things, is far more complex and meaningful than a mere momentary existence. The idea of an isolated individual who eventually dies a lonely death in the secularized biophysiological sense is not even a rejected possibility in the Confucian perception of human reality. A human being is an active participant of an agelong biological line, a living witness of an historical continuum and a recipient of the finest essences of the cosmos. Inherent in the structure of the human is an infinite potential for growth and an inexhaustible supply of resources for development. Ontologically a person's selfhood embodies the highest transcendence within its own reality; no external help is needed for the self to be fully realized. The realization of the self, in the ultimate sense, is tantamount to the realization of the complete unity between humanity and Heaven. The way to attain this, however, is never perceived as the establishment of a relationship between an isolated individual and God. The self as a center of relationships in the human community must recognize that it is an integral part of a holistic presence and accordingly work its way through what is near at hand. Mencius, in a suggestive passage [7A:4] observes: "All the ten thousand things are there in me. There is no greater joy for me than to find, on self-examination, that I am true to myself. Try your best to treat

others as you wish to be treated yourself, and you will find that this is the shortest way to humanity."[11]

In the next section we shall enter friendly criticisms of Confucian spirituality. Here let us put the best face on this interpretation of how Confucius and his tradition have told people to live. The first point to note is the attack on modern, individualistic views. The human being is not isolated from the biological or historical processes of evolution. We misrepresent the state of the human being if we fail to give lineage and connection to other living creatures their due. For Tu, the Confucian tradition has had no awareness of a secularized world, no sympathy for the modern Western vision of an individual standing against a flat, factitious biosphere. The implication is that Confucian spirituality has retained the Master's sense that nature is a congenial, instructive ambience for human development. The assumption is that human beings ought to tie their personal significance into the long line of natural and familial events that have not simply preceded them but have conspired to produce them. If they accept such implications and assumptions, individuals can look upon their lives as contributions to the future state of the cosmos and their lineage. They will become ancestors, and wise successors will view their lives as part of the prior history that constituted such successors' own present reality.

The second accent in Tu's view of how the individual ought to construe the ultimate reality of the human condition is what an Aristotelian might call "synthetic." The human being draws together and holds in itself the different orders of being. It is a crossroads or epitome of the inanimate, animate, and spiritual realms. To say that the human being is the recipient of the finest essences of the cosmos is to speak opaquely, but the most insightful explanation of this claim makes the world anthropocentric. Even though the Master retained the ancient sense that nature is much greater than humanity, his perceptions of how human intelligence grasps the order of the cosmos and the state pointed in the direction of making the realized human being the center of the universe. Inasmuch as reason came to expression in human beings, human beings were the place where the significance of the natural and social worlds could be found.

This sense of reason, spirituality able to raise the human being above the natural flux, grounds Tu's further claim that we have an infinite potential for development. What is infinite about the human being clearly is not its temporal span. All human beings are mortal and so finite through and through. But the human spirit can range beyond mortality, can escape from time. We see this when we watch human reason travel back in time, to write the history of people and ages that perished long before the specific writer came into being. We also see this when we watch astronomers map the heavens, theologians speculate about the existence of God (an infinite, unlimited existence). There is no stopping human creativity, because human spirituality is more powerful than human materiality. However much our bodies limit our brains and souls, our brains and souls can defeat our bodies on occasion, knowing things that seem to be imperishable.

The claim that human selfhood embodies the highest levels of being, is the greatest transcendence in reality, is bold indeed, and at this point Tu may be speaking for himself more than the Confucius of the *Analects*. It is far from clear that the Master's view of Heaven made it merely a function of human insight or spirituality. Heaven, like the Way of the ancients that ran nature as well as properly ordered human affairs, stands in the *Analects* as something beyond the control of human beings. That alone forces us to question any claim that human existence is the highest level of being in creation. Whether or not the human self can be fully realized through its own efforts depends on this questionable claim. If Heaven is not necessary for expiation, or existence, or proper order, or the explanation of reality, then the "place" to which human beings can move by themselves may be the farthest reach of existence and reason. If Heaven is necessary, then such a claim for human nature is fallacious.

On the other hand, Tu may merely be saying that it lies within the power of human beings, in virtue of their reason or spirituality, to sense what is beyond them ("Heaven" or the "Way"), and so that moving toward the highest viewpoint, that which most transcends the limitations of the natural world and human materiality, is not a supernatural act. It develops within the very makeup of the human being and so can seem to be its most distinctive achievement. Still, to speak of a complete unity between humanity and Heaven is to risk collapsing Heaven into human limitation. Unless Heaven transcends human limitation, it is not Heaven but earth—not the realm that gives humanity its measures but the realm that human beings themselves measure.

Tu's final thoughts, rejecting an individualistic interpretation of relations with God, remind us of the social orientation of human selfhood in the Confucian scheme of things. Always, the individual is a tissue of relationships. The primary relationships defining the self are familial, but relations with nature, the state, and groups apart from the family are also important. The implication of Tu's sense of holism may be that whatever relations human beings have with truly ultimate reality are corporate rather than individualistic. For him Confucianism would think of relations with the divine as matters for an entire family, or perhaps even the entire human community, to construe. Whether this does justice to the independence of the individual from social relations (the ways that social relations never define the self completely) is a difficult question. Probably it does not. For Western analysts, certainly, individuals have rights and duties before God that are as important as the rights and duties of their communities.

The advice to work one's way more deeply into the holistic presence of ultimate reality through attention to what is near at hand can be attractive. If such advice does not lower the ceiling of human potential to what is here and now in the sense of ephemeral, merely passing, it can encourage people to be utterly realistic about their spiritual commitments. In this vein, the Confucian argument or conviction would be that we only grasp what we can of ultimate significance by responding to the situation in which we find ourselves at a given moment. We should not construe Heaven or God as far away, apart from or even opposed to what is required of us at work, at home, in a friendship or even an antagonism currently absorbing us. The quotation from Mencius restates Confucius's own golden rule. Where the Master said that we should not treat others as we ourselves do not wish to be treated, Mencius urges us to treat others as we ourselves wish to be treated. Indeed, he says that this is the shortcut to realization as a mature human being. The first sentences in the quotation allow us to conjecture that being true to oneself (knowing where one stands in reality and acting upon this knowledge) would include fulfilling the golden rule. Everything that we know, of which we can be aware, lies in ourselves. Whether reality is more than the ten thousand things (a traditional figure for the totality of creatures) is another question, bound to be answered affirmatively by those who make Heaven something independent of human being. But that reality-for-us is only the ten thousand things is beyond dispute. There is no reality-for-us of which we are not aware. Only when we become aware of a reality beyond what we previously knew, and so not-for-us in significant ways, can we say that we do not possess the entirety of reality.

The upshot of this view of Confucian spirituality is a counsel to cultivate the self, though not in narcissistic ways. For the Confucians who would consider Tu accurate and authoritative, we can find the keys to realism, maturation, happiness, and success by studying human nature, in the first place as it occurs in ourselves. If we let our study expand as it presses to do, we can find that it reaches out to other people, the natural world, and the transcendent dimensions that Confucius suggested by "Heaven." This can then beckon as a lifelong pursuit of learning, in which what we learn is not so much facts as deeper appreciations of what it means to be human and what is required for full maturation. Thus, Confucian spirituality reveals itself to be a quest for wisdom, perhaps distinctive for its insistence on the social, holistic character of human existence. The self that moves forward is not alone, and the greater the progress it makes, the less alone it finds itself to be.

Friendly Criticisms

Obviously, there is in Confucian spirituality an immense amount to respect, cherish, and take to heart. When it comes to articulating the importance of tradition, social relations, rituals through which to socialize people toward maturity, the program that the Master established has few peers. Here, however, we come not to praise Confucius but to ask where his program is inadequate. With such a purpose in mind, several limitations seem clear.

First, the Confucian tradition has made little provision for the equality of women with men. At many points it has been misogynistic, and at no points has it gone out of its way to invite women to contribute

their distinctive gifts and shape Chinese culture toward the rich bisex-
uality latent in human potential. Second, Confucian spirituality has
been mute about transcendent divinity. If the differentiation of divinity
from nature, society, and the self represents a crucial advance in humanity's clarification of objective reality, then Confucian spirituality
remains backward in a significant regard. This is a serious charge, and
naturally Confucian spirituality has much to say in self-defense.

Whether we should differentiate divinity in the ways that the monotheistic traditions have done is a central question. Granted both the
difficulty of thinking clearly about a transcendent deity and the dangers of detaching such a deity from human experience of nature,
society, and the self, dialogue between Confucians and theists ought to
flow back and forth, with Confucians teaching as well as learning. Still,
because many contours of human existence only gain proper clarity
when one honors an Absolute not identifiable with the cosmos, or the
state, or the self, the lack of an adequate theology cripples Confucian
speculation about nature, political science, and human psychology at
many points. Inasmuch as without such a theology it is not clear why
people should sacrifice their lives for what is right—transcendently
beautiful or binding in conscience—Confucian spirituality is not so
persuasive to the outside world as it might be. Only those formed by
the Chinese or East Asian ethos are likely to find Confucian spirituality
intellectually adequate on matters of ultimate significance.

A third focus for criticism is the Confucian view of the self, inasmuch as that view is opposed to individualism. This is a complicated
question, and one bound up with the prior question of an adequate
theology. Many critics of contemporary Western cultures fault them as
being so individualistic that no commonweal is possible. In this context, Confucianism has much to teach the West. Some of such teaching
could be a reminder of Western ideals recently set aside, but another
part could be distinctively non-Western, rooted in the feelings about
nature and family life that have nourished China for millennia.

The question of an adequate understanding of the self reminds us of
the virtues that Confucians have tried to cultivate, and of the great
interest in developing mature selves that we find in the work of the
Master. To say that Confucian spirituality may not do the individual
justice is not to say that Confucians have not expended much energy on

the question of a mature, realized self. Again and again we find Confucius and Mencius concerned with analyzing the conditions, requirements, and constituent parts of human maturity. Again and again we sense that they realize how the process of maturation brings the individual face to face with the Way of the ancients, securing his (or her) distinctiveness.

On the other hand, it is hard to feel that the Confucian individual has rights equal to his or her duties toward the collectivity. It is hard, for example, to feel that the son or daughter stands on a level footing with the father or mother. Certainly, there will always be ways in which children should not be considered the equals of their parents, but there are other ways in which the rights of children should count for as much as their parents' wishes. One good example is the traditional arrangements for marriage. In the agelong Confucian scheme, marriage was arranged by one's parents. One's personal preferences as son or daughter were secondary. This is not to say that no Chinese married for love, but it is to say that the going ethos made love or other bases of personal preference peripheral to the will of one's parents. Ties between the families involved were the main consideration, along with concern to raise up another generation to carry on the family line and venerate the ancestors.

Inasmuch as modernity has spotlighted the rights of individuals to determine their own lives and make for themselves the judgments about love and faith crucial to human happiness, modern people are bound to consider Confucian spirituality suspect, perhaps even vicious. A wonderful debate lies in this opposition between traditional preferences for the good of the group and modern preferences for the freedom of the individual. Both sides have strong points to score. Only if ultimate reality individualizes human beings so that they are more basic sensoria of divinity than are the families and other groups to which they belong can the modern position claim victory. So how ultimate reality does in fact shape human beings, what mystical identification with the Way or God does in fact do to individuals and groups, becomes a capital issue.

The reality in the lives of the saints, Asian and Western alike, seems to be that they emerge from their peak experiences beautifully balanced. On the whole, they are willing to sacrifice themselves for the common good, but this willingness is no abdication of their rights or responsibilities as individuals. They feel free to oppose the group, when what it asks seems improper, let alone immoral, and they keep in their own hands the ultimate disposition of their free selves. However much they become servants and benefactors of other people, they retain a healthy independence. Inasmuch as Confucianism, like other spiritual traditions, has not always stood up for the rights of the individual (especially the individual who was female, or junior, or poor, or ordinary) and trimmed the rights of the community threatening to overwhelm the individual, Confucian spirituality now stands vulnerable to much proper criticism.

NOTES

1. See Laurence G. Thompson, *Chinese Religion: An Introduction*, 4th ed. (Belmont, CA: Wadsworth, 1989), pp. 3–35.
2. *Analects*, 2:4; in D. C. Lau, trans., *Confucius: The Analects* (New York: Penguin, 1979), p. 63.
3. Ibid., p. 72.
4. Ezra Pound, *Confucius* (New York: New Directions, 1969), p. 227.
5. Herbert Fingarette, *Confucius: The Secular as Sacred* (New York: Harper & Row, 1972), pp. 6–7.
6. Arthur Waley, trans., *The Analects of Confucius* (New York: Vintage, n.d. [orig. 1938]), p. 102.
7. Ibid., p. 97.
8. See Wing-Tsit Chan, "Confucian Thought: Foundations of the Tradition," in *The Encyclopedia of Religion*, ed. Mircea Eliade (New York: Macmillan, 1987), vol. 4, p. 19.
9. Wing-Tsit Chan, "Neo-Confucianism," ibid., p. 29.
10. See *Daedalus*, vol. 120, no. 2 (Spring, 1991), for essays on the current meaning of Chinese culture and tradition.
11. Tu Wei-Ming, "The Confucian Tradition: A Confucian Perspective on Learning to Be Human," in *The World's Religious Traditions*, ed. Frank Whaling (New York: Crossroad, 1986), p. 66.

CHAPTER 4

JESUS

Jewish Religion Before Jesus

The history of biblical Israel is hinted at in the three divisions of *Tanak*: the Law, the Prophets, and the Writings. When the Hebrew Bible came into quasi-canonical form, perhaps at the end of the first century A.D., these three groups of writings were enshrined as revelation. They contained texts accredited by the rabbis as trustworthy expressions of what Israel had been and ought to be, under the guidance of its God. We have no completely adequate way of separating a secular history of Israel from the religious convictions of the Hebrew Bible. The documents most important to traditional Jews are permeated by faith. The covenant that made biblical Israel the chosen people of God colored all reflection on how the Jewish people had evolved. What was most important to traditional Jews of Jesus' time was the conviction that the Lord of the Universe was guiding their destiny. As a pious Jew, Jesus grounded his life on this conviction. In this section we review key moments in the history that furnished pious Jews of Jesus' day with their confidence that God had called them to constitute a nation distinctively his own.

Although the Hebrew Bible begins with an account (two accounts, actually) of the creation of the world, the origin of the Jewish people proper begins with the call of Abraham (Genesis 12). Abraham is the monotheist, the professor of faith in a single God responsible for creation, who launches the Israelite people on their fascinating journey. In faith, Abraham accepts not only the existence of a single deity but that deity's promise that he and his wife Sarah will have descendents as numerous as the grains of sand along the seashore. The generations of the founding fathers of Israel (Abraham, Isaac, and Jacob) work out the first chapters in the story that Christians think gained a new direction in Jesus of Nazareth. By the end of Genesis what will be the Jewish people is sojourning in Egypt, under the providence of God that will give them Moses as the leader who mediates to them their historical destiny to live in a special, covenantal relationship with their Creator.

The biblical book of Exodus narrates the rise of Moses to leadership of the Hebrews sojourning in Egypt and their miraculous deliverance from slavery. In the desert to which they have escaped, the people receive the Law of the Covenant that ever-after will specify their relationship to their God. Moses is not only the deliverer of the people from bondage (the instrument of God, who is the real champion) but also the mouthpiece God chose to make known to the people how he wanted them to live. Though secular historians are bound to look upon the prescriptions of the Law (Torah) as largely compilations of tribal traditions, the Bible itself makes God the author. The Law is a code designed to make the people holy and so worthy of intimate contact with their holy God. The books of Leviticus and Numbers are shaped by this sense of the Torah as a code for holiness and the Israelite people as a nation called by God to be his (the biblical God is a patriarch) own holy portion. The book of Deuteronomy reworks the traditions about Moses and the Law, reenforcing the notion that the fate of the people will depend on their fidelity or infidelity.

These first five books of the Hebrew Bible, known as the Torah (Law, Guidance, Holy Teaching) or Pentateuch, are the holiest, most authoritative portion of Jewish scripture. Inasmuch as Abraham and Moses were the key figures in the constitution of the Jewish people, the traditions about them, along with the laws that the people were to observe in order to please God, occupied primacy of place in the Jewish imagination of Jesus' day. Also very important, however, were the writings and visions of the great prophets who succeeded Moses.

Under David, Israel had moved from being a loose confederacy of tribes to a unified Kingdom. Under David's son Solomon, Israel enjoyed a brief period of cultural brilliance. The historical writings sometimes called "The Former Prophets" continue the theme of Deuteromony that Jewish history is a function of fidelity or infidelity to the covenant. Although David was revered as a great religious hero, a favorite of God, the author of the Psalms, and a model penitent (because an all too human, sinful ruler), and Solomon was revered as a paragon of wisdom (the author of several works in the third portion of *Tanak*), the overall history recorded in the Former Prophets is a dismal story of infidelity. The division of the Kingdom into northern and southern portions in 922 B.C., the fall of the northern Kingdom to Assyria in 721 B.C., and the fall of the southern kingdom to Babylon in 597 B.C. all were, in the eyes of the biblical historians, disasters attributable to Israelite infidelity. Most of the kings were wicked, and the major defenders of the rights of God up to the exile to Babylon were charismatic figures known as prophets.

The most important early prophets, Elijah and Elisha, were enshrined in Israelite memory as heroes who kept true faith alive. The greatest literary prophets, Isaiah, Jeremiah, and Ezekiel, profited from the pressures of civil crises and worked out new, purified versions of Israelite faith. In memorable figures they (or the members of their "schools" who contributed to the books now associated with their names) reworked the demands of adherence to the one God, fidelity to the Mosaic covenant. In simplest version, their message was that the two key demands were a pure cult (the eschewing of all worship of foreign, largely natural deities) and social justice: concern for the poor, help for the widow and orphan. We find the words of Isaiah on Jesus' lips at the outset of his mission (See Luke 4:18–19, quoting Isaiah 61:1–2, 58:6), and the example of Jeremiah and Ezekiel must have been vivid in his mind, because they were great predecessors in his task of reforming Israel, to make it fit for the gifts of its holy Lord. The twelve "minor" prophets who fill out the second portion of *Tanak* offered variations on the themes of the need for a pure cult, social justice, and honest living worthy of the holy Lord of the covenant.

The final portion of *Tanak*, known as the Writings, contains disparate materials, among which what is known as "wisdom literature" stands out. Much of this material comes from after the Exile in Babylon, when those who returned reestablished Israel on a theocratic basis. Priests dominated this last period of biblical history, but the rather dour speculation of writings concerned with wisdom—the ways according to which God runs the world—also stood out. The result was a great concern with ritual exactness combined with a strong skepticism about human nature. Job and Qoheleth (Ecclesiastes) are the most famous such writings, but we also find Proverbs gathering together many of the prudential maxims that Israel was accepting from Near Eastern (largely Egyptian) influences.

Israel was in a period of cultural and military decline, reduced to being a minor player on the ancient Near Eastern scene. In this context, biblical faith becomes purified of many of the this-worldly ambitions it entertained in the period of the patriarchs and the kings. It becomes clearer that what God desires is very mysterious, and that people have to give God a blank check, if they are to measure up to the full implications of the covenant. Faith on the model of the quid pro quo implied in some portions of Deuteronomic theology is no longer adequate. After the Exile, in the aftermath of disaster, human beings have to let God be God: fully sovereign, answerable to no standards but God's own.

Jesus inherited this religious history, as well as the impact of movements that arose in the century preceding his birth. The Pharisees, a lay body interested in reviving adherence to the Torah in both letter and spirit, were influential in his time, and Jesus seems to have shared much of their program. The Sadducees, a priestly group concerned with limiting the Law to the first five books and maintain good relations with Rome, the pagan power ruling Palestine, had less influence on Jesus. The Essenes, a separatist group wanting to prepare the people to regain sovereignty by making them pure enough to merit being God's own portion, may have shaped the thought of John the Baptist, who clearly influenced Jesus at the outset of Jesus' public career. The Zealots, a group of political activists not above using terrorist tactics to make things uncomfortable for Roman leaders and collaborationists, seem to have had little appeal for Jesus. Apocalyptic prophets and writings circulated widely, proposing that God was on the verge of delivering his people from pagan rule.

The successful revolution led by the Maccabees, which gave Israel considerable autonomy from 167 to 63 B.C., served as the model for the more political apocalyptic writers. Along with the speculations of thinkers working with the traditions of biblical wisdom, the apocalyptic writers furnished many of the ideas that the writers of the New Testament used to characterize the person and career of Jesus. Cer-

tainly older ideas, related to Abraham, Moses, David, and images of
the prophets, such as Isaiah's Suffering Servant, were equally if not
more important, but for both Jesus himself and the early Christians
who composed the canonical interpretations of him the entire Jewish
tradition, as it lived in the first century of what came to be known as the
Christian era, was important. (This tradition had been in contact with
Greek culture since the time of Alexander the Great [died 323 B.C.],
but the influences of Hellenism, as such Greek culture is often called,
most significant for Jesus and the early Christians were all filtered
through Jewish faith or reworked by it.)[1]

The Life of Jesus

Because the documents of the New Testament are more confessions of
faith in Jesus and interpretations of his meaning than historical reports
about his birth, work, and death, they do not allow us to construct a
biography. On the other hand, they were composed within two generations of Jesus' death, when eyewitnesses could verify their substantial
accuracy, so the probability is that many of the details they report are
true—and may represent what Jesus actually said or did on a given
occasion. For the time prior to Jesus' public ministry, which probably
began when he was about thirty years old, we have only a few hints
about his biography. Tradition says that he was born of poor parents in
Galilee, a somewhat backward Jewish province. Christian faith asserts
that his birth was miraculous, his mother being a virgin impregnated
by the Holy Spirit of God. All probability is that he grew up in a pious
Jewish home, receiving a modest religious education (for example,
learning to read the scrolls of scripture). The so-called infancy narratives that we find in Matthew and Luke are at pains to present the child
Jesus as marked for great things. The earliest Christians were mainly
Jews who believed that Jesus had fulfilled the prophecies of a coming
messiah (christ)—a royal figure, anointed by God, who would lead the
people to political and religious fulfillment. The infancy narratives,
and many other parts of the gospels, are shaped by this belief.

When Jesus began his public work, he probably was under the

influence of John the Baptist, a charismatic figure who was preaching a message of repentance and preparation for the judgment of God. John would baptize people as a sign that they wanted to repent, cleanse themselves, and prepare for this judgment. Mark, which is probably the oldest of the four canonical gospels, places Jesus' baptism by John at the outset of Jesus' public career:

> John the baptizer appeared in the wilderness, proclaiming a baptism of repentance for the forgiveness of sins. And the people from the whole Judean countryside and all the people of Jerusalem were going out to him, and were baptized by him in the river Jordan, confessing their sins. Now John was clothed with camel's hair, with a leather belt around his waist, and he ate locusts and wild honey. He proclaimed, "The one who is more powerful than I is coming after me. I am not worthy to stoop down and untie the thong of his sandals. I have baptized you with water, but he will baptize you with the Holy Spirit." In those days Jesus came from Nazareth of Galilee and was baptized by John in the Jordan. And just as he was coming up out of the water, he saw the heavens torn apart and the Spirit descending like a dove on him. And a voice came from heaven, "You are my Son, the Beloved; with you I am well pleased" (Mark 1:4–11).[2]

In early Christian interpretation, John was the last of the prophets of the old covenant, and Jesus was the first of the prophets of the new covenant. Jesus was much more than this, the early Christians believed, but one of his key functions was to fulfill the promises that had gathered momentum from the time of Isaiah and came to a boil with John. After his baptism, Jesus withdrew to the desert, the New Testament says, apparently to absorb the impact of his baptismal experience and prepare for the mission that it implied. When he emerged from the solitude of the desert, having been tested by Satan, he set about proclaiming that the "Reign of God" was at hand.

This concept, the centerpiece of his preaching, was a rich metaphor for the opportunity that Jesus discerned in the present times. He apparently felt that God was about to liberate Israel from its oppressions and offer a new intimacy with the divine. The special beneficiaries of this great opportunity would be the poor, those living on the margins of established Jewish culture. Even "sinners," those despised as ritually unclean, would be able to step out of their bondage and enjoy intimacy with God, if they would repent and believe the good news that Jesus was proclaiming. Jesus repeatedly spoke about God in tones of great trust, calling him *Abba* (father). The New Testament's accounts of Jesus' preaching show him having great success among the general populace but raising opposition from the religious rulers, who feared that he would create chaos.

The gospels are written with extreme prejudice in favor of Jesus—indeed, with belief in his divinity. It is hard to know, in a detached way, how successful Jesus was (how many people he drew to his vision) and how great a threat the religious authorities perceived him to be. The fact that he was finally killed for his work suggests that, eventually, he was taken very seriously. This "work," in fact, included more than preaching and teaching. Jesus is portrayed as having been a great healer, exorcist, and thaumaturge (worker of miracles), as well as a compelling teacher. As the gospels portray his public life, people would bring to him their sick and demented, and he would make them whole. On several occasions he supposedly restored the dead to life, and the memories of him include many "signs" that he worked—deeds falling outside natural explanation and testifying to the God-givenness of his mission. Thus, the gospels say that he multiplied a few loaves of bread and fishes to provide food for thousands; that he walked on water; that he gave sight to the blind; that he cast out demons from those considered possessed. His speech was poetic, parabolic, amazingly moving. Those whom he converted to his vision were convinced that no one had ever spoken as powerfully as he. They thought that, as a spokesperson for God, he had no peers. At the least, he was a new Moses.

The teaching that Jesus imparted made love of God and love of neighbor (staples of Jewish religion) central. If one loved God wholeheartedly, one had nothing to fear, could walk through the world as a child of God. If one loved one's neighbor as oneself, one fulfilled the basic requirements of the Law. The point was to have faith, let the goodness of God permeate one's whole life, and so act as a child of God, trying to love everything good about life and one's neighbors, trying even to forgive one's enemies. One of the aspects of Jesus' ministry that most offended his opponents was his claim to forgive sins. This was a divine prerogative, so in claiming it he offended those sensitive to idolatry. As the logic of Christian faith worked itself out, Jesus' forgiving sins came to be considered one of the proofs for his divine status. He came to be considered the Son of God, the Word of God, in a strict sense—one that made him eternal and equal with God his Father.

The most famous epitome of Jesus' preaching is the "Sermon on the Mount," the fullest version of which occurs in the gospel according to Matthew. In the beginning of this sermon (Matthew 5:1–12) Jesus blesses those who most open themselves to the Reign of God:

> When Jesus saw the crowds, he went up the mountain; and after he sat down, his disciples came to him. Then he began to speak, and taught them, saying: "Blessed are the poor in spirit, for theirs is the kingdom of heaven. Blessed are those who mourn, for they will be comforted. Blessed are the meek, for they will inherit the earth. Blessed are those who hunger and thirst for righteousness, for they will be filled. Blessed are the merciful, for they will receive mercy. Blessed are the pure in heart, for they will see God. Blessed are the peacemakers, for they will be called children of God. Blessed are those who are persecuted for righteousness' sake, for theirs is the kingdom of heaven. Blessed are you when people revile you and persecute you and utter all kinds of evil against you falsely on my account. Rejoice and be glad, for your reward is great in heaven, for in the same way they persecuted the prophets who went before you.[3]

It is unclear whether Jesus actually spoke these words, or whether they represent an interpretation of his message composed after his death and supposed resurrection. Either way, they recall the end of Jesus' life, when he was crucified by the Roman authorities as a threat to the peace. Jesus had formed a core group of disciples, known as the twelve. One of their number, Judas, betrayed him to the Jewish authorities, who in turn handed him over to Pontius Pilate, the Roman authority. Before his betrayal, Jesus had celebrated a Passover meal with the twelve. This was the Jewish feast commemorating the Exodus of the Hebrews from Egypt. The symbolism in the New Testament is clear: Jesus is the paschal lamb to be sacrificed for the forgiveness of all people's sins—for the exodus of all humankind from bondage and to the freedom of the children of God.

The sufferings that Jesus underwent on the way to Calvary, where he was crucified, and his agony on the cross, have become for Christians, and many others, a summary of the entire vulnerability of human beings, especially those who challenge others to move from evil to goodness. The defeat of Jesus on the cross seemed to be the finale, the judgment that his message and person, however admirable, had succumbed to the wickedness of people determined to maintain the corrupt status quo. What changed the entire story of Jesus was the series of events known as his resurrection from the dead. His followers believed that, after truly dying, he had escaped from the tomb and appeared to them as fully alive. This experience convinced them that God had ratified everything essential to Jesus's message and person—that he was indeed God's premier prophet, messiah (christ), and even divine Son.

From their belief in the resurrected Jesus, his followers rethought everything that they remembered about him. It is this rethought version of their memories that we find in the New Testament. By the time that the first writings of the New Testament were collected (those attributed to the apostle Paul), Jesus was being worshiped by communities of his followers as the divine Son of God incarnate. Faith in him had become the gateway to a share in God's own life. A liturgical system of sacraments—sacred rituals—had arisen to celebrate key moments in a person's communion with God through and in Jesus the christ. Jesus had become a new thing in Israelite history, and when most Jews would not accept the interpretations that Christians made of Jesus, Christianity turned to the non-Jews, offering them admission to the Christian community, the church. Thus, the "life" of Jesus continued after his physical death. Jesus of Nazareth became the Christ, the messiah who had brought about a new relationship with the One God worshiped by the Jews, and subsequent Christian history became, in its inmost substance, the story of communion with Jesus, whom Christians considered to be the head of their church.[4]

The Personality of Jesus

The personality of Jesus was complex. As the New Testament presents him, he was both fiery and gentle, both sociable and solitary, both full of energy and subject to fatigue. Above all, he was both traditional and innovative—both a conservative and a revolutionary. Among his most distinctive features were his eloquence and his compassion. He spoke winningly, with an instinctive knowledge of what would make his message clear to his audience, how he could draw them to contemplate the Reign of God. His heart went out to the poor, the sick, children. He seems to have had a special affinity for women, making friends with them and winning their allegiance. (This was unusual for a Jewish teacher in Jesus's day. Men, above all rabbis, were not supposed to consort with women or teach them.) Manifestly, Jesus was a man drawn to prayer. We find him at home in the Temple, the center of Jewish worship, and inclined to private prayer, in which he might commune with his Father. There is no evidence that Jesus ever married. His sense of mission seems to have precluded a normal family life. It is probable that he believed that the Reign of God would come in his lifetime, perhaps at his death, to consummate ordinary history. He lived simply, on the alms of his supporters. He wandered from village to village, accompanied by his closest disciples, bringing the good news to all who would listen. At times the demands of the crowds for healing, or even for practical necessities like bread, threatened to overwhelm him. But he persevered, doing what he could, trying in every way that he knew to communicate the goodness and power of his God.

Jesus was also courageous. Before long it became clear that powerful forces were opposed to his message, seeing him as a threat. One of the fascinating threads running through the gospels is his debates with opponents, usually Pharisees, who challenged his interpretations of Torah. Indeed, they questioned the legitimacy of his mission. From these debates several capital aspects of Jesus' personality emerge. First, Jesus would not be cowed by such opponents, and he proved himself a formidable foe in debate. He was quick-witted, and he could turn opponents' supposed piety or orthodoxy against them, showing inconsistencies in their arguments. Second, Jesus did not care for the letter of the Law so much as the spirit. He was convinced that the Law was a humanistic patrimony, meant by God to ease people's lives, support people's best hopes and instincts. The heart of Jesus' message, clearest in the gospel according to John, was love. If people genuinely loved God and their neighbors, the details of the Law would look out for themselves.

Third, the main thing that Jesus asked of his hearers, and found lacking in his foes, was faith. People had to open themselves to the good news, if they were to appreciate its power. With faith, anything was possible. Faith could move mountains. Without faith, nothing that Jesus said or did could make a dent. By the end of his debates with the Pharisees, Jesus apparently had become convinced that they had no good faith, indeed were arguing in bad faith. Fourth, Jesus was willing to let the evidence of his teaching, works, and person be the basis for judgments about the authenticity of his mission. If he spoke well of God and did good for the people he met, especially the poor and the sick, he ought to be accepted as a genuine spokesperson for God. If he did evil or spoke badly, people could reject him rightly. He sought only his Father's will and glory, he claimed. His healings and exorcisms ought to be taken as signs that his Father was pleased with his mission, had verified it again and again.

These different facets of Jesus's personality dovetailed with many roles familiar to Jews of his day. People observing him could liken his work to that of the classical biblical prophets. They could also liken him to the rabbis who taught the Torah, the holy men (*hasidim*) who claimed to be inspired and worked cures, and the seekers after wisdom. Each of these roles was an accepted way for a religious Jew to behave. The early Christians added the role of messiah. To their mind, Jesus fitted the profile of the one whom God had promised would liberate Israel from bondage.

The distinctive feature of Jesus' messiahship, though, was that it was not political. It had political implications, but its roots lay in God's own initiatives to change the basic relations between human beings and divinity. By implication, such a change would open new possibilities for how human beings could relate to one another. If people felt themselves fully accepted by God, treated as beloved children, they could treat one another as beloved sisters and brothers. What Pauline theology called a "new creation" had occurred: humanity set free of the sin that had twisted its entire prior history, humanity rooted in a grace (a free gift of divine love and life) that incorporated it into the intimate relationship that Jesus had with God his Father. (So did the early Christians radicalize Jesus' significance.)

Jesus relied on such an intimate relationship to define who he was. The Spirit of God whom the gospels depict guiding Jesus consoled him

with reminders that God loved him, and that serving God was the
noblest, most fulfilling thing that anyone could do. Still, Jesus remains
a mysterious figure, a personality that we cannot fathom, not only
because all human beings finally escape our judgment, and not only
because the documents we possess are inadequate, but even more because the depths of his personality lie in the undecipherable relationship
he had with his Father. For Jesus to be was to be God's Son. This is now
orthodox Christian theology, expressing the Christian conviction that
the godhead is a Trinity of divine "persons" among whom Jesus is the
second, the Son and Word of God become flesh. But we find such a
theology latent in the evangelists' sketches of Jesus talking about God his
Father, praying to his Father, teaching the crowds in parables that depict
God as a loving parent. On the human level, Jesus seems filled with
concern for the needs of the poor people whom he encountered. On the
more mysterious, divine level, his sole concern seems to be to glorify his
heavenly Father.

Thus the personality of Jesus, as we find it construed after the
resurrection by the disciples who composed the New Testament, has
an inerradicable two-foldness. Jesus is manifestly, unquestionably human. He eats, sleeps, gets tired, gets frustrated, wants acceptance,
sheds tears, suffers when he is whipped and crucified. But he is also
more than human, unique among the human beings whom the writers
have known. The core of his personality lodges with his heavenly
Father. The signs that he works point beyond himself, are pregnant
with what can only be called divine grace. Even when he is attending a
wedding feast, or relaxing with his friends, his defining relationship
with his Father sets him apart. Even though he was not an ascetic but
seems to have enjoyed parties, wine, and food, one would never mistake him for an aesthete or a secular person beguiled by the world.

Indeed, the gospels never depict Jesus sinning. In their accounts, he
has no moral faults. This also sets him apart from the ordinary run of
human beings. He shows no agenda, no program, no edge that his
enemies can seize upon, no handle by which they can take hold of him
and turn him to their own purposes. His only purpose is to make
known the goodness of God—to make that manifest through his
several-sided proclamation of the Reign that is dawning. Wealth, pleasure, and power have no hold on him. He will not succumb to flattery,

nor to threats. He shows a sense of humor now and then. In the gospel according to John, he is often ironic. But his overall disposition seems serious, sad, absorbed in a mighty struggle. This does not make him self-important, but it suggests that no one could take him lightly. He was no comedian. He seems to have loved his friends deeply, and to have made himself vulnerable to them. When they did not believe, were obtuse, fled in his time of need, they hurt him deeply. Yet he was more interested in forgiving them than in holding their failings against them. He seems to have realized how weak most human beings are and to have asked God to take such weakness into account.

There must have been something compelling about the personality bearing all these traits. By the time of Jesus' "ascension to heaven," as his departure from his disciples after his resurrection was called, he had stamped many lives indelibly. Simon Peter and Mary Magdalene, the beloved disciples John and James—all his intimates felt that he had become the substance of their lives, the only treasure they cared about. The report of later Christian saints has been similar. The most intense Christians have felt that Jesus was their entire reason to be.[5]

Jesus' Teaching about Nature

Jesus has little that is distinctive to say about the physical world. He seems to have accepted without question the guidelines handed down through Jewish tradition. Those guidelines included, as a fundamental orientation, the refrain of the account of creation in Genesis that the Creator considered the world very good. Jesus never suggests that physical things—rocks, trees, animals, birds, the air, the seas—are a problem for human beings. Neither does he suggest that they interest him especially. He takes pleasure in their beauty, and he refers such beauty to his heavenly Father (in the spirit of the Psalmist), but his preponderant interest is the welfare of human beings. He is not a pre-modern ecologist. He does not share the instinct of some Eastern sages that nature is a more perfect reflection of ultimate reality than human beings.

Jesus also takes for granted the teaching of Genesis that human beings are images of God. Human beings have a special place in creation. They are the creatures in whom the Creator is most interested. They are the offspring called to special intimacy with God. Angels and Satan play only a small role in Jesus' worldview. He admits them, provides for them, but concentrates on human beings. Somewhat like Confucius, he is not a spiritualist, a shaman or diviner interested in the occult. Even when he exorcizes demons, he shows little curiosity about demons—little desire to study them or speculate about their significance. It is enough that they are hurting human beings and he has power to stop such hurt.

His Jewish view of creation, combined with his personal sense of God's care, makes Jesus a strong proponent of providence. Everything is open to God, unfolds according to God's will. Human beings cannot know the details of this will but, in faith, they can be sure that it expresses God's goodness and love. If God gives the lilies of the field their beauty, and provides food for the sparrows of the air, much more does he make provision for human beings, his people Israel. The images that Jesus spontaneously uses for God are not Master of the Universe, Lord of Creation, Maker of Heaven and Earth. They are images of paternity, parenthood, a ruler who can be stern when justice requires but more naturally is tender, loving, forgiving. The most famous parables of the New Testament, such as that of the Prodigal Son, depict God as more interested in the welfare of his children than any rights he might possess as sovereign Lord. If we human beings, evil as we are, know how to give our children good things, how much more will the heavenly Father give the best thing, his Holy Spirit, to the children who ask this of him? This is a rhetorical question. Jesus thinks that one can never exaggerate the goodness of God. Jesus thinks that both nature and human experience conspire to make the sanest stance in life giving God carte blanche.

The Israelite prophets had developed themes from the Deuteronomic history to make idolatry a great sin. If we accept the biblical historians' account of what happened to the people from the time of David to the exile in Babylon, worship of foreign, natural deities was a major failing. Apparently the people could not abide the simplicity, purity, and mysteriousness of the God revealed through Abraham, Isaac, and Jacob, the God who gave the covenant through Moses from

Mount Sinai. This God could not be represented. Nothing in human or natural experience could render divinity adequately, even appropriately. He was like a refining fire, but one could not call fire his inmost being. He was the source of all fecundity, but one erred greatly in worshiping sex or fertility. He was unique, sui generis, the original pattern rather than anything derived. One had to suffer his mysteriousness, in faith, never knowing the divine name, always struggling to believe that he would keep his pledge to be with Israel as he thought best. The covenant was like a marital relationship, an intimate sharing of being and life. But the spouse of Israel was a hidden God, a lover who held all the initiative and had to be trusted to show his love appropriately.

Jesus inherited this theology, yet he seems to have paid little attention to idolatry. He was not concerned that people would pay too much attention to sex or natural fecundity. He did not see nature as a competitor to his Father. If there is an idol that he attacks, it is human attachment to traditional ways of thinking. Specifically, it is the inclination of those who could not hear his message to make the Torah something static, something that could freeze relations between the people and their living God.

For example, Jesus honored the sabbath, taking it as a day for holy rest, but he would not absolutize it. When sick people came to him on the sabbath begging cures, he rejected the argument that curing them would be "work" violating the spirit of consecrating the sabbath. The sabbath was made for human beings, not human beings for the sabbath (Mark 2:27). How could curing someone offend the living God, whose whole concern was that human beings flourish, become healthy and whole? The inertia of human traditions raised more of Jesus' ire than overconcern with the forces of nature. Jesus thought that his great enemies were human fear, lack of imagination, above all lack of faith, not seductions of nature. Certainly, he did not have to face the idolatries possible since the rise of modern technology. He did not have to contend with a natural science that could seem more fascinating, and perhaps more powerful, than the study of God. But he had the entire polemical tradition of the Hebrew Bible to draw upon, had he wished to excoriate his contemporaries for an overesteem of nature. Either they sinned little in this way, or Jesus thought their greater problems lay elsewhere.

Implicit in Jesus' acceptance of Jewish faith, and in the way that he used material things, was a sacramental theology. For Christians, belief that the Word of God himself took flesh has been the deepest ground for a sacramental theology (one thinking that material things can mediate divine grace), but the example of Jesus has also been important. Jesus laid hands on the sick, to cure them. He blessed bread and wine, suggesting that these simple foods represented God's nurture of the human spirit. He spoke of his own body and blood as things precious enough to be sacrificed to God. He faced death bravely, if reluctantly, and so set physical life in the larger context of divine life: what God wanted human time to emphasize, how God provided meaning for mortal human beings. All this is sacramental, in the sense that all of it places divine activity within space and time. The material world is not alien to the dispensations of divine life. God, who is spirit, does not despise matter or flesh. Spirit and flesh have their religious antagonisms, as we find in the theologies of Paul and John, but they are not dichotomous, as much Greek thought tended to make them. The religious antagonisms between spirit and flesh come from sin, not a theology in which matter is evil, opposed to God, and spirit is godlike. The worst sins are spiritual: pride (love of self unto contempt of God, disobedience to God), hatred, lovelessness, lack of faith. The "fleshly" human being is one closed to God, ruled by sensuality or self-concern. The "spiritual" human being remains fully incarnate, fully called to love his or her body, yet makes God the center of existence—puts first things first.

The capstone to this view of nature, physical creation, is the Christian doctrine of resurrection. Jesus spoke of resurrection, rather than of immortality of the soul. He chose traditional Jewish categories, rather than Hellenistic ones, when it came to discussing the ultimate fate of human beings. The body would enjoy a new, perfected existence, in relationship with God, as much as the spirit would. The human being accepted into God's deathless existence would be the full matter-spirit, body-soul composite. Jesus simply assumed that the human being is an embodied spirit. He entertained no thought that death would liberate the essential part of the human being, a spiritual spark that alone was an image of God. Such a view, soon called heretical by his followers, was foreign to Jesus. And his own resurrection sealed the goodness of human flesh.

In triumph after his horrible death, according to the New Testament, he ate with his disciples, assured them that he was not a ghost, and led them to believe that, however much being taken to the bosom of God changed the human being, liberating it from many of the limitations suffered on earth, resurrection also perfected the human being, body as well as spirit. In principle, therefore, Jesus sponsored a profound humanism, and a profound appreciation of natural creation. By assumption, more than explicit teaching, he told his followers that it was natural and good for them to be in the physical world, love the sun and the rain, the fields and the flocks. The "world" they had to fear was the human culture, the human machinations, opposed to God. The lilies of the field and sparrows of the air were not threats but reminders of God's providential care.

Jesus' Teaching about Society

Just as Jesus assumed traditional Jewish views about nature, so he assumed traditional Jewish views about society. In general, he thought of Israel as an elect nation. Non-Jews were Gentiles, "the nations," *goyim*. They had their place in God's scheme of things, and the one God was their Overlord. But they were not partakers of the covenant, and Jesus thought that his mission was to Israel, not to them. Only accidentally, tangentially, did Jesus apply his convictions about the dawning of God's Reign to Gentiles. Only when Gentiles came to him with signal faith was he moved to cure their sick. The first plank in Jesus' social platform, then, was a traditional conviction that the main theater of God's operations was the people of Israel. What happened to outsiders was a secondary consideration.

The cement binding Jews together, Jesus further assumed, was Torah. The Law handed down from Moses was the "constitution" that made Israel Israel. Even when Jesus disagreed with his opponents about the proper interpretation of Torah, he never called Torah itself into question. He believed that Torah was God's guidance for the sanctification of God's people. His main quarrel with legalistic interpreters of Torah was that they missed its humanistic cut. God had not given Torah to be a burden for human beings. Ideally, it would liberate human beings so that they could be free of their false values and obsessions, so that they could find the basis of true fulfillment: living communion with holy divinity itself. Jesus accepted the institutions that had grown up in Jewish history—the Temple, the priesthood, the rabbinate—as a matter of course. He did not canonize these institutions, but neither did he attack them. They were as good or bad as their help toward the people's prospering under Torah. They were instruments, and as long as they performed their proper functions no one ought to quarrel with them.

Perhaps the most pregnant summary of Jesus' attitude toward the social realm was his statement about the relations between secular affairs (what one owed to "Caesar," the secular ruler) and ultimate affairs (what one owed to God). The entire context of this statement, as we find it in Matthew 22, bears study. Jesus is again debating with his regular opponents, Pharisees who in this case are trying to trip him up. Matthew's view is that such Pharisees feared the popularity that Jesus was gaining with the common people. They were more interested in defending their own power than in clarifying what God actually wanted them, or the common people, or Jesus to do. To Matthew's mind, the Pharisees soon realized that Jesus was a heavy threat, and they became increasingly determined to get him out of the way, not scrupling to entertain thoughts of murder.

Here is the substance of the exchange about what faithful Jews owed to Caesar (a volatile issue, since many Jews felt that having to submit to Rome was an abomination threatening the purity of their submission to God, the only Ruler to whom they ought to bow):

Then the Pharisees went and took counsel how to entangle him in his talk. And they sent their disciples, along with the Herodians [those supporting Herod, the Jewish ruler subject to Rome], saying, "Teacher, we know that you are true, and teach the way of God truthfully, and care for no man; for you do not regard the position of men. Tell us, then, what you think. Is it lawful to pay taxes to Caesar, or not?" But Jesus, aware of their malice, said, "Why put me to the test, you hypocrites? Show me the money for the tax." And they brought him a coin. "Whose likeness and inscription is this?" They said, "Caesar's." Then he said to them, "Render therefore to Caesar the things that are Caesar's, and to God the things that are God's." When they heard it, they marveled; and they left him and went away (Matthew 22:15–22).[6]

To say the least, this is not a fully helpful exchange. What are the things that are Caesar's, and the things that are God's? Jesus is wise enough not to answer this question. He probably knows that there is no definitive answer. Religious people have to determine, case by case, what their allegiance is to the temporal powers who keep the peace and to the divine power that holds their eternal destinies. Here the real point is that Jesus refused to let the Pharisees trap him. Had he said that it was lawful to pay taxes to Caesar, he would have offended those believing that Roman rule was an abomination. Had he said that it was not lawful, he would have been liable to the charge of being a revolutionary, a fomenter of civil discord. The hypocrisy of the Pharisees was that, in practice, they had struck a bargain with Caesar. The very money that they used (among other things, to pay taxes) was minted by Rome. It was a fairy tale to speak as though they were not subject to Rome, did not have to pay taxes.

Jesus was not interested in fairy tales. He did not care whether people paid taxes to Rome or to Jewish authorities. Presumably, he felt that the only function of such authorities was to keep civil affairs running smoothly. More important was what people owed to God: the center of their being, the substance of their selves. If they did not compromise this substance, they could pay all the taxes that Caesar required. If they did compromise this substance, no secular or religious absence of conflict would be honest. Jesus seems to have felt that Caesar, and other public authorities, had their place: their necessity, responsibilities, and so rights. He even implies that this is part of God's plan, and so that civil authorities are backed by God. But he also suggests, even more strongly, that all civil or secular authorities are limited. They cannot command the full allegiance of any human beings, let alone of Israelites blessed with the covenant. Temporal affairs are secondary, compared to heavenly matters. If people are not primarily servants of God, their entire lives will be disordered.

From such a conviction, Jesus gained immense freedom. He died at the hands of Roman authorities, Caesar's men, who apparently had been manipulated by Jewish foes such as the Pharisees. But he never fell into their captivity. In spirit, if not in body, he was the servant only of God. We sense this in the exchange between Pontius Pilate, the Roman authority, and Jesus. As reported by John, the exchange is loaded with irony. Pilate, who has capital power over Jesus, is the slave of public pressure. Jesus, who will soon be crucified by Pilate's decree, is free of all earthly pressures:

> He [Pilate] entered the praetorium again and said to Jesus, "Where are you from?" But Jesus gave no answer. Pilate therefore said to him, "You will not speak to me? Do you not know that I have power to release you, and power to crucify you?" Jesus answered him, "You would have no power over me unless it had been given you from above; therefore he who delivered me to you has the greater sin." Upon this Pilate sought to release him, but the Jews cried out, "If you release this man, you are not Caesar's friend; everyone who makes himself a king sets himself against Caesar." When Pilate heard these words, he brought Jesus out and sat down on the judgment seat at a place called The Pavement and in Hebrew Gabbatha. Now it was the day of Preparation of the Passover; it was about the sixth hour. He said to the Jews, "Behold your king!" They cried out, "Away with him, away with him, crucify him!" Pilate said to them, "Shall I crucify your King?" The chief priests answered, "We have no king but Caesar." Then he handed him over to them to be crucified (John 19:9–16).[7]

Jesus is crucified because he seeks to serve the will of God, which he will not identify with either Roman political authority or Jewish religious traditions. Only God is sovereign in his sight. In other places, Jesus makes it clear that, if people make only God their Lord, they will restructure their human communities. They will honor the poor, respect the suffering, care for the unfortunate. They will feel the rule of God as a pressure to make their human rules sources of mercy and mutual help. They will not abide worldly distinctions based on wealth, lineage, office, or even talent. This conflict between a radically faithful view of the human community and worldly views gave rise to Jesus' saying that the last will be first and the first last (Matthew 19:30, 20:16). It left his followers a permanent problem: how to coordinate allegiance to God with allegiance to Caesar. From the earliest Christian times, after the death of Jesus, Christians sought to prove that they were good citizens of the Roman Empire. Their faith made them gentle, peaceful, obedient, they claimed. But they could not worship the emperor. They could not swear that Caesar was Lord. Only their God, the Father of Jesus Christ, and Jesus Christ himself was Lord. All later Christian political theory reflects this early tension, which goes back to the teachings and example of Jesus himself. Because Jesus died as a criminal, his followers were bound to feel uneasy about the secular law, the powers that determine criminality and pass out capital punishments. That is how close readers of the New Testament have often reasoned.

Jesus' Teaching about Self

Jesus identified himself with God, his Father. The core of his selfhood lay in this bond of trust. Who he was, what he had to do, whence he derived his authority, where he wanted to lead other people—all this focused on his Father. Indeed, those seeking explicit assurances from Jesus that he considered himself divine are often foiled because Jesus pointed away from himself toward his Father. Only in the gospel of John, where the theological overlay is heaviest, do we find strong speech from Jesus indicating his own divinity. For John, the "I" of Jesus is reminiscent of the divine "I" echoing in Exodus 3, where God gave Moses the divine name yet withheld it. The most dramatic Johannine instance of this reflection of the divine "I" in the personhood of Jesus occurs in chapter eight. Even there, however, it is clear that Jesus is more concerned with the Father than with any glory of his own:

> "If I glorify myself, my glory is nothing; it is my Father who glorifies me, of whom you say that he is your God. But you have not known him; I know him. If I said, I do not know him, I should be a liar like you; but I do know him and I keep his word. Your father Abraham rejoiced that he was to see my day; he saw it and was glad." The Jews then said to him, "You are not yet fifty years old, and have you seen Abraham?" Jesus said to them, "Truly, truly, I say to you, before Abraham was, I am." So they took up stones to throw at him; but Jesus hid himself, and went out of the temple (8:55–59).[8]

Whatever the historical basis for this Johannine interpretation of Jesus' own psychology, it is clear that Jesus thought of human selfhood and destiny as a function of a person's relations with God. Neither work, love, family life, patriotism, nor money merited serious consideration, when it came to describing the treasure on which people ought to set their hearts. No status or source of pride, no worldly accomplishment, could compare. Thus we may say that Jesus took a mystical view of the self, as long as we understand this term correctly. He thought that the significance of the self was hidden in God, but this did not make him otherworldly. In his understanding, intimate relationship with God facilitated good relations with one's brothers and sisters. God was not the enemy of social concern or warm, familiar love. The closer that people drew to God, the closer they could draw to one another. Indeed, Jesus' hope for the community of his disciples was that they would become like fellow branches grafted into one vine. He was the vine. They were the branches (see John 15). Together, they shared a common, organic life. The sap of that life, we might say, was their faith and love. If they committed themselves to him, they could grow closer than what any worldly ties or ties of blood could effect.

It follows that Jesus' view of the self was relational. The self was not a monad existing in isolation. Jesus was no champion of individualism, if that word means a neglect of social ties. Jesus wanted people to love their neighbors as they loved themselves. He thought that serving other people—feeding the hungry, curing the sick, visiting those in prison, giving alms to the poor—was serving God. This view reflected his legacy from the Israelite prophets. What was new in his sense of the self was the trust and intimacy that he urged people to seek with God, their Father. Jewish tradition of his day was not as bold as Jesus on this point. It believed in God's love, and could quote wonderful lines from the prophets and Deuteronomy. But Jesus stood out for the passion of his trust, the audacity of his commitment of himself into his Father's keeping. So strong was his trust that Jesus called people to live at what seemed an impossible level of idealism. In retrospect, it seems that only if the Spirit of God (the experiential sense of God's power) held people up could they sacrifice themselves for God and neighbor as Jesus urged them to do.

Consider, for example, the counsel to love one's enemies. Jesus wanted his followers to move beyond their natural instincts of retaliation, move beyond even their sober sense of justice. As he depicted God, God was much better than what human desires for justice intuited. God operated by a "justice" quite unlike human instincts. For example, God might pay workers hired late in the day the same wages he paid workers who had labored since sunup (see Matthew 20). God was generous beyond human calculation. He would never cheat anyone (the workers who had labored since sunup would get all that he had promised them), but he would surprise people, especially the humble and repentant, with his largess.

This was true in the moral realm, with special vigor. God would forgive sinners, accepting them back into the divine embrace even when they had been offensive. They had no right to be received back into God's favor, but God did not care about rights. God cared about the heart, what people really felt, where their love lay. If people repented from the heart, God would forgive any sin. The famous parable about the prodigal son (Luke 15) includes a lesson for the dutiful, represented by the elder son. The father goes out of his way to welcome the prodigal back, not because he despises the faithful service of the elder son, but because his heart tells him that the younger son was lost and now wants to come back to life. God cares more about saving a child who might easily have been lost than about standing on legalistic proprieties. The elder son will not lose because of the father's generosity toward the younger son. The elder son has yet to learn that love is more important than duty and justice.

This call of the self to live beyond itself, in imitation of how God lives beyond human expectations, may be the greatest challenge in Jesus' psychology. How can one understand this supernatural view of human possibility? What happens when people's idealism crashes? Is it reasonable to expect people like the elder brother or the workers hired early not to feel resentful when ne'er-do-wells or latecomers receive as much if not more than they? Yes, but only if such people experience, on a regular basis, the goodness of God toward themselves. If they really feel that they are sinners or underachievers who have received far more from God than they deserve by any strict accounting, they may be able to leave justice to God and strive to treat other people as generously as they can, on the model of God. They may be able to take to heart the

startling verses from the Sermon on the Mount in which Jesus depicts
God as universally benevolent (and so urges his followers to forgive
their enemies):

> You have learnt how it was said: You must love your neighbour and hate
> your enemy. But I say this to you: love your enemies and pray for those
> who persecute you; in this way you will be sons [children] of your Father in
> heaven, for he causes his sun to rise on bad men [people] as well as good,
> and his rain to fall on honest and dishonest alike (Matthew 5:45–46).[9]

Finally, we may note that Mary Magdalene, one of the most important New Testament saints, was celebrated in Christian piety for her
great love of Jesus, which more than compensated for her sins. Because
of her love, she merited to see the Risen Lord before any of the other
disciples, including Peter, their leader. The Magdalene stands for the
disciples who most took to heart the psychology that Jesus preached.
She stood by the cross, refusing to be intimidated by the Roman
authorities or the ugly crowd. She was utterly bereft, but a part of her
seems to have kept hoping, even kept believing, that not even death
could take away her beloved Lord. Whatever the actual happenings at
the source of the New Testament's accounts of Jesus' resurrection, love
like that of Mary Magdalene has to have played a significant role.

The final basis of Jesus' prescriptions for the self was his understanding of God as love. Through communion with God, the human personality could become dominated by love. With such a dominance,
human potential could expand beyond measure. People might even
love their enemies, and so make new starts. They might become
content with their lot in life, no matter how difficult, because they were
able to interpret it as a dispensation of God's love. They might live in
hope of an eternal fulfillment, since the love of God is deathless. They
might sacrifice themselves on the model of Jesus, who showed there is
no greater love than laying down one's life for one's friends. Jesus' way
of dealing with passion, then, was different from that of the Buddha.
Jesus' way was to deepen passion. In effect, Jesus told his followers to
take their greatest loves and set them in the mystery of God. There,
believers could find themselves completely transformed—taken into
the divine life and divinized, as Jesus himself had been.

Jesus' Teaching about Divinity

We have seen that Jesus' relation with his Father was the center of his being. Nothing else competed for his allegiance. The closest thing to a rival for his love of God was his concern to help his fellow human beings, especially those who were suffering. But this concern was probably a function of the understanding Jesus had of the nature of his God. To his mind, the Father was surpassingly good. It was mere logic (if one can ever speak of love in such terms) to treat one's fellow human beings as well as one could, because that was how God had shown divinity to be: universally benevolent. If human beings were images of God, they ought to, in a way had to, imitate God. They did this best by showing one another selfless love. As God had poured out the divine being in making the world, so Jesus felt he had to pour himself out for the welfare of the needy men and women he met.

This conviction about the goodness of God did not prevent Jesus from showing to God the reverence and honor traditionally inculcated by Jewish piety. If Jesus presumed to deal with God intimately, with the confidence of a child in its mother or father, he still attended public worship, bowed low in his private prayers, and in all ways acknowledged the sovereignty of his Father, who was also his Lord. The only difference between the worship that Jesus offered to God and that of other human beings stemmed from his sinlessness. As the New Testament writers present him, and later Christian theology made axiomatic, Jesus was like his fellow human beings in all things save sin. If he did have no stains on his conscience, no feelings of guilt, he did not have to come to God in a mode of repentance. On the other hand, he did have to come as a limited creature. He did have to acknowledge that everything in his human makeup derived from God and testified to God's sovereignty over him.

Though acknowledging such sovereignty is not the primary accent of Jesus' prayer, it does run through his whole bearing toward his Father. The Father always holds the priority. Jesus is concerned to glorify his Father, serve his Father. He is not concerned to equate himself with his Father. The doctrine of the Trinity is founded on statements one finds in the New Testament, especially in the writings of John and Paul. But the full elaboration of that doctrine only comes after the New Testament period. Jesus speaks of the Father and the Spirit in ways that ground the Christian sense that they are equally divine, but he does not preach about the Trinity or teach about the equality of the divine persons.

In the spectrum of the world religions, it is the accent on love that distinguishes the teachings of Jesus from those of other great founders. Muhammad, as we shall see, was eloquent about the sovereignty of God. One could also argue that Muhammad never doubted the complete goodness of God. But Jesus says much more about God's love than what we find in the Qur'an, and Jesus does not have the reserve about ultimate reality that we find in the teachings of the Buddha and Confucius. For Jesus, God is love. God is also life, light, power, and a dozen other things. But love is the best analogy. The Father made the world in love, and the Father cares for all the things in the world more intensely than human beings can imagine. Not a leaf falls without the Father's awareness and consent. Every hair on the heads of the faithful is numbered. Jesus is convinced that God runs the world directly. Jesus is not formed by the scientific mentality that points out all the proximate causes of the phenomena of nature and history. He shares with his Jewish forebears the sense that God makes the rain fall, the sun rise. If that raises problems about God's responsibility for the bad things that happen in nature or history, such problems do not trouble Jesus very much.

It is impossible for us to capture the experiences that gave Jesus such confidence in his Father. Christian theologians are tempted to say that, as divine, Jesus naturally knew the full extent of the Father's goodness and so could depend on it completely. But we are not dealing with Jesus here as though we were Christian theologians. We are dealing with him as we have dealt with the Buddha and Confucius, and as we shall deal with Muhammad. It is the human being Jesus of Nazareth who concerns us, not the Word become flesh. Admittedly, the sources that we have about the man Jesus are filled with theological convictions about his more-than-human status. Admittedly, we have no images of Jesus or narratives about his experience that prescind from Christian faith in his messiahship or even divinity. But, in principle, we might have reports about the man Jesus that allowed us to glimpse the source of his apparently complete confidence in the goodness of his Father. In principle, we might be able to point to times and places when Jesus was so overwhelmed by the goodness of God that the evils of the world could never become a great challenge to his faith. In fact, however, we have no such evidence. We can only conjecture that what Jesus felt at his baptism by John, or during his sojourn in the desert, or perhaps even earlier, in boyhood or adolescence, primed him to entrust himself to God without reserve.

How did Jesus reconcile himself to the evils and injustices of the world? How did he handle his own painful fate—the rejection of his message and person? We cannot say for certain, but there are signs that he attributed hatred and the other free acts that mar history to human sinfulness, and that he assumed that natural disasters were part of a cosmic providence that lay outside human ken but had to be God's way of making all creatures testify to the divine goodness. As Jesus speaks about his foes, they emerge as lacking faith. Because of this, they cannot grasp the full import of his words—cannot sense the Father's advent, the dawning of the Reign of God. How culpable they are is not clear. Often Jesus seems to charge them with bad will, a blindness that they should not have—would not have, if they were honest. But other times Jesus implies that people's ultimate dispositions are mysterious. Unless God gives them help, grace, they remain in their blindness, their sin.

At one level, God gives faith to whom God wishes. There may be no merit in having faith, since God could raise up children of Abraham from stones (Matthew 3:9). Yet this implies that God is capricious, and such an implication runs against the whole grain of Jesus' presentation of his Father. Again and again, Jesus implies that God is a better guarantor of people's rights—even their rights before the divine majesty—than anything human, including the codifications of God's laws, could be. If we ask God for bread, he will not give us a stone. If we ask him for an egg, he will not give us a serpent. If we have faith, we can see the glory of the lilies of the field and realize that, if God takes care of them, his care for us must be immeasurably more intimate, significant, powerful. There is more joy in heaven over one sinner who repents than over ninety-nine just securely on the path to salvation. This argues that nothing in human experience can tell against God's goodness. As much as Jesus hated the prospect of his own suffering and death, he abandoned himself to his Father's will. Death itself could not shake his confidence that, somehow, God would make all things turn out well.

One can call this view of God, this theology, irrational, or one can call it an interpretation of God based on passionate love. Jesus seems to have moved beyond reason, when it came to his relationship with his Father. He shows no signs of having doubted his God. That also distanced him from other human beings, perhaps almost as much as his reputed lack of sin. To Jesus' mind, the two could not be separated. Lack of faith was a species of sin, because sin includes distrust of God, lack of love of God, unwillingess to surrender one's creaturely self into the keeping of the infinite Creator. How Jesus could live so far beyond the darkness and doubts of the average human being is impossible to say. Once again, a humanistic approach has to assume that he had experiences justifying the blank check he gave to his Father.

The edges of his trust, where one can see how he might have been tempted to discouragement, come into view when he is disappointed with human beings, including his disciples. They do not understand what he is preaching, why he is likely to suffer and die, how God has construed the Reign that is dawning. They are slow, thick, torpid. More than once, Jesus seems tired of having to battle their obtuseness. On occasion, he is even shocked by the lack of faith in the crowds that come to him, their venality in wanting material things. So we must distinguish sharply between what Jesus expected from God and what Jesus expected from human beings (despite his faith that God was working in all human beings). Jesus could be completely hopeful about God without expecting much from the average people who listened to him. Perhaps his joy at finding apparently genuine faith is a measure of how unimpressive he found the general run of his fellow human beings to be. It is clear that he believed that any significant fulfillment of his mission had to come from his Father, and that increasingly he found "success" very paradoxical.

Christianity after Jesus

The New Testament comes after Jesus, of course, but most commentators think that the writings presently included in the New Testament were all composed by about A.D. 100 (sixty-five years or so after the death of Jesus). The apostle Paul, who had not known the historical Jesus, felt that he had encountered the resurrected Christ, who gave him what ultimately became a mission to preach the gospel to non-Jews. The Pauline writings of the New Testament represent the first phase in a transition from a Jewish Christianity to a Christianity concerned to interpret Jesus for Gentile audiences. By the close of the New Testament era, it seemed clear that the future of the Church lay with Gentile converts, since Israel as a whole had rejected the claim that Jesus was the messiah.

The second and third centuries of Christian existence required the Church to consolidate its teachings and establish the disciplines necessary to maintain order. Order included doctrine, liturgical practices, and morality. The leaders in the Church's efforts to gain control of its doctrine, liturgy, and morality were the bishops who headed local churches. The great external tasks included defending Christian claims against both Jewish and Gentile detractors, and convincing secular authorities that Christians were not seditious—posed no threat to Roman rule. The fall of the Temple in Jerusalem in A.D. 70 seemed to many Christians a symbol of God's having rejected Israel because of its rejection of Christ, while the majority of the early apologetic efforts sought to convince educated Gentiles that Christianity was the path of salvation and wisdom for which they had been looking.

With the rule of the emperor Constantine early in the fourth century, Christians came out from under the imperial suspicion that had blocked their efforts to grow. Constantine paved the way for Christianity to become the most favored religion in the empire, and after him persecutions of the Church, which had on occasion been bloody, significantly decreased. The martyrs who had died witnessing to the faith during such persecutions established one of the most important paradigms for Christian holiness. Indeed, by the fourth century much Christian spirituality followed the motif of dying to the world, either for the faith in actual death or through ascetical practices. As the Church gained favor in the Roman world, ascetical practices gained momentum.

From the third century significant numbers of Christians renounced the world, thinking that the Church's prosperity was more dangerous than persecution had been. What is known as the monastic movement organized this impulse to flee the world. By the middle of the fourth century not only had solitaries escaped to the desert to seek God in simplicity but communities of men and women had arisen, bound to a revered elder supposed to direct their spiritual development. Before long vows of poverty, chastity, and obedience defined what later became known as the "religious" life, in contrast to the "lay" life in which people were free to manage their material possessions, marry, and run their affairs as they chose.

The age of the great Church councils began with the assembly of bishops at Nicaea in 325 to discuss orthodox understandings of the nature of Jesus. Arianism, the view that Jesus was only the foremost creature and not the strictly divine Son of God, was the first great heresy rejected by a full assembly of bishops. From earliest times (within the New Testament era itself) there had been doctrinal controversies, but from the time of Nicaea such controversies commanded more formal responses. Dissidents tended to continue to push their views (the Aryans did so successfully for centuries after Nicaea), and the entire history of orthodoxy and heresy is complicated by political factors, some of which stemmed from outside the Church itself (for example, the desires of emperors).

The fall of Rome in 430 was a great shock to all members of the empire. From that time the fate of Western Christianity lay with various efforts to accommodate to the cultures of pagan European tribes. Eastern Christianity better maintained its sovereignty (until the rise of Islam in the seventh century), but East and West grew apart. A major reason was linguistic: the East spoke Greek while the West spoke Latin. By 1054 the two portions of Christendom had become so antagonistic that each declared the other to be in schism.

Byzantium, as Eastern Christian culture is often called, was characterized by the symbiosis of what we now name "church" and "state." The emperor claimed much control over church affairs, in the name of his own Christian status as a leader appointed by God. The great sees (administrative jurisdictions) in the early Church were those of Rome, Constantinople, Jerusalem, Antioch, and Alexandria. Obviously, four were in the East. Nonetheless, Rome increasingly claimed special status (as the center of the Empire at the time of Jesus and the apostles, and as the church founded by Peter and Paul). The papacy (rule of the bishop in Rome) was the most effective force in Europe during the period after the barbarian invasions, and beginning with the rule of Pope Gregory I (590–604) what we call the medieval era began to take shape.

In the West the glories of the medieval period included the development of theology known as scholasticism and the rise of several important religious orders. The popes were fairly successful in maintaining the freedom of the Church from intrusions by secular rulers, and missionaries completed the Christianization of previously pagan Europe. The era of the councils had dovetailed with the predominance of theologians later known as the "Church Fathers." The greatest among them (Augustine in the West, Origen and Gregory Nazianzen in the East) developed the first full articulations of Christian faith, often by writing voluminous commentaries on the scriptures. The scholastics introduced the new logic that had become available through Arab translations of classical Greek texts (especially those of Aristotle). Where the Fathers had blended preaching, exegesis, doctrinal speculation, and mystical writings, the scholastics wanted to be more rigorous, applying philosophy so that faith might gain a better understanding. Indeed, developing a notion of Augustine, the Western scholastics came to define theology as "faith seeking understanding."

Following the medieval era, the end of which saw the corruption of the papacy and much irregularity among the clergy, came several centuries of great confusion. The plagues that ravaged Europe led, in the fourteenth and fifteenth centuries, to a mood of deep depression, while the corruptions in the church led to cries for reform. In the wake of such significant predecessors as John Wycliffe in England and John Hus in Bohemia, Desiderius Erasmus, Martin Luther, Ulrich Zwingli and other reformers made the sixteenth century a period of both creativity and tumult. Eventually what became known as the Protestant Reformation split Western Christendom. By the middle of the sixteenth century, when Roman Catholics regrouped at the Council of Trent, battle lines were drawn that would result in terrible religious wars and the antagonism of Protestants and Catholics down to the twentieth century.

Paradoxically, perhaps, the sixteenth century was also a time when Christianity began to become a truly ecumenical, worldwide religion.

In the wake of the explorers who discovered the "new world" of the Americas and brought Asia into Christian consciousness, missionaries planted the cross on new ground. Two medieval religious orders, the Franciscans and Dominicans, and one order founded during the Catholic Counter-Reformation of the sixteenth century, the Jesuits, furnished many of the most successful missionaries.

While much of Eastern Christendom languished under Islamic rule, Western Christianity found what we now call the modern centuries a great challenge to traditional faith. Such movements as the Reformation, the Renaissance, the Enlightenment, the rise of modern science, modern political revolutions, eventually the Industrial Revolution, colonial incursions in the Americas, Asia, and Africa, the application of critical intelligence in matters of history and textual analysis—all these together brought the death knell of the medieval synthesis of faith and reason, church and state. The political revolutions in North America and France at the end of the eighteenth century changed the face of both North America and Europe. The secular thrust to both ventures relegated Church authority to the margins in political affairs, just as the new physical sciences were doing in many educational circles.

These trends continued in the nineteenth and early twentieth centuries, as theories of evolution, psychoanalysis, relativity, and quantum mechanics destroyed the final remnants of the medieval views of the cosmos and the human being. Protestant Christians split into those who tried to appropriate the findings of the new movements, both political and intellectual, and those who retreated into a sacrosanct world of biblical piety. Catholic Christians, following the conservative lead of the papacy, tended to condemn most of modernity as godless and yearn for the thirteenth century. Only after two world wars did the climate of Western culture begin to change, and with it the future for religion.

The Christian churches made some progress in the first part of the twentieth century toward overcoming the effects of the split between East and West, and then the split of the West during the Reformation. The Second Vatican Council (1962–1965) consolidated many of these gains and brought Roman Catholics into the modern world. Presently there is great interest in Christian spirituality, in part because of a new appreciation of the spiritualities of other world religions, and in part because of the many signs that modernity, as highlighted by the Enlightenment, has itself broken down. What many call a postmodern era, characterized by the globalization of economics and politics, ecological crises, the horrendously destructive capacities of modern arms, the great poverty of large parts of the world, and greater sensitivities to race, sex, and religion is now begging clarification. Few intellectuals are still confident that science and technology will solve all of humanity's problems. Many people, both intellectuals and lay folk, sense that a reform and renewal of the human spirit itself is the great need, and so the great challenge to Christianity and the other traditional sources of wisdom and holiness.

Christian Spirituality

The heart of the spirituality of Jesus was love, of God and of neighbor. With the elevation of Jesus himself to the status of divinity, subsequent Christian spirituality became love of an incarnate deity, with immensely sacramental consequences. That is to say, Christian spirituality had to take special pains to love the historical Jesus, love actual human beings in their here-and-now specificity, love God through rituals that consecrated matter as a channel of grace. The sacred writings that spoke of Jesus and the first generations of church life became the great guidebook of Christian piety. The New Testament colored Christian interpretation of the Jewish bible, inasmuch as Christian commentators thought that Jesus had fulfilled prophecies about the messiah. From the incarnational center of Christian faith came a mandate to make history, the earth, human culture fit to house divinity. The flowering of Christian culture in medieval times gave the fullest indication of what Christian spirituality could be like, for both weal and woe.

When filled with traditional, "catholic" (universal) Christian faith, human culture aspired to find God in all things. This was a motto of the Jesuits, but virtually every other Christian spiritual school felt the same way. Because the Word of God had taken flesh, everything decent in human existence could carry the touch of God. Certainly, human beings were sinful—disordered, weak, self-centered. Nothing proved this more dramatically than the crucifixion of Jesus. But where sin had abounded, Paul said (Romans 5:20–21), grace had abounded the more. In principle, the victory had been won. The resurrection of Christ proved that. So, no matter how suspicious they might become of human motives, orthodox spiritual masters had to believe that human nature had not become fully corrupt. The image of God still worked in the human spirit. The divine Spirit, given by Christ to all who believed, could polish this image more and more, so that eventually believers became holy—full of God's own life.

Art, music, science, politics, sport, marriage, education—nothing was foreign to the Spirit of Christ, or the aspirations of Christian humanism (Christian spirituality convinced that the Incarnation meant a commission to sacramentalize all areas of human experience). Sex was problematic, but not dirty. Money was dangerous, but not intrinsically corrupting. The great sins were pride and unbelief, which closed the human heart to God. As long as the human heart stayed open to God, human culture would remain healthy. The tragedy of the modern centuries, in the eyes of traditional Christians, was the atheistic revolt of much of the intelligentsia. Closing themselves to the transcendent sources of order, both personal and political, the intelligentsia were nearly bound to pave the way for mass murder and tyranny.[10]

The transcendence of God justified "religious life." To leave the world, take vows of poverty, chastity, and obedience, made no sense unless there were a God beyond the world in value as well as being. At its best, Christian culture balanced religious and lay spiritualities, producing a mirror of the Incarnation itself, where divinity was the personal center of human flesh. Just as Christ was both beyond the world and fully immanent in the world, so the overall Christian spirituality produced by the religious and lay vocations was a matter of both/and. On the eve of the Protestant Reformation, however, the lay vocation had been denigrated as second class. The vast majority of Christians lived in fear of hell and aspired to little perfection. When one added the corruption of many clergy, both diocesan priests and religious men and women, one had an intolerable situation. In the name of what we might now call a viable Christian spirituality (a faith that people could take to heart without blushing), Erasmus and Luther attacked clericalism (the assumed spiritual superiority of the clergy) and tried to revive the faith and morals of ordinary Christians.

Protestant Christianity has done the lion's share of work on the matter of a lay Christian vocation. In good measure this has dovetailed with the Protestant stress on Scripture. In the New Testament, one finds little distinction between clergy and laity. The entire community is considered holy, called to share divine life. Most of the apostles were married. Jesus himself lived in the world, was remembered to have worked as a carpenter. The Reign of God meant the renewal of the real, physical, truly historical environment in which human beings suffered and exulted. It meant the transformation to the core of the hopelessness that afflicted pagan culture, the opening of beautiful new vistas. Even when Christianity had long accepted the fact that the Parousia (return of Jesus, to consummate history) expected in the New Testament was as much a symbol as an object of realistic expectation, it continued to think that Jesus had brought an "eschatological" (definitive, consummating) salvation.

Through the Incarnation of the Word, the life, death, and resurrection of the Son of God, history had changed. Indeed, for Paul the very cosmos had changed. Salvation—the radical healing of creation—was present right now, as well as not yet fully achieved. Eschatology was another instance in which mainstream Christian faith sought a balance, an attitude of both/and rather than either/or. Because they believed that faith brought them the very life of God, with the possibility of experiential relations with all three divine persons, astute Christians found present times more gracious than sinful. Because present times obviously included much suffering, including increasing awareness of human mortality, present times could never be confused with "heaven," the direct communion with God that faith said Jesus had entered upon through the resurrection. Heaven was more important than earth, as God was more important than human beings. But no healthy believer could despise the earth, or human beings, or the flesh that Jesus had consecrated, on penalty of rejecting the mysterious way that God had chosen to enter time and open it to eternity.

More acutely than any other spirituality sponsored by the world religions, Christian spirituality has focused on the conjunction of time and eternity, flesh and divine spirit. The center of its entire enterprise has been the God-Man, Jesus Christ. To deny the full humanity of Jesus was to fail the truth and lose the anchor of salvation, the guarantee that it had really transformed space and time. To deny the full divinity of Jesus was also to fail the truth, and to lose the substance of salvation: God's own deathless love, joined so intimately to humanity that it became humanity's inmost meaning. One had to say "both fully human and fully divine." One had to seek a love that stretched as wide as heaven yet did not neglect the smallest bit of human flesh. One had to follow Jesus, make the "imitation of Christ" the actual, if not fully articulated, center of one's Christian spirituality. For Paul, to live was Christ and to die was gain—because through dying one could find more of Christ: union not marred by human weaknesses. For John the trick was for the branches to abide in the vine: human beings to live in the love that constituted the being of the triune godhead itself. These have been representative, paradigmatic Christian spiritualities.

Friendly Criticisms

It is difficult for people raised in Christian cultures to think critically about Jesus, as it is difficult for Muslims to criticize Muhammad, Buddhists to consider where Gautama is wanting, Chinese to think that Master Kung could have fashioned a better social theory. One contrast between Jesus and these other great religious founders is his relative youth. He died before he reached thirty-five. On Christian theological grounds, this is insignificant, inasmuch as his divinity provided all the holiness and wisdom requisite for his work of revelation and salvation. On human grounds (and Christian theological grounds regarding the full humanity of Christ), however, the relative youth of Jesus is worth pondering. Is it possible that, with greater experience, he would have stressed detachment more than passionate involvement, been less prophetic and more sapiential?

This is a speculative question, of course, but the answer may certainly be yes. Jesus knew enough about human folly to make him leery of committing himself to any human enthusiasm, yet had he lived another thirty years he would have learned much more. The center of his life, the overwhelming goodness of his divine father, was the primary source of his independence and detachment (what human, earthly good could compare with the Father?), yet had Jesus begun to feel the effects of aging, come to know from inside the certainty of his death because he was forced to confront the slowdown of his own biology, such detachment might have gained a different flavor. For the Buddha and Confucius, enlightenment about the intrinsically painful nature of all reality, and long experience of the Way, produced a detachment redolent with the wisdom of old age. Jesus never had the opportunity to suffer such experience. He died in his prime years, unaware that more experience might have tempered his passions, reconciled him more biologically to the limitations of everything human.

This relates to the unreality, or romanticism, as some critics have named it, that Jesus' teaching can seem to exhibit. Christian believers are bound to challenge any notion such as this, of course, and humanistic readers of the New Testament are wise to pause before passing judgment on what was unrealistic in Jesus' message and what realistic at a level beyond ordinary human understanding. Still, when one reads the Beatitudes, Jesus seems so otherworldly, so much lifted above ordinary human existence by the divine Spirit, that the possibility, the practicality, of his religious program becomes questionable.

Certainly, one has to take account of the semiticisms of Jesus' speech and rhetoric. Exaggerations, hyperboles, were stock in trade in his neighborhood, and have remained so to the present day. Nonetheless, Jesus preached the definitive coming of salvation. He said that something never seen in history before was dawning. God would transform human nature from the core. He himself was the witness to this present, uniquely gracious reality. The success of Jesus depended on his making good on his claims. He was a credible witness, not the least because he performed deeds (miracles) of such power that people were bound to wonder whether the Reign of God wasn't dawning. Yet Jesus himself intuited that such deeds or signs were not the main point.

The main point was that whenever people gave themselves over to God completely, vastly different possibilities opened. Jesus tapped the wellsprings of human faith, hope, and love. He got to the most creative parts of the human personality, where the self-censoring that usually limited people to what they had known in the past fell by the wayside. Still, the question remains: How realistic was it to think that the experience of the Reign of God or the Spirit of God would remain so vibrant that the poor would be blessed, suffering would become privileged?

The history of Christianity itself suggests that Jesus expected more of human beings than they were likely to be able to deliver. The Church that Jesus founded has shown itself to be all too human: often sinful, arrogant, forgetful of higher things because it has been preoccupied with its own power or wealth. This is not to say that many saints did not keep the ideals of Jesus burning. It is not to say that the fault has not lain more with faithless Christians than with their Master. But it is to say that the detached observer of Christian history has to wonder whether the relatively young man Jesus knew how idealistic his hopes were. Perhaps things would have been different, had the New Testament been formed by a Jesus preaching and teaching in old age or, even more, after his passion and death, fully aware of how stubbornly sinful human beings resist divine grace. We can never know.

At the least, though, we are left with a two-way challenge. The history of Christianity, and much other data about human nature, suggest that only the few will ever open themselves to the Holy Spirit and so realize the possibilities that Jesus pioneered. On the other hand, the example of Jesus, the Christian saints, and analogous holy people from other traditions suggest that the only problem with Jesus' program is that so few people have embraced it wholeheartedly. Nietzsche said that the last Christian died on the cross—a cynical saying, but still provocative. How realistic Jesus was depends on the spiritual status of any who would judge him.

We cannot pretend to stand outside the fray. We cannot cut Jesus, Muhammad, the Buddha, or Confucius down to our own size and pontificate about their achievements without opening ourselves to the accusations of bad faith. Admittedly, much academic work on the great founders stands wide open to this charge. Admittedly, the supposed detachment and objectivity of many scholars become a farce, when the question is personal credentials to teach a way of salvation. Nonetheless, the youth of Jesus remains a pregnant datum. What would the second half of the lifecycle have taught him? How would he have ended his teaching about the service of God, his modeling of human perfection, had he lived to be seventy? Or are we to conclude that no fully genuine spokesperson for divinity is likely to survive to old age? Should we conclude that all people who stand up for their ideals, preach the Reign of God without flinching or compromise, are bound to be dead before forty? Speculative questions, perhaps, until one thinks about what speaking the truth, doing the truth, has tended to mean in the recent China, USSR, or Latin American dictatorships, as well as in supposed democracies.

A final friendly criticism focuses on the harshness that one finds in some of the speech placed in the mouth of the New Testament Jesus. If this speech is faithful to the historical Jesus, he often saw things in black and white terms. Those who did not believe in him would be condemned by God. Those who were not for him were against him— and also against God. Certainly, there are other sayings attributed to Jesus that are more nuanced and kindly. Certainly, we are told that he condemned zealotry among his disciples and said that those who were not against him could be for him. Still, Jesus seems fixated upon the response of his fellow Jews, their decisions for or against his preaching of the kingdom. Meanwhile, a wide world of non-Jewish humanity suffered and played, lost battles and triumphed, under the eye of the One God. Was Jesus' Jewishness a source of myopia, monomania, unawareness of the grander designs of God? Did he limit himself catastrophically by accepting Jewish notions of election, convenant, as being the center of the history of salvation?

These are grand questions, requiring far more space then we have available. They suggest, though, that Jesus the limited human being could not fully manifest the range of the Logos, the infinite Word of God. In submitting to the vicissitudes of history, Jesus opened himself to the criticism that his incarnation of God was too small, partial, parochial, patriarchal—too limited to be revelation *tout court*, without remainder. The beguiling likelihood is that the Risen Christ would have said, "Yes. That is so. That is what a full incarnation of divinity entails."

NOTES

1. See John Tully Carmody, Denise Lardner Carmody, and Robert L. Cohn, *Exploring the Hebrew Bible* (Englewood Cliffs, NJ: Prentice-Hall, 1988), and John Riches, *The World of Jesus* (New York: Cambridge University Press, 1990).
2. *Holy Bible: New Revised Standard Version* (Nashville: Thomas Nelson/Cokesbury, 1990), p. 35.
3. Ibid., p. 4.
4. See John Tully Carmody, Denise Lardner Carmody, and Gregory A. Robbins, *Exploring the New Testament* (Englewood Cliffs, NJ: Prentice-Hall, 1986), and Howard Clark Kee, *What Can We Know About Jesus?* (New York: Cambridge University Press, 1990).
5. See Gerard Sloyan, *Jesus in Focus* (Mystic, CT: Twenty-Third Publications, 1983); Monika K. Hellwig, *Jesus: The Compassion of God* (Wilmington, DE: Michael Glazier, 1983); Lucas Grollenberg, *Jesus* (Philadelphia: Westminster, 1978); Denise Lardner Carmody and John Tully Carmody, *Jesus: An Introduction* (Belmont, CA: Wadsworth, 1987).
6. *The New Oxford Anotated Bible, Revised Standard Version* (New York: Oxford University Press, 1977), p. 1201.
7. Ibid., pp. 1314–1315.
8. Ibid., p. 1300.
9. *The New Testament of the Jerusalem Bible* (Garden City, NY: Doubleday, 1966), p. 23.
10. See David Walsh, *After Ideology* (San Francisco: Harper San Francisco, 1990).

CHAPTER 5

MUHAMMAD

Arab Religion before Muhammad

In beginning an overview of Islam, Fazlur Rahman, a distinguished
historian, notes two broad elements in the immediate religious background of Muhammad's reception of the *Qur'an* (which we may consider the start of Islam). One element was the native Arab culture. The
other element was the presence of Jewish and Christian notions in the
Arabian Peninsula. Although the *Qur'an* (41:37) refers to the worship of
stars among natives (bedouins), on the whole these Arabs were secular,
in the sense that they paid little attention to an afterlife.

The bedouins did create sanctuaries where people could worship
"fetishes" (tokens of spirits), and Rahman thinks that from this worship
may have developed a full-fledged idolatry. He spends more space,
however, on the following cultural qualities:

> The bedouin Arabs believed in a blind fate that inescapably determined
> birth, sustenance (because of the precarious life conditions in the desert),
> and death. These Arabs also had a code of honor . . . that may be
> regarded as their real religious ethics; its main constituent was tribal
> honor—the crown of all their values—encompassing the honor of
> women, bravery, hospitality, honoring one's promises and pacts, and last
> but not least, vengeance. . . . They believed that the ghost of a slain
> person would cry out from the grave until his thirst for the blood of
> vengeance was quenched. According to the code, it was not necessarily
> the killer who was slain in retaliation, but a person from among his kin
> equal in value to the person slain. For reasons of economics or honor,
> infant girls were often slain, and this practice, terminated by the *Qur'an*,
> was regarded as having had religious sanction (6:137).[1]

Southwestern Arabia had developed a culture more sophisticated than the bedouins' since well before the birth of Muhammad. There trade and agriculture flourished. Indications are that originally people venerated stars in that area, but later accepted monotheistic tendencies, including the worship of a deity known as *al-Rahman* (the Merciful). This latter worship may have been a strong native influence on Muhammad, for *al-Rahman* is one of the most important names of *Allah*, the God who dominates Islam. Shortly before the work of Muhammad, Jewish and Christian ideas had become influential in southwestern Arabia, and *al-Rahman* had come to be applied to the First Person of the Christian Trinity.

Ismail and Lois al Faruqi, in their encyclopedic work *The Cultural Atlas of Islam*, downplay the dependence of Islam on Jewish and Christian predecessors:

Were the contribution of the Judeo-Christian tradition to that of Islam to be measured by the co-existence in both of identical religious personalities, events, ideas, and principles, it would be enormous. But co-existence is not contribution; and the fact that Islam came later in history than either Judaism or Christianity constitutes no proof of same. Western scholars, however, not only affirm such contribution but even call it a "borrowing," thus exacerbating Muslim dissatisfaction with Western interpretations of Islam. It is repugnant to speak of "borrowing" between any two movements, an earlier and a later one, when the later sees itself as a continuation and reform of the earlier. The same scholars do not speak of "borrowing" by Christianity from Judaism, or by Buddhism from Hinduism, or by Protestantism from Catholicism [the al Faruquis may be wrong here, at least in some instances]. Yet that is precisely how Islam sees itself regarding Judaism and Christianity, namely, as their very same identity but reformed and purged of the accumulated tamperings and changes of their human leaders and scribes. Islam does not regard itself as a new religion but as the oldest religion—indeed, as the eternal religion of God, of Adam in Paradise and on the earth, of Noah and his progeny. It sees itself as the religion of Abraham and his descendants, of all the prophets God had sent to the Hebrews as well as to other peoples, and of Jesus, the son of Mary. Moreover, Islam assumes the religious legacy of Mesopotamia as its own and does so rightly, since Mesopotamian civilization was the product of

Arab migrants from the Peninsula as they settled in Mesopotamia and were reinforced by the continuous flow of humans from the desert into the Fertile Crescent.[2]

Thus far, this suggests that Arab Religion before Muhammad was a rich, complex entity. Traditions from the southern portion of the peninsula, from the wandering bedouins, from Judaism, from Christianity, and from Mesopotamia all had shaped the people to whom Muhammad came with a message from Allah. Rahman has suggested some of the native Arab components, stressing the tribal code of honor. The al Faruqis stress the biblical line that locates true religion in the posture of the first human beings in paradise, and then takes up the story of the patriarchs and prophets. Abraham becomes a great figure in Islam, as do Jesus and Mary. What most impressed Muhammad, however, was the monotheism of both native and Judaeo-Christian traditions. From the viewpoint of Muslim faith, this monotheism—the soleness of Allah—was branded in the Prophet's soul through the revelations that were assembled into the *Qur'an*. From the viewpoint of possible pre-Muhammadan influences, both Judaism and Christianity are strong candidates, though the monotheism of Judaism was simpler to grasp, due to Christian notions of the Incarnation and the Trinity. Islam has condemned the latter, pruning them from Christianity in what the al Faruqis see as its reform of Christian prophecy.

Related to Islamic monotheism is the phenomenon of prophecy itself. Abraham and Jesus, to mention only two, were predecessors of Muhammad in the line of prophecy that led to the *Qur'an*. They were authentic spokesmen for God, but their message became corrupted. Inasmuch as Muhammad purified the original message, he restored what Abraham and Jesus had proclaimed. The problem was not with the proclamation given to Abraham, Jesus, or any of the other prophets who preceded The Prophet. The problem was that human beings are weak, prone to forget, inclined to dilute or distort the pure Word of God. Still, the tradition that God had called men to proclaim the divine will stood Muhammad in good stead. When he went to his countrymen with the message of the *Qur'an*, they could fit him into a well-known category. Eventually Muhammad became the new paradigm of the prophet, forcing Muslims to realign the ingredients of that category.

When they proclaimed him the "seal" of the line of prophets stretching back to the beginnings of revelation (to Adam), they added the notion that what had gone before him had found its consummation with him. Just as Christians had thought that Jesus had fulfilled Jewish expectations and raised them to a higher level, so Muslims looked on Muhammad as the purifier, reformer, fulfiller of Jewish and Christian prophecy. After Muhammad there could be no further revelations, because what God had given through Muhammad was complete, perfect.

The Mesopotamian aspects of the pre-Muslim Arabian culture were more problematic for Islam than helpful. Certainly, the ancient Mesopotamian accounts of creation appear to have influenced Genesis, but the popular Mesopotamian religion was polytheistic—structured by a pantheon of natural forces like the wind, the sun, the rain, and the seas that shaped people's lives and so required veneration. The most that one can say about such a polytheistic religion, in light of Muhammad's reforms of Arab religious culture in his own day, is that it served as a good example of what Allah was not and could not be: "shared" in any way across a spectrum of locations; parceled out so that he (if given a pronoun, Allah is masculine) is anything less than infinite, wholly complete. Like the pre-Muslim code of honor that Muhammad tried to reform, by making the community of believers more basic than the different tribes, pre-Islamic polytheism served as the point from which the Prophet wanted to move forward, purifying traditional Arab culture in the name of the pure divinity of Allah.

The Life of Muhammad

Muhammad was born about A.D. 570, and he lived about forty years before being transformed into a prophet (The Prophet). Although hard information about his family is sketchy, it seems likely that he was a member of the Quraysh tribe, which was a powerful family in Mecca, and the clan known as Banu Hashim, which was less powerful but had a good reputation. Muhammad was an orphan. His father died before he was born, and his mother died when he was about six. This fact seems to have made him sensitive to the plight of marginal people, and when he began to legislate for the community that Allah wanted him to form, he took care to provide for widows and orphans. Tradition says that he was sent to the desert as an infant, to a wet nurse. His time with a bedouin tribe provided not only physical but also spiritual nourishment. The bedouins were regarded as speaking the purest Arabic and, later, one of the "proofs" for the legitimacy of the Qur'anic revelations that Muhammad had received was the purity of the Arabic in which the Word of God was cast. Also working in the background of this tradition is the notion that Arab culture was born in the desert, and so that contact with the ways of the bedouins (in contrast to the ways of the citified Arabs of Mecca) was a return to the roots of Arab culture—a drink at the wellsprings.

When Muhammad's mother died, he passed into the care of his grandfather. For two years he enjoyed this oversight, which apparently was loving, but then further tragedy struck, because his grandfather also died. By the time that he was eight, then, the future Prophet had experienced a full measure of human mortality. He had never had a chance to know his biological father, his mother had died before he came into reason, and his grandfather too had left him. Did that prepare him to think of God as his only sure, reliable comfort? At the death of his grandfather, his uncle assumed the responsibility for rearing him. Like his grandfather, his uncle also seems to have been kindly. Indeed, when Muhammad first began to preach, his uncle defended him against his detractors, many of whom were polytheists in control of much power in Mecca.

Popular Islamic lore concerning the birth of the Prophet says that his mother had received a revelation that the child she was carrying would become the leader of his people. Other legends say that a Christian holy man noticed the young man Muhammad and pointed him out as a coming prophet. At that time Muhammad was a lowly baggage-handler, so the insight of the monk was taken to be divinely inspired. To protect the youth from troubling experiences, further stories of his adolescence say, God arranged to divert him from nights on the town in Mecca. As Frederick Denny has summarized this legend:

Some stories even tell of Muhammad's being prevented in interesting ways from leaving his flocks to go into Mecca for a "night on the town."

Once he is said to have been distracted from such a goal by a rustic wedding being held on the outskirts. Joining in the festivities, he soon fell asleep. Muslims view Muhammad as sinless and remember such stories as evidences of God's providential arrangement for Muhammad's innocent youth and manhood until he was ready to begin his prophetic career.[3]

Muhammad developed a reputation for being especially honest and trustworthy. By the time that he had come to young adulthood, he was familiar with the caravan business. He came into the employ of a wealthy widow, Khadija, managing her caravan. She noted his good work, liked his upright moral bearing, and proposed marriage. Khadija was perhaps fifteen years older than Muhammad, and by marrying her he gained not only economic stability but the counsel of a mature woman. Indeed, she and his uncle became the first to believe in his call to prophecy when, at about age forty, he began receiving revelations. One story says that the Prophet himself was uncertain about such revelations, even feared for his sanity. Khadija and his uncle helped him to see the vocation that God was giving him. With Khadija Muhammad had six children, four daughters and two sons. Neither of the sons survived to adulthood (which later complicated the question of succession to Muhammad in leadership of the Muslim community).

In his thirties, Muhammad had developed the habit of seeking God in prayer, and at the time that he began to receive the Qur'anic recitals he would sometimes go into the desert night in search of solitude. As reflected in the much-praised but rather flowery translation of the *Qur'an* by A. J. Arberry, Muhammad's visions were dramatic indeed:

By the Star when it plunges, your comrade is not astray, neither errs, nor speaks he out of caprice. This is naught but a revelation revealed, taught him by one terrible in power, very strong; he stood poised, being on the higher horizon, then drew near and suspended hung, two bows-length away, or nearer, then revealed to his servant that he revealed. His heart lies not of what he saw; what, will you dispute with him what he sees? (53:1–11).[4]

The celestial figure is an angel, probably Gabriel. Tradition says that the fact that Muhammad did not flinch from this encounter confirmed his worthiness to receive what followed after it—the later revelations.

The text seems to reflect a time when Muhammad came to some companions to explain what had happened to him and met with skepticism. His insistence on the veracity of his account, along with his description of the angelic being commissioning him, may have been designed to counter such skepticism.

The gist of Muhammad's first preachings, which soon followed his acceptance of the angel's commission and the first of the revelations filled with the message of Allah, dealt with the goodness and power of Allah, the need for Arabs to turn to Allah (the sole God) in anticipation of his coming judgment, the need for worship in response to both the divine goodness and the coming divine judgment, the claim of Arabs on one another for generous help (including the practical help of alms), and Muhammad's own status as a messenger chosen by Allah.

This initial proclamation troubled many Meccans, because turning from their customary gods to worship a single God Allah meant changing their work as well as their accustomed beliefs. Many were involved, directly or indirectly, in religious business directed to spirits or lesser deities. Accepting Muhammad's preaching rendered these spirits insignificant, if not evil: the soleness of Allah wiped them out. Similarly, the social program that soon became prominent in Muhammad's preaching threatened the long-standing tribal structure. Muhammad was saying that loyalty to Allah formed a new community more basic than ties of blood and prior tradition. There were large financial, political, and emotional implications in this assertion. Third, the call to prepare oneself for divine judgment seemed ominous to many and so was unwelcome.

So at first his fellow Meccans rejected the Prophet. Some scholars conjecture that it was while he was trying to understand this rejection that Muhammad learned of Jewish and Christian traditions about the fate of those whom God calls to prophecy, and that such traditions consoled him. His first converts, members of his own family, stood by him, but some of the most powerful clan leaders opposed him vigorously. Muhammad probably began to preach around 613. In 619 he received a double blow, because both his wife and his uncle died. He was gaining converts, but prospects were so unpromising, or dangerous, that in 622 he left Mecca. People in Yathrib, later named Medina ("Town of the Prophet"), asked him to mediate a dispute, and his success gave him a new base of power.

Muslims consider the move of Muhammad from Mecca to Medina, known as the *hejira*, the turning point in his career. Through it he left the old order of Mecca and established a new, Muslim order in Medina. There his revelations often concerned practical matters—things he needed to legislate for the community he was forming. Once in control in Medina, Muhammad began to harass his old foes in Mecca, mainly by disrupting their trade. He was convinced that he had a holy mission, and those who would not accept Allah's word became his enemies. In 624 he won a victory that his followers considered miraculous, defeating a much larger army. Before long he had won several other battles, and then he triumphed in the decisive confrontation known as the Battle of the Ditch. Mecca fell in 630, though more by the Prophet's diplomacy than by military arms, for throughout the war Muhammad had worked hard to convince the Meccan tribes of the rightness of his message and the practical benefits that accepting it would bring. As soon as he was in control, Muhammad cleansed the old Meccan shrines of their pagan paraphernalia. He crushed the final challenge to his power in a skirmish at the town of Hunayn, near Mecca, thereby gaining unchallenged rule of the Arabian heartland.

In the final two years of his life, the Prophet expanded the blueprint for government that he had developed in Medina. His main concern was to educate the people he was leading, to show them the full implications of the faith they had embraced. So well did Muhammad begin this work that shortly after his death in 632 Islam was strong enough to embark on a course of expansion and conquest. By the end of the seventh century it was the dominant force in the Near East.

The Personality of Muhammad

Muslims consider Muhammad the exemplar of Islam. Though it is abhorrent to consider him divine, because Allah does not share divinity with any creature, Muhammad is the best indication of the holy life that Allah requires. The core of Muhammad's personality was his relation with Allah, just as the core of Jesus's personality was his relation with his divine Father. Muhammad became *the* Prophet through the revelations that God gave him. It was his disposition to receive these revelations that most marked his personality. His nocturnal sojourns in the desert for prayer suggest that he was hungry for revelation, needed to experience the power, majesty, and beauty of Allah. Through God's inscrutable choice, he came away more than satisfied. Indeed, he came away completely changed: commissioned to reform his people and place in the world a purified version of the religion that God had wanted from the beginning, when he first made Adam and Eve.

We could say, then, that the core of Muhammad's personality was religious, but if we said this with modern overtones, it would miss the point. There was nothing not religious in the worldview that Allah disclosed. Islam has always fought any distinction of reality into the secular and the religious, the profane and the sacred. Allah is the Lord of all creation: Muhammad had that message burned into his soul. It followed that his conception of leadership in the *Ummah*, the community of Muslims, was holistic. There was nothing incongruous about standing at the head of his people at the hour of prayer and then riding at the head of their army to conquer their foes. Similarly, there was nothing incongruous about spending much time in prayer and heading an extended family, with several wives and children.

Islam is a worldly faith, in the sense that it considers all human experience Allah's domain. It has never approved of celibacy, for either men or women. The Sufis, who have best represented mystical aspects of Muslim faith and culture, have not formed monastic communities. Their "orders" have been headed by sheiks who were married. Thus the exemplary character of Muhammad's personality has included his completeness and balance. He was a man dedicated to Allah but also at home in the world. He could deal with political, military, and family matters, as well as with theology. His prophecy aimed at transforming the whole of traditional Arab culture, in light of the new revelations of God. The body and the spirit, the individual and the community, sexual intercourse and contemplative prayer, food and study—each had its place. Balance, harmony, came from seeing each, dealing with each, with a heart, a soul, open to God.

Traditions about the Prophet, known as *hadith*, were collected from shortly after his death. After the *Qur'an*, they are the most important authority in Muslim culture. Muslim scholars have developed detailed, sophisticated rules for judging the authenticity of a purported remembrance of the Prophet. When considered reliable, a given *hadith* has considerable influence. For example, a practice such as facing Mecca when praying goes back to how Muhammad organized prayer in the earliest community (see the *Qur'an* 2:144). An inquiry into the virtues that holy living requires has to deal with stories about how the Prophet comported himself. For instance, one day Muhammad saw Abu Bakr, his second-in-command, beating a pilgrim (on his way to Mecca) who had let his camel stray. Muhammad smiled in irony: Abu Bakr was a pilgrim in life, still far from his goal of union with Allah. Had he not strayed from the path now and then? Other stories suggest that Muhammad was shy, gentle, gracious, humble. Though he was filled with courage, willing and able to lead Muslim armies, mediate disputes, and stand before God representing his people, he did not swagger or push himself forward. Descriptions of his bearing as a husband and father make him warm, loving, approachable.

The simplicity of the basic Muslim religious program, which goes back to Muhammad, suggests that the Prophet was also clearheaded. The five "pillars" of Islam comprise an eminently practical, wise set of basic responsibilities: reciting the Creed, praying five times a day, fasting during the month of Ramadan, giving alms, and making a pilgrimage to Mecca. The Creed itself is brilliantly concise: "There is no God but God, and Muhammad is God's Prophet." At a stroke, the Creed establishes the radical monotheism of Islam and the full authority of Muhammad. By ordering prayer five times a day, Muhammad ensured that his people would maintain steady contact with Allah, the root of their existence. By legislating fasting during Ramadan, he gave Muslims a regular reminder that all healthy religion has an ascetic component. Almsgiving expresses the solidarity of all Muslims, their responsibility to look out for one another. Pilgrimage to Mecca reminds all Muslims of their center, their founding traditions.

Each of the pillars may be honored simply or profoundly. One can say the Creed with superficial understanding and acceptance, or one can say it after having meditated for years on its implications. The same with prayer, fasting, almsgiving, pilgrimage. By keeping the letter of the obligation, Muslims support their tradition, their community, and remind one another who they are. By penetrating deeper into any of these obligations, fulfilling it with great love and wisdom, individuals enrich the community by reminding it how infinite are the riches of faith in Allah. To have conceived of such a program (how explicitly is not clear), Muhammad must have possessed much insight into both the requirements of monotheistic religion and human nature. By blending faith and practice, he must have realized the mutuality of soul and body, individual and community, understanding and doing. So perhaps the best word for the personality of the Prophet is: beautifully balanced and complete. Muhammad was not eccentric, a genius one could admire but not emulate. His uniqueness lay in the holy worldliness that familiarity with God, being chosen by Allah, gave him.

Muhammad's Teaching about Nature

Inasmuch as the *Qur'an* is the greatest authority in Islamic life, we naturally look to the *Qur'an* for Muhammad's teaching about key elements of reality. The problem with this approach is that it runs counter to Muslim intuition. For Muslims, Muhammad has no Qur'anic teaching not given to him by Allah. The *Qur'an* is not Muhammad's book but Allah's. Indeed, traditional Sunni Muslims think the *Qur'an* is uncreated. It has existed with Allah in heaven as long as Allah has been. Heaven has no time, no before or after. Heaven is eternity: the constant presence of Allah infinitely. Thus the spoken words and written text of the *Qur'an* that human beings use express an unchanging heavenly original. Muhammad did not compose the *Qur'an*. God dictated its contexts, either directly or through angelic intermediaries. Muhammad was the receptacle, the repository, of this dictation. As the *rasul*, the messenger sent by God to humankind, he gave voice to what he had heard. But his speech was no human creation. He did not think up the teachings he announced as coming from Allah. The *Qur'an* rather is the revelation by Allah of what Allah wanted human beings to hear. Muslims submit to its teachings not as to human wisdom, but as to divine self-expression.

That said, the humanistic stance that we have taken throughout this work, and the need for symmetry in our treatment of the great religious founders, compels us to consider the *Qur'an* the main source for Muhammad's views on nature, society, the self, and divinity. For our purposes, Muhammad either functioned as a fully human creative agent in the construction of the *Qur'an*, perhaps completely subordinated to Allah, or he made his own—the basis of what he taught—the revelations that he had received utterly passively. In either case, the *Qur'an* became the basis of the message he had to proclaim, the work he had to accomplish. It represented his mandate, his letters patent. He subscribed to it entirely, and if asked for his views, he certainly would have pointed to it for what he considered God's views set into his mind, heart, soul, and strength. In all these ways, the *Qur'an* was his teaching, and we are justified in going to the *Qur'an* for the positions the human founder of Islam held about the basic zones of reality.

Surah 10, verses 4–7, suggests the Qur'anic view of creation, and so of the natural world:

> Lo! your Lord is Allah Who created the heavens and the earth in six Days, then He established Himself upon the Throne, directing all things. There is no intercessor (with him) save after his permission. That is Allah, your Lord, so worship Him. Oh, will ye not remind? Unto him is the return of all of you; it is a promise of Allah in truth. Lo! He produceth creation, then reproduceth it, that He may reward those who believe and do good works with equity; while, as for those who disbelieve, theirs will be a boiling drink and painful doom because they disbelieved. He it is who appointed the sun a splendour and the moon a light, and measured for her stages, that ye might know the number of the years, and the reckoning. Allah created not (all) that save in truth. He detaileth the revelations for people who have knowledge. Lo! in the difference of day and night and all that Allah hath created in the heavens and the earth are portents, verily, for folk who ward off (evil).[5]

First, we note that Allah is recognizably the biblical God, who according to Genesis made the world in six days. This is a good instance of the general Muslim claim that we considered at the outset: Islam is not a new religion but rather the purification and final form of the prophetic faith begun with Adam and developed through Abraham, the Jewish prophets, and Jesus. God is the director of all that transpires in heaven and on earth. He sees all, and all follows his will, moves according to his plan. Far from thinking of material creation as autonomous, either always having existed or having been created by God and then left on its own, the *Qur'an* is at pains to affirm the constant Lordship of Allah. All things return to Allah. Human beings at death, the rest of creation at its consummation—everything that God has made ends where it began. Allah is the final cause as well as the first cause. He is the *telos*, the consummating end, as well as the beginning.

Second, the sun and the moon come from Allah. The *Qur'an* gives no hint of a doctrine of evolution, in the modern sense. It thinks of the heavens and the earth as having their present forms as the result of Allah's direct activity. There is no suspicion of a Big Bang, and then an unfolding of the astral entities to the production of galaxies, solar systems, or moons. The changes in the moon, which form the basis of the traditional Muslim calendar (for instance, Ramadan is a lunar month, and so sometimes is hot and sometimes cold), come from Allah. He gave them so that human beings could measure time, orient themselves through duration. His creation is truthful (that seems the gist of the tortuous translation in verse 6) and may be relied upon. What he does in making the universe is like what he says to the Prophet: utterly truthful.

Third, the sun is a splendor: something to draw the eye, and also the mind. What does such splendor signify? The wise will ponder this question. The moon is a light. What does its beauty suggest? Why has Allah placed it above human beings, made it draw their admiration? The concluding verse suggests the answer. The difference between day and night is a portent. The alternation of light and darkness, the unfolding of the days into months and years, tells human beings something about Allah and his purposes for them. If they have eyes to see, minds to understand, they will sense the power and control of their Creator. They will trust that the world and history stand under his control. They will admire the beauty, the intricacy, the mysteriousness of his creation, above all the play of light and darkness. Everything in heaven and on earth is a portent. Everything bears the imprint of Allah.

St. Augustine taught the same message to Christians: all creatures are vestiges of God—footprints, showing where God walked, something of what God is like. If people take such portents to heart, they will be able to ward off evil. Evil comes from forgetting the complete sovereignty of God. Evil comes from failing to believe that only Allah is in charge of the world and deserves complete obedience. Wise people, people of deep faith, need only to contemplate the sun and the moon, the change of the seasons, to recall how mighty is their Lord, and how wonderful it is that one so mighty should also be compassionate and merciful.

In explaining how Muslim theology tended to regard creation, an article in *The Concise Encyclopedia of Islam* emphasizes an instantaneous act (what Christian theology means by both "creation from nothingness" and "continual creation"):

> Creation . . . is not a process but an instantaneous act; and the changes which natural and human history imply are the successive revelations of that act in time, which, along with extension, number, and the other conditions of existence, exist for man, but not for God. The links between apparently "successive" creations may appear to be cause and effect on the "horizontal" human plane, giving rise to the theory of evolution, for example; but not *in divinis*. On the earth night becomes day, continents form, mammals appear, empires rise and fall, Alexander conquers as far as the Indus, Napoleon retreats from Moscow. These are events over millennia; for God they are all in the eternal present, along with Adam's Fall and the end of the world.[6]

This description expands the horizon of Muslim thought about creation from what we find in the text of the *Qur'an*, so that it includes later Muslim speculation. Still, the point is valid for Muhammad himself. Creation comes from God as a single, instantaneous act. It derives from the divine nature, which is not subject to the vicissitudes of space and time. Human beings are bound to periodize time and map space. But their work, even though blessed by God (encouraged, for example, by the alternation of day and night that Allah has established in the heavens), does not encompass the foundations of the natural or human worlds.

Only God is the foundation of these worlds. Nothing exists apart from God, and nothing acts apart from God. Nothing develops except as God has determined. We shall consider the problem of human freedom that this creates in the section on the self. Here it is enough to realize that physical creation has served Muslims primarily as a proof of the divine sovereignty and providence. Allah has put nature into humanity's keeping, in the sense that human beings have the need and right to develop the earth's resources. But human beings never become the full, ontological possessors of creation. They cannot, because creation stems from the Creator, the sole source of being and ultimate meaning. Human beings are God's "vice-regents," standing in for God in the rule of subhuman creation. But this vice-regency has a limited significance. Much as it dignifies human beings, it detracts not a whit from the lordship of the Lord of the Worlds.

Muhammad's Teaching about Society

There is much social teaching in the *Qur'an*, but little political theory. Muhammad assumes that humankind forms a unity. In the creative plan of God, human beings were one "nation" (10:20), but they became dispersed into different groups after the Fall. The Prophet also assumes leadership of the "House of Islam," the community of believers. His right to this leadership is unquestioned: God has given him the role. Just as human beings are vice-regents of God in creation, ruling over subhuman beings, so the Prophet rules over the community of believers—is Allah's representative.

After the death of Muhammad, the question of rule in the Muslim community became vexed. Muhammad died suddenly, without having made provision for a successor. Two traditional Arab views of succession came into conflict. One view was that blood relatives ought to ascend to power. The other was that the most capable person left behind ought to rule. Arab tribal custom blended both views. If the closest blood relative (eldest son; daughters were not considered) of a sheik were competent, he would succeed. If his competence were questionable, tribal elders could choose someone else. Thus, the situation after the death of the Prophet was ripe for dissent.

In fact, the major schism in Islam, the rift between Sunnis and Shiites, began with the death of the Prophet. The Sunnis are the descendents of those who put Abu Bakr in power. The Shiites are the descendents of those who thought that Muhammad's closest male blood relative, his son-in-law Ali, should have succeeded. Abu Bakr was a longtime associate of Muhammad and his second-in-command, as we have seen. Ali was the husband of the Prophet's daughter Fatima, but unimpressive to many of the Prophet's inner circle. So Abu Bakr became the first caliph (ruler of the Muslim community, after the Prophet). Later Ali got his chance, but internal strife resulted in his assassination, and then the assassination of his sons, making the rift between the two factions irremediable.

Apart from the notion of the caliphate, which later gave way to the sultanate (a term originally designating temporal, especially military power, but later becoming more comprehensive), Islam has elaborated few political institutions. In this it has reflected the Prophet himself. The lawyers who developed the *Shariah*, the body of Muslim religious legislation, always exerted great influence. This continues today, inasmuch as the mullahs and ayatollahs of Muslim theocracies wield much political influence. Muslim society has been patriarchal, so women have seldom been official leaders, teachers, lawyers. Women have been influential saints, and Islam has considered the roles of wife and mother full of dignity. But in the Prophet's day, polygamy and the subordination of women were the rule, and Islam held to this rule until, in some Muslim countries, modern secular ideas took hold.

For the *Qur'an*, a man may have up to four wives, as long as he can provide for them, both materially and emotionally. The witness of one man is worth that of two women in a court of law, and female children do not have the same rights as male when it comes to inheritance. A man may divorce a woman almost at whim: if she displeases him. Divorce for a woman is more difficult. A Muslim male may marry a non-Muslim, but a Muslim female may not marry a non-Muslim. In the case of a divorce, children remain with the father. The rights of women to education have been markedly less than men's, and in many periods women have not been welcome in the mosque. The *Qur'an* lays a foundation for such practices as veiling and purdah (the seclusion of women, including that of several wives to form a harem), and in general it fears the exposure of females to males, for both their own safety and the lust they may incite.

Muhammad actually improved the lot of women, compared to what it had been before the *Qur'an*. Polygamy was not simply a matter of male lust, it also served some longstanding social needs, such as how to provide for poor women who could not assemble a dowry or women who could not attract a man. They could become second, third, or even fourth wives. Though competition among wives was always possible, wives sometimes cooperated and became friends, supporting one another in the social isolation their culture could impose. Women were supposed to concentrate on pleasing their husbands and raising their children well. Those were their tickets to paradise (the Garden). Sometimes the tradition said that women were to obey men the way that men were to obey God. This is not found in the *Qur'an*, but the *Qur'an* does set men over women, because this is the divine plan and men have to provide for women materially. At its best, then, Muslim culture encouraged men to provide for women generously, so that women could raise the next generation well.

As the requirements to give alms to the poor and make the pilgrimage to Mecca suggest, Muhammad was concerned about the solidarity of his followers. Traditional Arab culture had made family members close. He wanted to help Muslims think of all fellow believers as brothers and sisters. The alms, which was not optional, concretized the duty each Muslim had to consider the welfare of others, especially the unfortunate. Widows, orphans, the poor, the sick, the handicapped—all were the responsibility not just of their closest relatives but also of the entire community. Obviously, early Muslim cultures had no insurance, institutionalized health-care, homes for the elderly, the mentally ill, or the orphaned. The community had to meet these needs. The alms was a way of gathering some of the material resources necessary to do so.

The symbolism of the pilgrimage to Mecca (*hajj*) ran in the same direction. Pilgrims were to wear the same garb, go through the same ceremonies, consider race, nationality, even sex secondary to their common faith. Mecca became the international center of Islam, the navel point. Psychologically, it was the place to which Muslim imaginations went, Muslim hearts turned, when the desire was to feel at one with the whole body of believers. By requiring the daily prayers to be said in the direction of Mecca (each mosque has a niche showing this direction), Muslim leaders kept faith with Muhammad's original instincts. The Prophet had created a religion and scripture for the Arab people. They could compare themselves favorably to the Jews and Christians, who were also "peoples of the book," all the more so when Muslims considered Qur'anic religion the purification and perfecting of biblical religion. Muslims would also have a capital comparable to Jerusalem and Rome or Constantinople. They would be able to feel themselves united, in spirit if not legal, geographical identity.

We have noted the reluctance of Islam to make distinctions between sacred and secular zones. Put more positively, Muslims have thought that laws and customs ought to derive from the *Qur'an*, directly or indirectly, so that all of culture could be pleasing to Allah. Thus, marriage, inheritance, education, and business were shaped by traditions generated through reflection on the surahs of the *Qur'an*, the practice of the Prophet, the teachings of the leading schools of Muslim law, the consensus of the community, analogous reasoning (to bridge the way from past traditions to new circumstances), and similarly religiously grounded sources of authority.

In the twentieth century some Muslim countries adopted secular constitutions, based on Western models, but with the upsurge of fundamentalist forces in recent decades, such constitutions have come under heavy attack. Iran, Egypt, Iraq, Pakistan, and India, to name only a few countries that have tried to modernize, have all suffered, in different ways, in the process of trying to work out a viable accommodation between legislation based on religious traditions and legislation suited to a secular, religiously pluralistic society.

Muhammad's Teachings about Self

For the Qur'an, the self cannot be separated from nature, other people, or, especially, Allah. Allah made human beings from dust and a clot of blood. Allah is the direct creator of the soul. So the first relationship the self has to establish correctly is that with Allah. A person who stands

right with Allah is successful. A person who offends Allah is ruined.
At the Judgment, people will pass to the Garden or the Fire based on
their faith. If they have believed in Allah, and carried out his precepts,
they will be saved. If they have not believed, have lived disobediently,
they will be condemned. Allah is merciful, above all in having made
clear the path to success, salvation, pleasing him, gaining the Garden.
He was merciful in making creation full of portents testifying to his
power, but his greatest mercy was to give a line of prophets to call
humanity to the right path. The consummation of this revelational
mercy was the gift of the *Qur'an* through Muhammad. Now that they
know what is required of them, human beings have no excuse for not
carrying it out.

A major issue in the history of Muslim theology has been the freedom of the human being. A text such as surah 57:22 could call such
freedom into question:

> Every misfortune that befalls the earth, or your own person, is ordained
> before We bring it into being. That is easy for Allah: so that you may not
> grieve for the good things you miss or be overjoyed at what you gain.[7]

This is predestination, in the sense that for Allah everything is worked
out in the eternal present of the divine mode of existence. Allah knows
at any instant (as human beings imagine the divine existence to occur;
in fact Allah does not have instants, in the sense of discrete moments
forming a sequence of past, present, and future) the entirety of his
creative plan and work. The spiritual consequence of accepting this
priority, oversight, and execution of the divine plan should be acceptance. People who bow low in prayer as a genuine expression of their
submission to the complete sovereignty of Allah should not grieve at
misfortune or exult at good fortune. What happens is the will of Allah.
They have to struggle to believe that whatever comes is a blessing of
Allah, meant for their benefit. That benefit may emerge through chas-
tisement, to purify their faith and detach them from worldly things. Or
it may come through bounty, allowing enjoyment of the good things of
creation, so that people may feel the generosity of Allah. Either way,
the point is to submit to Allah, to be a genuine Muslim: one concerned
only to accept what Allah disposes.

Does this mean, however, that human salvation—the fate of human beings after death—has been worked out "ahead" of any acts that a person performs? Orthodox Islam, basing itself on the call of the Prophet for specific kinds of behavior, has answered no. Human beings have sufficient freedom to be responsible for their destinies. They have the power to say yes or no to the revelations of the *Qur'an*. Allah does not force them to accept the divine will and carry it out. They can become unbelievers, sinners, even criminals. Precisely how they can have such freedom when everything stands under the control of Allah is not clear. It cannot be clear, and no other religious tradition has made it clear. The issue of human freedom in concert with divine predestination asks us to coordinate two realms of being, the infinite and the finite, which we cannot link. We do not understand the relations between infinity and finitude, and so we cannot say how God can be fully in charge of the cosmos and human beings still free to choose to obey or disobey God.

The *Qur'an* suggests that both sides of the relationship—God's full control and human freedom—have to be maintained. It would make no sense to castigate people for their unbelief and sins if they could not do otherwise. Even in this Qur'anic text, the implication is that people can accept their fortune, good or bad, or reject it, fight against it. They are free to respond to suffering or success, can determine their own psychological state. We may say, then, that Muslim psychology counseled people to choose freely to accept the divine disposition of their lives. When pious people said, "as God wills," they were choosing to dispose themselves to God's intentions.

The social relations of the self are strong in the *Qur'an*. Muhammad is much concerned with the care of children, the treatment of unbelievers, the relations between men and women, how to handle inheritances, when to go to war. His followers constitute a unified community. They do not pray or believe, work or raise children, alone. They are separate from unbelievers, separate even from Jews and Christians, who are not unbelievers but also are not Muslims. Muhammad wants Islam to spread to all peoples, but those who refuse to accept his message retain God-given rights. They have to submit to Muslim rule, but they do not have to become Muslims. Indeed, when many conquered peoples wanted to convert to Islam, the community had to figure out ways to integrate them into the still tribal social structures of Arab culture.

The Muslim self is not an unhappy tension of spirit and matter, as Greek psychology tended to depict it. The teaching of Muhammad assumes that human beings have both physical and spiritual needs. The spiritual are more important, but the physical are fully legitimate. Islam does not teach a doctrine of original sin. Human beings have not been wounded in the ways that Christian theology, following St. Augustine, often has depicted them. Human beings are weak. They tend to forget the goodness of Allah and his precepts. But they are not alienated by fallen nature from God and so in need of a savior. Jesus did not really die on the cross. He only seemed to die. It could not be that God would allow a great prophet to be treated so badly. The self will only find its fulfillment in communion with Allah, through obedience and faith, but this fulfillment is compatible with life in the world. The Muslim saints, often basing their practices on traditions about the Prophet, have urged moderation in sensual matters: food, drink, clothing, sex, housing. They have lauded prayer, both communal and private. But they have not promoted any world-hating asceticism. The most they have said is that right order, proper priorities, enjoin that one's religious duties come first.

When it came to mystical claims for union of the self with divinity, Islam drew a cautionary posture from the clear teaching of the *Qur'an* about the transcendence of Allah. One could never bridge the gap between Creator and creature. No union could become an identification. Thus the famous mystic Al-Hallaj was put to death as a heretic for claiming to have become God (lost his identity in God). Relatedly, the *Qur'an* denies that God has a Son. Nothing material, finite, or created can share the divinity. There could be no Incarnation, as Christians claim. That is a blasphemy. So the self does not have any potential to be called into a share of the divine life. The Garden is not any substantial participation in the life of Allah. It is a reward for fidelity to Allah, and it offers closer forms of communion with Allah, enjoyment of Allah, than are possible on earth. But it does not abrogate the chasm between creature and Creator. The self is always finite.

The greatest passion of the Muslim religious self, according to the *Qur'an*, is faith. Some of the Muslim saints have spoken eloquently about the love of God, but love—romance, marriage, friendship, parent-child affection—is not the central analogue for the successful relation to Allah. Faith and obedience are more central. Awe before the majesty, power, goodness, or mercy of God is more appropriate than love. The great insight of Muhammad was that God is God—unique, exalted. The correlative anthropological insight was that human beings should bow low, submit, obey, even think of themselves as God's slaves—because this is simply the way that things are, the utterly holy reality. Certainly, the pious person feels great gratitude toward Allah. He who could have been only a frightening judge has chosen to be compassionate and merciful, very good. But he is not the lover of the soul, the passionate bridegroom, or the intimate and so in some ways equal friend. Later Muslim piety might veer toward some of these relations and analogies, but the mainstream loosed by the *Qur'an* was plain: Master/servant, Creator/creature. The self would find its greatest fulfillment in living humbly, gratefully, as a servant overwhelmed to be admitted into the palace of the Great King, overjoyed to be able to respond with praise and service.

Muhammad's Teachings about Divinity

We have implied many of the most salient features of Muhammad's theology strictly so-called. Allah is personal, a being of unlimited intelligence and will. Allah can be described using characteristics familiar from human behavior: compassionate, merciful, full of power, knowing everything. Allah is the source of all that exists. History, both natural and social, unfolds as Allah has decreed. Allah is alone in divinity. No other being shares his estate. Relatedly (as Muhammad understood Christian teaching), Jesus is not the divine Son of God. God is not a trinity of divine persons. As Islam has understood Christian theology, three "persons" are incompatible with the uniqueness, the simple soleness, of God. God dwells in eternity. How God produced effects in time is beyond human understanding, but not beyond divine understanding and power. God is the upholder of the moral law. God's Judgment will mete out to sinners and saints their just deserts.

Muhammad is the mouthpiece or spokesperson for God. God chose Muhammad, for God's own reasons, to recite the message of coming Judgment and mercy that God wanted to impart. Angels serve God's Will, but they do not share divinity. Wicked spirits exist by God's permission, but their power is limited. God wants a pure response from human beings. As noted, faith and obedience are the hallmarks of true religion. Only God himself can be the center of true religion. All sorcery, witchcraft, divination, and idolatry are wicked. The worst sin in the Muslim catalogue is unbelief. Idolatry is a form of unbelief. To focus one's ultimate concerns on a limited, non-ultimate object is ruinous. For that reason, orthodox Muslims have condemned the modern humanistic movements, such as Marxism, that would replace God with human progress or well-being.

Very important for Muslim culture has been the Qur'anic prohibition on representations of God. Pre-Muslim Arab religion had been idolatrous, representing many spiritual powers to which people could pray. The safeguard against such idolatry was to prohibit pictures of divinity. The episode of the Golden Calf in the Bible (Exodus 32:1–35) stood as a permanent warning. Thus, Muslim art became nonrepresentational. The safest ornamentations for mosques were linear embellishments that suggested the endlessness of God. Artists could decorate Qur'ans (the books), and such decoration through elaborate calligraphy became a much-prized art. But always one had to refrain from picturing God. Pictures of God, idols, were the great deceiver. God was pure spirit. To materialize God was to fall into grave error.

How could one avoid idolatry when using the Word of God? Did not sound have as much potential for drawing people astray as sight? Islam has tended not to think so, yet it has also been leery of sacred music, though chanting verses from the *Qur'an* could become a high art. Pondering the text has been the major way of praying and studying. Gnostic influences sometimes led Sufis to give Qur'anic words numerical values and to work out codes to inner meanings, but the mainstream of Muslim theology and law has opposed such practices. The best context for theology, in the sense of understanding Allah, has been the emptiness, the nakedness, of the desert. There the voice of Allah could sound in all its primordiality. The more quiet human beings could give to the Word of God, the more strongly it could form their souls. The literal words of the Qur'an were to be prized, but deeper Muslims knew that these came forth from an absolute mystery.

The best way to understand what human beings could understand about Allah was to approach the divine majesty in the spirit of the first surah of the *Qur'an*. N. J. Dawood has called this surah an "exordium": a challenge to set one's soul in good order. The text itself says:

> In the name of Allah, the compassionate, the merciful. Praise be to Allah, Lord of the Creation, the Compassionate, the Merciful, King of Judgement-day! You alone we worship, and to You alone we pray for help. Guide us to the straight path, the path of those whom You have favored, not of those who have incurred your Wrath, nor of those who have gone astray.[8]

The enterprise of reading the *Qur'an*, hearing it recited, opening oneself to its directions—all this ought to transpire "in the name of Allah." Indeed, many Muslims would say that every human enterprise ought to transpire "in the name of Allah." That intention would keep people from doing wicked things, and it would affirm the plain fact that there is nothing irreligious—nothing that does not stand under Allah's scrutiny, depend on his power, proceed according to his plan. What are the first attributes of Allah that the believer should call to mind? His compassion and mercy. One should come to him in hope, more than fear. One should think of him as inclined to favor rather than punish.

As with other profound religions, Islam has made praise and worship central. Muhammad's responses to Allah in the *Qur'an* ring with praise and worship. Again and again the Prophet veers away from exposition to laud the godness of Allah, the majesty of Allah, and offer the praise that Allah deserves. Worship is the complete submission of the rational creature to its Creator. Worship means acknowledging the godness of God, loving the godness of God, aspiring to serve the godness of God. The note that Allah is King of judgment day reminds all readers of the first surah that the *Qur'an* is about serious matters—the most serious possible. Allah will require an account of how people have used the lives he has given them, what they have done with the message he has vouchsafed to grant through Muhammad. Allah is the only one whom Muslims can worship, the sole source of help to whom they should recur. To seek spiritual help, deep meaning, from any other source would be to sin gravely. To worship any other deity would be to commit idolatry.

What is the straight path, the way walked by those whom God has favored? The implication is that it is the existential way laid out by the Prophet. One may formalize this way in terms of the Five Pillars, but the inner substance is more difficult to attain. The true Muslim, walking the right path perfectly, has become a complete submitter to, embracer of, the divine will revealed in the *Qur'an*. The *Qur'an* holds the place in Islam that Jesus holds in Christianity: exemplification of the will of God, the nature of God; guide that gives truth and life. The path of those who go astray is manifold: any unbelief, idolatry, sin that denies the lordship of Allah, the prophecy of Muhammad. Complete fidelity, then, is the goal of Muhammad's teachings about Allah. Those teachings were markedly practical, not at all speculative. Muhammad was not interested in thinking about God for intellectual pleasure. His passion was to understand God rightly so that Muslims could praise and serve God as God deserved.

Islam after Muhammad

When the Prophet died in 632, he left his community bereft but well-founded. Abu Bakr took charge, and the probability is that he carried out plans that Muhammad had formulated rather clearly. For its basic resource, the community had the revelations given to the Prophet. Quickly the records of what Muhammad had experienced in receiving the *Qur'an* were organized into manuscripts. The principle of organization was simple: the longest accounts went first, the shortest accounts went last. Scholars have since formed hypotheses about the dating of different surahs. The basic distinction they have observed is that between revelations received in Mecca and revelations received in Medina.

Although close analysis suggests that one can assign different verses within a given surah to each of the two locales, the major thematic difference seems to be that the revelations associated with Medina are more practical: concerned with the matters for which the leader of a newly founded community would have to legislate. The revelations associated with Mecca, at the beginning of Muhammad's prophetic career, tend to be more dramatic: concern for Judgment, tremulous experience of the majesty of Allah, worry about how the message will be received. Combined, though, the Meccan and Medinan surahs produced a comprehensive scripture. Muslims could find in it both reasons to pray ardently and starting points for a faithful resolution of practical problems in family life, dealings with non-Muslims, regulating fasting, and the like.

In addition to the *Qur'an*, the community had its memories of Muhammad himself. As noted, how he had comported himself, what he had said on such and such an occasion, how he had bowed in prayer, what he had taught about women and children—all this was treasured, recorded, taken to heart as a model for later leaders. The community knew that Mecca would be its center. It knew that the one God, Allah, would be its sole treasure. It brimmed with excitement at the prospect of offering to all Arabs a pan-tribal identity. It rejoiced in the purification of the traditional shrines in Mecca, which included the *Ka'bah*, the central precinct, and its ancient black stone (perhaps a meteorite), long reverenced in the area. The program of the Five Pillars lay ready to hand, though how crisply formulated is not certain. The sense that Allah had solved the problems of how Arabs were to live, what guidance they were to follow, where their future greatness lay gave Muhammad's successors great energy.

Abu Bakr had to deal with efforts by tribes forced into the Muslim community to break away. Shortly after his death in 636, however, the community was sufficiently united to expand into areas nominally controlled by Byzantium and Persia. By the end of 636 Muslim armies had gained control of Jerusalem and Damascus. After that, their record continued to be one of nearly unqualified military success. Many of the peoples adjacent to the Arabian peninsula were restless—unhappy with Christian or Persian rule. They were ripe for conquest, and some welcomed the new religious vision that the Muslims offered.

Thus, by 649 all of Persia lay in Muslim hands. In the early 640s the Muslims had success in Egypt, taking control of both Cairo and Alexandria. Quickly transposing themselves from desert-based forces to maritime powers, they gained control of the southeastern Mediterranean at the same time. By 648 they had conquered Cyprus. In 655 they held control of the waters around Greece and Sicily. They also moved quickly on land, conquering Berber regions around Tripoli in 643 and shortly thereafter the Nubian capital of Dongola. In 661 the Umayyad caliphate gained control, and this Muslim dynasty directed even more ambitious expeditions. Muslims traveled to India, China, and western Europe. Islam moved into Afghanistan, Armenia, Iraq, and eastern India; by 800 all these areas lay under Muslim control.

Shortly after 800, the Muslim domain extended westward from Palestine to the Atlantic. Islam controlled the southern two-thirds of the Iberian Peninsula, and Muslim soldiers had advanced into France as far as Orleans. Two generations earlier they had taken charge of southern France. In the ninth century they crossed into Switzerland, eventually controlling many of the Alpine passes. Until 1050 southern Europe was a Muslim preserve. Had earlier incursions of Huns not weakened the Muslims, the Normans who drove them from Europe in the second half of the eleventh century might well have failed.

Concommitant with this military expansion went a broadly based cultural development. Partly as a result of the internal logic of the Islamization of Arab culture, and partly through contact with newly conquered or contacted peoples, Muslims produced impressive scientific, artistic, literary, and religious innovations. Fertilized by Greek and Persian sources, their scientists, philosophers, astronomers, and physicians composed new treatises. Muslim scholars produced translations of classical Greek and Persian texts. Muslim architects elaborated the principles for building huge, often gorgeous mosques, which became the patterns even for nonreligious buildings. Cairo, Baghdad, and such Spanish cities as Cordoba and Toledo became centers of Arab learning and culture. In Spain Muslims, Christians, and Jews coexisted relatively peacefully, often debating religious issues with tolerance and mutual profit. Speaking about the medieval period generally, apart from Spain, we may say that the writings of such giants as the Muslims Averroes and Avicenna, the Jew Maimonides, and the Christian Thomas Aquinas share many similarities, including large debts to classical Greek philosophy and the conviction that reason provides a basis for cross-religious dialogue.

The major religious development during the centuries after the death of the Prophet was the rise of Sufism. Just as Christian monasticism had arisen as a reaction against the dangers of worldly success, so did Sufism. The Sufis were concerned that the spirit of Islam, the desire for living contact with Allah, would get lost among the practical concerns of administering a rich array of new territories. They also feared that the lawyers, who were elaborating the seeds sown in the *Qur'an* and *Hadith* into a full corpus of Islamic law, would miss the simple religious center. The various Sufi orders developed distinctive religious practices—for example ways of meditating, including the dances of the dervishes. Common to most orders, though, was direction by holy men in the ways of the interior life. Most Sufi brotherhoods or lodges established a succession of such spiritual masters. Pious men would move to the neighborhood of their chosen master and take regular direction from him, even as they continued to work to support their families.

Sufis developed an extensive literature exploring the mystical life. Although they claimed to revere the tradition, and to base their practices on it (above all, on the *Qur'an*), many staid Muslims came to fear that the Sufis would infect Islam with superstition. To this day, opinion divides concerning the benefits that Sufism brought to Islam. Those hospitable to the mystical life tend to see them as heroes, while those wanting a plainer adherence to the simple program couched in the Five Pillars tend to see them as having deflected Islam from its more practical, reliable, and so better beginnings.

The embrace of Islam by such peoples as the Turks and Mongols brought new, non-Arab traditions into creative friction with Qur'anic culture. Persia became a center of a glorious Muslim (but non-Arab) culture, one especially renowned for its poetry. In India Muslims interacted with Hindus, beginning a long history of antagonism that continues to the present day. The conflict there, as in many other places where Muslims came to rule, lay between Islamic prohibitions on idolatry and native religious practices that represented various gods. Until the modern period, when European forces (especially French and British) bent on colonial expansion took power away from Islam in the Middle East, India, and Africa (Muslims having lost control of southern Europe earlier), Islam resembled a system of epicycles. It had no single political center, and several cultural centers vied for influence: Egypt, Turkey, Iraq, Persia, Northern India.

As modern European ideas penetrated, in the wake of European military power, many Muslim countries had to consider updating their political, philosophical, scientific, and technological outlooks. At first intellectuals tended to be open to Western ideas, but by the middle of the twentieth century a religious backlash was beginning. Modern European and American culture, for all its technological prowess, seemed to many Muslims godless, and so destructive of the wellsprings of a healthy culture. As pressed most forcefully by fundamentalists, this impression stands atop the agenda for future Islamic development.

Muslim Spirituality

In introducing a volume of studies on Islamic spirituality, the noted Muslim scholar Seyyed Hossein Nasr begins as follows:

> The Spirit manifests itself in every religious universe where the echoes of the Divine Word are still audible, but the manner in which the manifestations of the Spirit take place differs from one religion to another. In Islam, the Spirit breathes through all that reveals the One and leads to the One, for Islam's ultimate purpose is to reveal the Unity of the Divine Principle and to integrate the world of multiplicity in the light of that Unity. Spirituality in Islam is inseparable from the awareness of the One, of Allah, and a life lived according to His Will. The principle of Unity (*al-tawhid*) lies at the heart of the Islamic message and determines Islamic spirituality in all its multifarious dimensions and forms. Spirituality *is tawhid* and the degree of spiritual attainment achieved by any human being is none other than the degree of his or her realization of *tawhid*. For the Word manifested itself in what came to the be Islamic universe in order to declare the glory of the One and to lead human beings to the realization of the One. The central theophany of Islam, the Quran, is the source *par excellence* of all Islamic Spirituality. It is the Word manifested in human language. Through it, knowledge of the One and the paths leading to Him were made accessible in that part of the cosmos which was destined to become the abode of Islam.[9]

It is not clear what the Spirit means in this context, but it seems closely related to divinity. What is clear is Nasr's conviction that unity is the first name of the Muslim deity. Allah is One, in the sense of unified in himself, having no parts or peers, and existing as the sole divinity. Everything finds its source and reason to be in this unity. Allah is the sole font of creation, the sole explanation of why things are as they are, and also of why their being as they are is good. To be a Muslim of lively faith, a Muslim with a vibrant spiritual life, one must be striving to grow in one's awareness of the divine unity. Equally, one must be striving to do the divine will, as a way of uniting oneself with the One God. For Nasr the criterion of spiritual accomplishment is the degree to which such striving has succeeded. The deeper the Muslim's realization of the Oneness, the Unity, of Allah, the greater his or her sanctity.

Let us reflect on the implications of this position. First, it gives reality a stark clarity. One point of reference determines all meaning. Allah is the source of everything that exists. Without Allah there would be no creation, no humanity, no meaning. Common sense therefore dictates that people refer the totality of their lives to Allah. The bottom line in every significant calculation ought to be, How does this square with the Unity of Allah? Is it compatible with his unique lordship? The many things of the natural world, and the equally many things of the diverse human cultures, are radically alike in being subject to these questions, this bottom line.

For the pious Muslim, literally nothing stands on its own, apart from Allah. Every physical being, every thought, every moral evaluation transpires under the umbrella of the divine presence, will, plan. That is why unbelief is so disastrous. Not to accept the bottom line in the equation of human existence is to ruin such existence. Not to honor the One Lord who determines all significance is to be foolish, ungrateful and abhorrent. Relatedly, to put anything in the place of Allah is to err grievously. Idolatry is not a benign mistake, a simple failure to move from tangible forms of the divine presence to the single pure form. It distorts the entire universe. It throws one's whole perception of reality out of kilter. This was the realization that crashed through to Muhammad with such power. This was the burning center of the Qur'anic revelation. There is *no* God but God. There is no thing independent of God.

The description of the *Qur'an* as the central theophany of Islam suggests the complementary portion of Muslim spirituality. If asked where to learn about the Unity, the Divine Principle, Allah, the Muslim is bound to point to the *Qur'an*. We have noted the parallel between the *Qur'an* and Jesus, the Incarnate Word. The *Qur'an* is the divine Word of Allah. It gives form, a kind of materiality, to the divine mind. What Allah has chosen to say in human language reposes in the *Qur'an*. The Bible has its validity, since it gathers together the testimony of estimable prophets who preceded Muhammad. But only the *Qur'an* is the adequate expression in human language of the divine Word. Only Muhammad mediated the final, consummate revelation of Allah, after which there can be no more. Clearly, then, Muslims seeking spiritual guidance ought to recur first to the *Qur'an*. Clearly, no Muslim spirituality hoping to reach the Unity or wanting to keep faith with Islamic tradition would look in any other direction, let alone dare to contravene Qur'anic teaching.

We glimpse how this attitude has functioned in the history of Muslim piety in the following reflections from a study of Muslim prayer:

> It should be noted that the recitation of the Quran and the keeping up of prayer of remembrance (*dhikr*) of the Blessed Name *Allah* converge upon one and the same focal point, that is, the development of man's [the human being's] awareness, which is fostered by meditation upon the revealed Word of God and is fortified by obedience to what God wants him to do. For the believer, the revelation of the Quran is an act which is itself evidence of the Mercy of God, in that it was revealed to man for his benefit and to help him to cope with the problems of life. Continual and constant remembrance of God's Name or recitation of his revealed Word is one sure way of acquiring nearness (*qurb*) to Him. Prayer acts as a constraining influence upon the animal impulses of man and keeps him away from things that are foul, ugly, and unclean.[10]

First, we note that recitation of the *Qur'an* is a primary form of Muslim prayer. Simply saying the words reverently reaches out to

Allah, honors Allah, as "prayer" intends. Second, remembrance of the divine name is facilitated through use of the *Qur'an*. The *Qur'an* is where the divine name is most available, has its beauty and significance best displayed. Third, the goal of prayer (of spirituality as a whole)—awareness of God—is fostered by meditation on the revealed Word of God: the *Qur'an*. Meditation alone is not enough (one must also obey the divine Word), but meditation prepares the way for obedience. Those most familiar with the Word of God are most apt to carry it out.

Fourth, the proper attitude with which to approach the *Qur'an* is one of gratitude, based on the perception that the *Qur'an* is a great evidence of the mercy of God. What greater gift has Allah bestowed than revealing to human beings who he is and what he requires of them? Fifth, pious use of the *Qur'an* is perhaps the best way to draw close to God. Since drawing close to God, becoming one with the One, is the goal of Muslim spirituality, pious use of the *Qur'an* has long been the central method or discipline of Muslim spirituality. Last, this author chooses to underscore the constraining influence of prayer (and, no doubt, pious use of the *Qur'an*). In addition to curbing people's lower appetites, however, both prayer and pious use of the *Qur'an* elevate the human personality, giving it experience of its highest appetites. For when Muslims commune with Allah, they know the gist of their tradition's wisdom, the heart of their tradition's promise. They experience oneness with the One, and so, at least for the moment, know how all might be right with the world.

Friendly Criticisms

The spirituality initiated through Muhammad has developed many saints and inspired great cultures. Muslim mystics command respect in all comprehensive anthologies of mysticism, while comparative studies of religious law have to contend with the enormous influence of the *Shariah*. We have noted the warm memories that Muslims maintain of Muhammad, and we should dismiss as vicious propaganda most of the negative characterizations of Muhammad that arose in the Christian

West. Nonetheless, Muhammad was not divine, as Muslims themselves are the first to emphasize. Only Allah is without flaw. Thus both the Prophet and the tradition he inaugurated are fitting subjects for friendly criticism.

Two matters arise in virtually all objective discussions of Muslim spirituality: treatment of women, for which polygamy often stands as the epitome, and advocacy of holy warfare (*jihad*). Recently a third matter, fundamentalism, has become a popular focus for criticism. Let us examine these three topics.

Muhammad himself had numerous wives, and several concubines. Even when one admits that this was permissible in the Arab culture of his day, and that he married several of his wives to help them out of difficult circumstances, the question of the inherent fairness of polygamy (which in fact usually means polygyny [having many women], since polyandry [having many men] is rare in Islam) remains. Even if Muhammad uplifted the status of women, compared to what it had been in pre-Muslim Arabia, did he not fail to recognize the basic equality of the sexes, the detriments that a plurality of wives was nearly bound to bring to many women, and so the injustice of a polygamous system?

These questions raise hackles in Muslim quarters, though many modern Muslim countries have outlawed or greatly discouraged polygamy and most current Muslim spiritual writers propose monogamy as the ideal. The questions seem to import Western standards into Islamic cultures, where such standards can be foreign. The same applies to such matters as the veiling of women nowadays and the *purdah* (seclusion from public life) of women in past ages. More aggressively, Muslim commentators are apt to criticize Western morals, noting the proliferation of divorce, broken families, pornography, prostitution, and other social ills that injure women more than men. What moral standing enables the West to pass judgment on Muslim traditions?

Obviously, there seems to be truth on both sides of the controversy, and the best result, for people interested in spirituality, would be for Muslims and non-Muslims to speak charitably of one another, in an effort to generate greater understanding. One cannot import foreign ideas simplemindedly. On the other hand, one cannot suppress criticisms that seem warranted by hard facts. The hard facts include the historical record, according to which Muslim women have had many fewer rights, both secular and religious, than men, have suffered from such practices as child-marriage, and have had little defense against physical abuse, as well as limited access to education, public office, and religious leadership. In some countries this pattern continues today, compounded (for example, in Africa) by the acceptance of originally non-Muslim practices such as clitoridectomy. A retrospective view of the Prophet, and so of Muslim spirituality at its foundations, suggests that, despite his manifest love for wives such as Khadija and A'ishah, Muhammad might have done more to secure the wellbeing of female Muslims. (This is a judgment that we might also bring against the Buddha, Confucius, and Jesus, realizing that, as with Islam, we must tread a fine line between being anachronistic and accepting without criticism deficiencies in an original vision.)

The second matter for criticism is the institution of *jihad*. While this word can refer to struggle against oneself, and so be taken to heart by ascetics, it has also meant struggle against those deemed enemies of Islam—a judgment that ought not to be made lightly but, throughout Muslim history (including very recent years), sometimes has been. Muslims claim from the *Qur'an* (for example, surahs 2, 4, and 9) the right to clear a space so that their message can be heard. If opponents should try to thwart this, they become enemies. If a people permits them entry, Muslims should not war with it. But if a people resists, Muslims should take up the sword.

This is not the same as saying that Islam spread by the sword. *Jihad* was not a wholesale justification for any Muslim expansion. But it reveals at the heart of Islam a conviction about a mission from God that did not refrain from using violence. Indeed, the promise to Muslim warriors that if they died in a *jihad* they would go straight to paradise sealed the religious legitimacy of holy warfare. The obvious problem has been the easy abuse of this outlook. Anyone opposing a Muslim regime ran the risk of becoming an opponent in a holy war. In recent times, terrorists have claimed to justify their actions as legitimate in holy wars, and respected Muslim leaders have refused to condemn terrorism outright.

Muhammad probably expected restraint in these matters, but the *Qur'an* opens the door to abuses. Underneath the doctrine of *jihad* lies the sense of superiority that Christians can recognize from the abuses of the Crusades. When recourse to violence becomes an easy way to deal with perceived evils, and distinctions between what is a legitimate opposition to proselytizing or political takeover and what is a suppression of perhaps innate rights to proclaim one's opinions or offer one's alternate leadership go neglected, the stage is set for great abuses. An irony in the Muslim case, as in the history of Christianity, is that (to this day) many Muslim countries forbid any religion other than Islam to proselytize. (In the Christian case the Inquisition sometimes forbid even being Jewish or Muslim. People had to convert, or risk death or expulsion).

This relates to the third of our foci for friendly criticism. The fanaticism that the prophetic religions, especially Islam and Christianity (Judaism seldom had the military or political means), have regularly indulged raises serious questions about their moral health. The intellectual equivalent of military fanaticism, often present even when no actual *jihad* is intended, is an aggressive fundamentalism. Those who read their scriptures so that outsiders become enemies, people lesser in the sight of God, divide the world into two zones, of light and darkness. They themselves are the creatures of light. Their opponents—whether unbelievers or infra-Muslim or Christian antagonists—are creatures of darkness. The Puritans of Oliver Cromwell, continuing a medieval tradition clear in the Cathari, thought this way, and so have many fundamentalist Muslims. To this day, fundamentalists in Iran do not scruple to wage holy war against Baha'is, or against supposedly heretical writers such as Salman Rushdie, seeking their death, while fundamentalist Muslims in India match fundamentalist Hindus in their willingness to murder for their views. Any time that people think they have the Word of God contained between covers, along with exclusive rights to its interpretation, great danger raises its head. Muhammad was a creature of his time, when there was no critical tradition to oppose fundamentalism. But the openings that the *Qur'an* gives to fundamentalists and zealots redound to his responsibility, as well as to the responsibility of Allah.

NOTES

1. Fazlur Rahman, "Islam: An Overview," in *The Encyclopedia of Religion*, ed. Mircea Eliade (New York: Macmillan, 1987), vol. 7, p. 303.
2. Ismail al Faruqi and Lois Lamyaal al Faruqi, *The Cultural Atlas of Islam* (New York: Macmillan, 1986), p. 60.
3. Frederick Mathewson Denny, *An Introduction to Islam* (New York: Macmillan, 1985), p. 68.
4. A. J. Arberry, *The Koran Interpreted* (New York: Macmillan, 1955), p. 244.
5. Mohammed Marmaduke Pickthall, *The Meaning of the Glorious Koran* (New York: Mentor, 1963), p. 157.
6. Cyril Glasse, *The Concise Encyclopedia of Islam* (San Francisco: Harper & Row, 1989), p. 219.
7. N. J. Dawood, trans., *The Koran* (Baltimore: Penguin, 1971), p. 107.
8. Ibid., p. 15.
9. Seyyed Hossein Nasr, "Introduction," in *Islamic Spirituality: Foundations*, ed. Seyyed Hossein Nasr (New York: Crossroad, 1987), p. xv.
10. Allahbakrsh K. Brohi, "The Spiritual Dimension of Prayer," ibid., p. 134.

CHAPTER 6

FURTHER
QUESTIONS

The Relation between Buddhism and Hinduism

In this chapter we consider further questions nibbling at the edges of our four square treatment of the great religious founders. By dealing with these questions, we hope to suggest the wider horizon within which it is most profitable to locate the spiritualities of the men we have studied. Our first reflection bears on how we should locate the Buddha.

Hinduism thinks of Buddhism as its offspring. Hindu lists of *avatars* (material manifestations of great divinities such as Vishnu) frequently include the Buddha, and even though Hindus and Buddhists have traditionally disagreed on several fundamental questions, for Hinduism Buddhism makes no sense except as a heterodox reaction to the form of the Hindu tradition prevailing at the time of Gautama. Inasmuch as many Hindus take a broad and benign view of revelation and the ways of salvation, Hinduism often seems tolerant of Buddhist ideas and practices (more tolerant, for example, that it is of Islam).

Buddhists may agree to the characterization of their spirituality as heterodox by Hindu standards, since they do not accept the Vedas as the prime source of divine revelation. However, even when they find much in the Upanishads akin to the searches of Gautama, they have to insist that something distinctive occurred in the enlightenment of the Buddha. That event was a watershed, dividing a new epoch from an old. The hallmark of the Buddha's preaching was his experiential conviction that he had answered the great question of existence, had

171

solved the problem that had defeated him as a Hindu. On his own, he learned, to the depths of his being, the source of suffering and, equally, how to overcome suffering. The rest was commentary, elaboration, exemplification. Inasmuch as Hindus had no such singular, decisive, "eschatological" experience to which to refer all their rituals and doctrines, they differed from Gautama.

Taken less doctrinally, more culturally, the question of the relation between Hinduism and Buddhism is simpler. Both are recognizably Indian religions. In both the core spirituality is yogic. In the next section we consider how Buddhism changed when it emigrated to East Asia. Here, restricting ourselves to the first centuries of Buddhist existence, we must stress that Hinduism and Buddhism shared the same geography, history, cultural presuppositions, sense of the priority of the spiritual over the material, drive to undercut distraction and preoccupation by the senses, concern to step out of the cruel cycles of *samsara* and gain release into a realm of unconditionedness. Buddhist social thought was marked by caste nearly as completely as Hindu. Even when Buddhists opted to step out of the prevailing social structures, by opening the monastic life to all castes and making caste incidental to salvation, they still tended to use "brahmin" as a synonym for "noble," as we see in the beloved scripture called the *Dhammapada.*

The Buddha broke with Indian notions of the sexes when he finally admitted women into the Sangha, but tradition says that he did this reluctantly. Inasmuch as the basic Indian convictions about karma remained strong in Buddhism, many of the longstanding ways of thinking about the influence of karma also remained. Because prevailing Indian culture said that being born female was the result of bad karma, the Buddha had to overcome a cultural prejudice against women before he could admit their potential for enlightenment.

The great divide between Hinduism and Buddhism occurred over the question of divinity. Hinduism depicted holy ultimate reality as something distinguishable from the world, something to which the *atman* could unite itself or from which, in final perspective, the *atman* could not be distinguished. Hinduism also allowed for innumerable manifestations of divinity—the rich pantheon of Hindu gods and goddesses. Buddhism said that there was no divinity or holy ultimate reality apart from or behind ordinary reality. Nirvana occurred in the midst of *samsara*. Buddhism also said that there was no *atman* to be distinguished from ultimate reality or to be identified with ultimate reality. All entities were painful, fleeting, and selfless. All were empty of ultimate significance. The correct way to picture reality was as a flux, a constant stream. Buddhist spirituality called for people to move with the stream, discard essentialist or substantival thinking.

Indeed, influential schools such as Zen urged people to drop ordinary thinking completely. When they meditated, people did well to seek the original mind below the dichotomies of the ordinary, workaday mind. They did well to drop their customary moral distinctions as well, not bothering about the value of what they were involved with at the moment, trying rather to attend wholeheartedly to what the task at hand happened to be. That is why the tea ceremony, archery, sweeping the yard, walking in the monastic portico—any assigned duty, any current obligation, could be good, even holy.

In enlightenment Gautama learned that all things are good in themselves. Each entity is intrinsically lightsome, enlightened in the sense of luminous in itself. The trick is to let this luminosity shine forth. The trick is to take oneself, and all other things, as one finds them to be—to accept their "suchness." Until we are enlightened, we tend to impose on entities, our selves included, much that they are not. We fail to let them be themselves, are always trying to manipulate them or fit them to preconceived forms in our own minds. The serenity of the Buddha came in part from letting all such preconceptions fall. He had no agenda for other beings. There was nothing he wanted from them or for them. It was enough for him to be himself before them, and to encourage them, invite them, to be themselves before him. Until people escaped from their thrall to sensation, ego, desire, they would not approach such a dispassion. They would not know the peace of detachment. And they would not be able to see things clearly, appreciate other beings or themselves in their suchness.

One can find equivalents to this view of wisdom in Hinduism, including its call to detachment, but something distinctively Buddhist remains. The Buddhist sense that selfhood is an illusion (so that one must drop the most primary attachment of one's being, attachment to one's own "I") is different from the Hindu sense of self-denial and self-knowledge. What is alike in the two spiritualities, however, is the instinctive conviction that yoga—spiritual discipline—is the best way to liberation. India has developed pathways (*margas*) of action (Hinduism more than Buddhism), but these do not dominate the image of the holy person as the interior yogas do. The discipline of the body, the senses, the imagination, the mind, the will, and finally even the consciousness that one finds in the classical Hindu yogic texts suggests an ideal of complete self-control.

The conviction is that by going to the depths of the self, below consciousness and even sleep, one can enter upon a state of profound peace and autonomy, where no waves of desire or pain make more than a glancing impact. This state (*samadhi*) is the acme of the classical yogic path sketched by Patanjali. Buddhist yoga differs in thinking that the core of the personality is empty, and so that enlightenment consists in accepting and becoming one with the flux of *dharmas* (items of experience and being). Buddhists, like Hindus, expended much energy on the analysis of psychological states. The Buddhist Abhidharma literature testifies to the strength of this interest in Indian Buddhism. Yet Buddhist meditation was but a means to the realization of the illusions of selfhood. In meditation the serious Buddhist came closer and closer to realizing the truth of the explanations of reality given in the wisdom literature—above all (for Mahayana) the Prajnaparamita sutras concerned with the "wisdom that has gone beyond" *samsara*, that can speak from the viewpoint of nirvana.

This viewpoint was dialectical: nirvana was nowhere and everywhere, in the midst of *samsara* and beyond *samsara*, the same as the buddhanature and distinguishable from it, both empty and full of the experiences of living beings. From the perspective of enlightenment (to reach which human beings had to practice meditation and obey the common moral precepts), the world was both one and many, neither one nor many. All speech failed, miserably and radically. All conception and ratiocination broke down, could not do the job. The experience of enlightenment came as a simple, holistic, irrefutable intuition. One's prior sense of self and being tipped over, and everything took on a new shine, even as it stayed the same.

Before enlightenment, trees were trees and rocks were rocks. During enlightenment, one realized that none of this had to be, all trees and rocks were up for grabs. After enlightenment, trees were again trees and rocks were again rocks, but as beings full of buddhahood, intrinsically perfect and lightsome. Hinduism seldom talked in these accents (which, admittedly, come from East Asian Buddhists more than Indian Buddhists). Hindu *moksha* was not so concrete, quirky, fleeting or empty as Buddhist *nirvana*. Gautama had made a difference. His spirituality had set Buddhists apart from their Hindu brothers and sisters.

The East Asian Transformation of Buddhism

After the seventh century A.D., Buddhist influence in India declined. Hinduism was winning the battle for India's spiritual loyalty. Buddhism remained predominant in Ceylon, but its future lay eastward. The Theravadin tradition did best in Burma, Thailand, and other countries relatively close to India. The Mahayana tradition flourished still farther to the east: in China, Japan, Vietnam, Korea. Tibet developed interesting schools unique to itself, blending native shamanistic practices with Indian Buddhist philosophy.

The most dramatic transformations of Indian Buddhism occurred in China and Japan. Because of its massive cultural influence, China was the land where Buddhism could work out quite new angles of vision, could gain quite new feelings. Nature meant more in China than in India. China was more materialistic, less preoccupied with interior, spiritual problems. The Chinese were not by inclination ascetic. They had little native appreciation for celibacy or poverty. There was no native Chinese monasticism. There was a Chinese philosophy (recall that the Buddha and Confucius were contemporaries), but it was more practical than speculative, more interested in ethics than metaphysics.

The Chinese introduced the notion of clans into Buddhism. Just as Chinese families were preoccupied with lineage, and revered ancestors going back for generations, so Chinese Buddhists established lineages for spiritual masters. One belonged to the lineage, in effect the clan, of the founding master (whose relation to Gautama might or might not be clear). The Chinese reverence for old age and the wisdom of the elders took the form of honoring the line of descent through which the present master had received enlightenment, wisdom, mastery of the tradition, and so existential authority to hand the tradition on.

Several centuries into the Common Era (A.D.), when Indian Buddhist monks, traveling as missionaries to spread the Dharma, gained the attention of Chinese interested in deepening or intensifying their spiritual lives, the problem arose of how to translate Indian terms into Chinese. The language best suited seemed to be the terminology developed by the philosophical Taoists. Although they were not as metaphysical as the Indian Buddhist philosophers, the philosophical Taoists had pondered such questions as the relation between the Tao and nature, the relation between the human spirit and the Tao, the relativity that came when the human spirit got lost in the Tao—aesthetic and mystical issues cognate to Indian Buddhist metaphysical ones. The terms, concepts, images that Taoists such as Lao Tzu and Chuang Tzu had created served as the translators' starting point. Eventually East Asian Buddhists created their own language, but at the outset the Taoist influence was strong.

The less speculative schools, such as Ch'an (Zen, in Japan), often seemed to produce masters little different from Taoist sages. Both were earthy, holistic, aware of the place of the body, leery of the ratiocinative mind. Both instinctively drew on naturalistic analogies, tended to think that the spontaneity of nature, its unreflective perfection, was a good model for the enlightened personality. Both were hospitable to the arts, thinking that painting, poetry, the cultivation of gardens, creating or listening to music that summoned running water or singing birds could serve spiritual development. Both loved wit, puzzles, freedom from pretense, a light rather than a heavy touch in personal interactions as well as conceptions of the self.

All of this made East Asian Buddhist spirituality different from Indian Buddhist spirituality. Certainly the two geographical areas continued to hold much in common. Certainly the three jewels—the Buddha, the Dharma, and the Sangha—were a common treasure, and many East Asian sects were transplants of originally Indian sects. But East Asian Buddhist meditation, morality, and wisdom sought to fill native needs different from those of Indians. It provided for lay people, sexuality, art, nature, and many other aspects of culture on models much shaped by Confucianism. So it felt different: more concrete, less abstract; more practical, less speculative; lighter, more humorous, more artistic. We should not exaggerate these contrasts, of course, because similar doctrinal convictions and meditational experiences kept the two Buddhisms recognizably fraternal or sororal. But we should appreciate them, because they show the ability of Buddhist spirituality to adapt to quite different cultural settings. As well, they show the genius of Gautama—how well he had cut to the heart of the personal religious matter.

The following selection from an account of the enlightenment of a contemporary Japanese Buddhist layman can serve as a case study concerning this matter of the transformations of the tradition worked by East Asians:

> At midnight I suddenly awakened. At first my mind was foggy, then suddenly that quotation flashed into my consciousness; "I came to realize clearly that Mind is no other than the mountains, rivers, and the great wide earth, the sun and the moon and the stars." And I repeated it. Then all at once I was struck as though by lightning and simultaneously, like surging waves, a tremendous delight welled up in me, a veritable hurricane of delight, as I laughed loudly and wildly: "Ha, ha, ha, ha, ha, ha!" The empty sky split in two, then opened its enormous mouth and began to laugh uproariously: "Ha, ha, ha!" Later one of the members of my family told me that my laughter had sounded inhuman.[1]

The man is sleeping at home, alongside his wife. He is not a monk sequestered in a monastery (though he has recently returned from a retreat at a Zen monastery). The change in consciousness that produces enlightenment comes suddenly, as a notion that has been boiling in his depths bursts forth. He realizes, in an intuition so powerful that it shocks him into delighted laughter, that reality is not dual. Mind and physical reality are not opposites, dichotomies. Enlightenment has no reasoning, and ultimate reality is not reason-able. It is not discrete, separated into solid units, as the unenlightened mind tends to think. And this is delightful. The experience brings relief, pleasure, fulfill-ment, great joy in the presence of great beauty.

Later the man will weep with gratitude that the tradition has proven true, the masters have not let him down, there is a wonderful coherence to reality, one so simple and lovely that he can only feel immensely grateful for the privilege of having perceived it, felt it, been drawn into union with it. The line about the empty sky illustrates the wild, poetic, illogical, yet gripping imagery characteristic of Zen approaches to meditation, enlightenment, the substance of the spiritual quest. The quest can be painful, but its end and fundament is delightful. Enlightenment brims with freedom, light, a sense of having moved from illusion and sadness to realism and joy. Reality itself seems to laugh, to be happy. The teachings about the intrinsic goodness and light of all things seem verified eminently. Something inhuman, in the sense of not limited by ordinary conventions, of having broken out of what chains most people in much ugliness and depression, appears, takes over, raises the person to a new kinship with the animal world, the simple suchness of nature.

The style of this account would never be mistaken for an Indian Buddhist treatise on realization. It is concrete, funny, passionate, energetic as few Indian parallels would be. This does not make it better or worse than its Indian equivalents. It simply exemplifies how Buddhist spirituality changed, when it entered the substance of East Asian cultures such as the Chinese and Japanese. It simply shows that East Asians made the Dharma wholly their own.

Confucius and Lao Tzu

Analogous to our question about the relation between Hinduism and Buddhism is the question of how Confucianism relates to Taoism. The difference from the Indian question is that the Chinese question doesn't bear on genesis. No one disputes that "Hinduism," as a generic term for the native Indian tradition that arose after the invasion of the Aryans (beginning about 2000 B.C.), preceded Buddhism and was the soil in which it grew, the *ancien régime* against which it revolted. The genesis of Buddhism involves the recombination of Hindu elements, spurred and changed by new insights of Gautama. In China, Confucianism determined Taoism much less. Taoism drew on native, pre-Confucian elements, as well as an aversion for Confucian formalism. Lao Tzu and

Chuang Tzu claimed kinship with the oldest Chinese intuitions about spirituality, just as Confucianism claimed to preserve the wisdom of the ancients about politics.

Consider the following text from chapter 32 of the *Tao Te Ching*:

> The way is for ever nameless. Though the uncarved block is small, no one in the world dares to claim its allegiance. Should lords and princes be able to hold fast to it, the myriad creatures will submit of their own accord, heaven and earth will unite and sweet dew will fall, and the people will be equitable, though no one decrees. Only when it is cut are there names. As soon as there are names, one ought to know that it is time to stop. Knowing when to stop one can be free of danger. The way is to the world as the River and the Sea are to rivulets and streams.[2]

This text concerns the same Tao that Confucius lauded, but with significant differences. Here the Way is more metaphysical and naturalistic. Certainly, it is the Path that human beings ought to follow, by reference to which they ought to clean up and order their acts. But in the first place it is simply itself: something primordial rather than derivative, a judge rather than a being liable to human judgment. It can never be named, because it is the closest thing to the source of language. It exceeds our linguistic ability. We cannot pin it down, fence it in by references to things like it, things different from it. When we think we have named it well, we are most deeply deluded. When we admit that it names us, we are closest to wisdom.

The uncarved block is human nature without cultural adornment. It is small, in the sense that we can take it for granted, because we can think it is merely what we ordinary men and women are. Yet who can claim to have mastered it, understood it, brought it to his or her side, like a domesticated animal or a trustworthy servant? It escapes all attempts to rule it, define it once and for all, put it in service. It has a quicksilver quality, as attests every leader who thought he knew his subjects but learned on his way to the gallows that he did not.

Lao Tzu is like Confucius in thinking that the way to lead human beings is through virtue. But the virtue that Lao Tzu stresses is a mystical appreciation of how the Tao forms human nature. The prince who could hold fast to the uncarved block—original, unspoiled human nature—would rule without effort. His sway would be nearly magical, for he would have mastered the fulcrum of political persuasion. Indeed, those who hold fast to original human nature bring heaven down to earth, establish a sacrosanct harmony. To be fully human, as nature intended men and women to be, is to know the equipoise of creation, to be oneself a prism through which all the beauty and power of creation reflect. Obviously, Lao Tzu has a powerful faith in the goodness of unspoiled human nature. He shows an early magical trust that, could they shovel away the detritus of bad culture, men and women would regain their lost harmony with nature, would reenter paradise. The fall of sweet dew from heaven would signal heaven's blessing. The holy powers above us earthlings want only that we be what we could be, what we most deeply are. This includes being free from concern about social conventions. It implies the ability to enjoy life spontaneously, without the fetters of education into orthodox views of good and bad, beautiful and ugly. If any leader could reach the original blessing spoken into human nature, he or she would have no need to rule by decree. The mere presentation of a sound human nature would bring other people to obedience, harmony, cooperation. Simply from enjoying the presence of a whole human being they would become much less divided themselves.

We may consider this mere poetry, or an imagination better suited to fairy tales than philosophical analysis, but we should realize how regularly the more estimable spiritualities have wrestled with the question of why it is so hard for human beings to be human. What Lao Tzu is intimating in this chapter is little different from the dramatization in the Christian gospels of what happens when Jesus, a uniquely whole human being, speaks to the crowds, commands the forces of nature, brings into creation a brand new thing: a true specimen of humanity, an unflawed instance of our kind. He heals people miraculously. He commands the wind and the rain. He speaks as no one before him has, with a personal authority putting Torah in the shade. He even defeats death—first with Lazarus, then in his own person.

The Christian scenario includes an important difference from the Taoist, of course. On the way to resurrection Jesus passes through a dreadful suffering caused by the rejection of his model of humanity, the hatred of his wholeness. Lao Tzu does not reckon with the animus that acculturated and so deformed human beings are bound to show toward anyone clinging to the uncarved block, exhibiting original human nature. In that regard, he is much less historical than the Christian gospels.

The cutting of the uncarved block is what gives the Way names. The acculturation of human beings limits their potential, and the metaphysical price is loss of the holistic character of the pathway through reality. Every decent education brings many benefits, but it also carries serious dangers. The greatest danger is loss of immediate access to the mysteriousness of existence. The deepest formation that people need is the orientation that opens their souls to the beyond, the infinite, what moves in consciousness as its sovereign norm. Granted this orientation, human beings are essentially sane, rightly ordered at their foundations.

When socialization distracts people from this foundational ordering or, even worse, denies that such ordering is significant (compared to making money, or marshaling facts, or running a state office, or leading religious rituals), the uncarved block of human potential is whittled away disastrously. Original vigor lies strewn on the ground like a spray of woodchips. Lao Tzu will not forgive Chinese civilization (which thought itself the acme of human refinement) for taking away the native vigor of the human personality. He will not forgive the Confucians for concentrating on form and frequently neglecting substance. His intuition of the Tao tells him that it devastates the pretensions of superficial acculturation. The "names" that human beings use, all their bookkeepings, do them in, make them pygmies. When naming becomes the great passion (for example, when newspapers and television programs shape popular consciousness), it is time to stop. The experiment in developing human nature has revealed its deadly vector. Any with eyes to see can realize their culture is on course to crash.

Still, the great thing about human nature (the amazing continuing influence of the uncarved block) is that as soon as we recognize spiritual disaster we take a giant step back toward health. We stand free of self-mutilation whenever we say no to the media of our day, the babbling politicians, the canting preachers—whenever we hear our soul's pain and move back into silence. Like a person finally revolted by rock music, the Taoist after Lao Tzu's heart reclaims his or true humanity by saying "No! I am made for harmony, not senseless noise. I prefer quiet to sound that slashes or suffocates my soul."

Finally, Lao Tzu shows us the radical reason why our change of soul, our conversion to the silent primacy of the Tao and the uncarved block, is healing. The bare truth is that the Way, the divine measure, is the Source and End, while we, along with all the stuff of our accultura-tions, are but tiny derivatives. It is the River and the Sea. We are but rivulets and streams. The original human nature buried deep under our bad education hungers to return to the Sea, honor the oceanic being that could make us significant. Inasmuch as the Confucians denied this basal truth, or pretended that cultural norms, rituals and traditions, were more than rivulets and streams, Lao Tzu saw them as the enemies of true human prosperity and so mortally dangerous.

Japanese Spirituality

We have noted the kinship between Taoism and Zen Buddhism. Fol-lowing the example of China, Japan took Buddhism to heart, and Zen became very influential, especially among the warrior class (samurai). Previously, Japan had opened itself to both Confucian and Taoist influences. The Confucian impact sharpened the native Japanese ven-eration of ancestors, patriarchy, interest in ritual and manners, adding a sense that good public order required a docile bureaucracy. The Taoist impact sharpened the native Japanese affinity for nature, inclina-tion toward a clean, stripped aesthetic, and conviction that paradox is at least as true as straightforward prose.

Receiving these influences, Japan also heightened its awareness of its native spiritual traditions, which became articulated as Shinto: the way of the *kami*. The *kami* are the gods or spirits pervasive in the landscape. Tradition says they number 800,000. Any striking natural phenome-non, and also any extraordinary human being, can be a *kami*. The *kami* come to tall trees, winding streams, the regalia associated with the emperor. They have an affinity for fertility, reposing in rocks shaped like phalluses or vulvas. They favor salt, as a cleansing astringent.

They call for purity of mind as well as body. The ancient Japanese mythology tells how they formed the islands and are connected with the imperial line. The Japanese emperor is divine inasmuch as he represents this line and so himself becomes a *kami*.

Along with the fascinating sociology of Japan, the traditional Japanese love of nature holds the key to Japanese spirituality. The sociology derives from millennia of organization into clans. Today Japanese businesses draw on this background, treating employees as members of a clan and expecting clan loyalty. Relations between men and women also derive from the centuries when clans arranged marriages and legislated sex-specific tasks. As in most other traditional cultures, women came to specialize in raising children and supporting the adventures of men. In turn, men left domestic affairs to women and concentrated on gaining food, security, power.

The love of nature is expressed in the theology that located *kami* throughout the landscape, but it also runs hand in hand with a deflating view of human nature. Animals and plants, even rocks and waters, are what they are perfectly. Human beings have to struggle to become human. This is not a new perception, but Shinto and Zen currents in Japanese culture made it highly influential. Certainly, one can point to the pride of the samuri, and other classes, and admit that Japanese people could be as egocentric, proud, or willful as any others. Equally, one has to allow for the changes that have come with exposure to Western modernity, especially Western technology. Nonetheless, the naturalistic orientation of traditional Japanese culture, along with the pressures from Japanese sociology to conform to one's assigned role, have reduced the Japanese estimation of individuality. Zen masters certainly were vibrant individuals, and Japanese captains of industry can have mighty wills. But Japanese spirituality as a whole has proved fertile ground for Buddhist teachings about egolessness and emptiness.

Because (as we Western analysts are bound to see things), for Japanese spirituality the individual is less significant than a more perfect nature, and also less significant than a more primordial clan, the individual should seek fulfillment in the loss of self-concern, the attunement of consciousness to deeper, broader rhythms. Thus, the family man who came to enlightenment saw that reality ultimately is not plural. There is no self that stands out from the whole or ought to place itself over and against the whole. When one loses self-centeredness, the grandeur of the cosmos, of buddhahood, of the beautiful world run by the *kami* becomes apparent. The way to joy is to lose self-concern, drop the mentality of "me and them." The way to holiness is to surrender to the bigger forces in existence, love the simple "isness" of what is natural, longstanding, basic. Currently Japanese culture is a battle-ground on which these venerable spiritual instincts struggle against Japanese versions of Western preoccupations with ephemeral problems and pleasures. The result is a laboratory for spiritual scientists—scholars interested in how historical changes alter human nature's foun-dational orientation to transcendence.

Jesus and Moses

Leaving the zone of further questions about Eastern spiritualities, let us take up some further questions about Western spiritualities. The first is the relation between Jesus and Moses. Nowadays it is virtually a dogma of New Testament studies that Jesus was a Jew of his time and cannot be appreciated accurately without making this fact central. He did not set out to found a new religion. He never imbibed at other, non-Jewish spiritual fonts. The changes that he wrought on Judaism, and that he inspired his disciples to bring about, stemmed from his under-standing of the God of the Jews. His "Father" was the God of Abraham, Isaac, and Jacob. No new God came to Jesus in prayer, revealed himself to Jesus in the Transfiguration (Matthew 17, Mark 9) or Resurrection. Still, Jesus' understanding of his Father clearly of-fended many of his contemporaries. They thought he was betraying the heritage passed down from Moses, if not from Abraham. What, then, should we think about the Jewishness of Jesus? How did the spirituality of Jesus differ from that of Moses? How did Jesus himself differ from Moses, especially in the eyes of Jesus' followers?

The Jewishness of Jesus was unthinking, in the sense that Jesus seems never to have contemplated being anything but Jewish. Salvation was from the Jews. His family, friends, and disciples were all Jews. If he healed Gentiles on occasion, that was accidental, though revealing.

Gentiles too were children of God, objects of God's care. But his own mission was to Israel. Even Samaritans held little interest for him, though when he met the Samaritan woman at the well he dealt with her lovingly.

On the other hand, Jesus was not Jewish in an uncritical way. He felt free to castigate his fellow Jews, when he saw them failing the standards of his Father. Like the biblical prophets, Jesus had a keen eye for failures in justice and mercy. He showed little concern for matters of pure cult, in the sense of feeling it necessary to warn people not to hanker after false, pagan gods, but he did say that one cannot serve both God and mammon. On the question of healthy worship, pure cult, Jesus stressed honesty, humility, and solidarity with one's neighbors. God doesn't want formalistic babble. God wants prayer and repentance from the heart. Thus, the publican who approaches God humbly goes away justified, while the pharisee who trumpets his own virtue does not (Luke 18). Similarly, God wants people who come before him to be reconciled with their neighbors. If their brother or sister has a grievance against them, they should settle this—make peace—before expecting God to hear them. God will not tolerate a worship that is insincere. Only a transparent conscience, an utterly honest manifestation of soul, can please the divine majesty.

Thus, again like the prophets before him, Jesus was a free-spirited Jew. He did not confuse loyalty to his people with unthinking approval of everything that they or their leaders did. The injustices of his day, and the spiritual obtuseness of many of his contemporaries, offended him. Both cried out to God for change. When forced to choose between what seemed to be God's truth and outmoded or inauthentic traditions, Jesus chose God's truth. That should have endeared him to honest, wise Jews. That it seems to have enraged some powerful members of the Jewish establishment suggests that they were spiritually bankrupt, if not corrupt.

It is hard to know whether Moses himself was punctilious about the Torah, in the sense of the Mosaic law stemming from the covenant struck on Sinai, after the Exodus from Egypt. Certainly the spirituality of Moses, as we might try to extract it from Exodus and Deuteronomy, suggests that he had experiences of God bound to make him relativize any legal code. Obedience to the law of the covenant could not have been in his eyes something slavish. If the biblical portraits reflect the historical actuality, Moses learned from painful experience that his people needed discipline and were prone to forget the benefits that the Lord had bestowed upon them. The Torah would be a safeguard for them, to keep them from abandoning the pathway of life. On their own, without clear guidance about what they ought to do and how they ought to think, they might easily lose the great treasure that God had offered them: to be God's own holy people. But this awareness probably inclined Moses to think of the Torah as a minimal sketch of a faithful response to God. The majestic God of Sinai could never be satisfied, honored adequately, by a merely literal execution of the Torah. Only love of God, with whole mind, heart, soul, and strength, could approach offering God what human beings were privileged to offer.

Jesus seems to have taken a similar tack. He honored the letter of the Mosaic law, but he was more interested in the spirit. On such matters as keeping the sabbath or a kosher diet, he shows himself respectful but not scrupulous. The sabbath was made for human beings, not human beings for the sabbath (Mark 2:27). God is not a legalistic God, or a God anxious about his dignity. The sabbath ought to be a time when God's mercies toward human beings are especially evident. What could be better evidence than healing through God's power people long held captive by sickness? To miss the deeply religious significance of such healing and pontificate about breeches of the law would be to show oneself a bad lawyer, not a good believer.

The Torah had no function except to honor God and benefit human beings. When the Torah became an end in itself, it turned into an idol. The spirituality of Jesus was profoundly Mosaic in being deeply opposed to idolatry. Only the honor and love of the living God, whom Jesus experienced to be a Father, captured the rightly ordered human heart. People so wrapped up in their traditions, their casuistries, that they missed the lovely humanism of the Torah were little better than idolaters. Indeed, sometimes they seemed to be haters of God, in that they rejected witnesses to God's living, much-more-than legal reality.

The best of the Pharisees agreed with Jesus on this point. Their desire to reinvigorate the Law stemmed from a hunger to make all of life instinct with God's holy, healing presence. But the time-servers and pedants, those threatened by the largeness of the living God or jealous that someone other than themselves seemed to be gifted with God's healing power, departed from the best of the Pharisaic tradition. The best way to read the New Testament's accounts of the controversies between Jesus and "the Pharisees" is to understand the writers of the gospels as focusing on the inauthentic, bastardized group.

Last, the great personal difference between Jesus and Moses, as Christians saw it, was the divinity of Jesus. Moses was a great religious hero, the medium of God's amazing grant of the covenant. But Jesus was a new Moses, and considerably more. He gave a new Law, that laid greater stress on love. He fashioned a new covenant, soon opened to the Gentiles and communicating a share in God's own life. He died a sacrificial death, in the lineaments of Isaiah's Suffering Servant, and this death was the means through which God repaired the deep ruptures of human nature, the pervasive alienations, that we now associate with original sin.

It is difficult to extricate the human Jesus from this divine figure, as we have mentioned previously. The entire New Testament presents Jesus in light of the Resurrection and the growing clarity of the Christian community about his divinity. Still, the picture of Jesus that we find in the gospels does not alienate him from Moses. He believes that the Reign of God is at hand. He thinks that the messianic era is about to dawn. He considers his own work the vanguard of this enormously significant event. But none of this makes him turn his back on the Mosaic covenant or repudiate the Mosaic spirituality centered in wholehearted love of God (and neighbor).

Jesus feels the pressure of the Law and the Prophets, and this is congenial. Moses and the prophets were great servants of God, in whose footsteps he walks. On the other hand, their heritage has tarnished, and something new is dawning. His own intimacy with the Father takes him beyond the spirituality we find in Exodus and Deuteronomy. Moses is the friend of God, the intimate with whom God will converse, but Moses is not the beloved child, the utterly trusting offspring who never doubts the Father's love. The human Jesus suffers more than Moses did (which is not to minimize the sufferings of Moses). His death as a criminal becomes throughout Western culture the great symbol of innocent human suffering—the great claim upon

God's justice. There is no resurrection of Moses, as there is a resurrection of Jesus through which God honors this claim. So speculating about Jesus, puzzling out his spirituality, requires categories beyond those needed for Moses.

Jewish and Christian Spiritualities

Inasmuch as Jewish spirituality has placed less emphasis on an afterlife than Christianity, and has been less influenced by Hellenistic dualism (tendency to make matter and spirit antagonistic), Jewish spirituality often appears more at home in the world and joyous. The goods of the earth are given by God to be enjoyed. Asceticism is not as important as a spirit of gratitude, a willingness to work in the world for the flourishing of creation and humankind. Judaism has never approved celibacy. It has made the family the center of the quest for God. Taking the command to increase, multiply, be fruitful and fill the earth seriously, Jewish spiritual masters have helped their disciples feel that sexual love and parenting can be the marrow of a vibrant spirituality. Money and power, though dangerous, can also be gifts of God. Sinfulness is a factor, but not one to dominate estimates of human nature. People enjoying riches and influence have the obligation to use them for the good of the entire community. If they do, they deserve the honors that the community bestows on them. Prosperity includes a responsibility to help the unfortunate. Torah, marriage, and good deeds make a trinity of spiritual treasures. The person who honors the Law, creates a warm family life, and helps neighbors in need is a model Jew.

Christian spirituality has affirmed all these virtues, but with different overtones. Christian incarnationalism could sponsor a this-worldliness, a humanism or sacramentality, as attractive as the Jewish, but Christian asceticism stood by to counterbalance such this-worldliness. The ideal Christian lived on a razor's edge between time and eternity. The ideal Christian psychology balanced "now" and "not yet." Now the substance of salvation, the very life of God in grace, was available, had come into people's midst. But salvation was not yet fully achieved. How could one think that it had been, when so much injustice, suffering, and sin remained?

What people possessed at present through faith and grace strained to achieve consummation through vision and glory. Heaven was the only adequate, complete expression of salvation. Only when people saw God face to faith and enjoyed the fulfillment of their every decent longing would the proportions of Christ's victory be clear. Thus something tentative or skeptical shadowed Christian humanism in many ages. Something cautionary rang in the teachings of many spiritual masters. The only way to keep one's balance was to deny oneself. The power of sin was so strong that it was prudent to postpone most pleasures, even many spiritual satisfactions, until the fulfillment of one's earthly course.

The institutional form for this cautionary attitude was monasticism, and the other species of religious life that evolved from it during Christian history. By fleeing the world, taking vows of poverty, chastity, and obedience, and fixing their sights on God alone, monks and nuns hoped to proclaim, to both themselves and their fellow human beings, that God alone is the substance of all human fulfillment. God is worth the sacrifice of wealth, family life, autonomy. Active, apostolic religious orders tried to combine this witness with a self-spending service of other people. By attending to the sick, teaching the ignorant, preaching the gospel, offering spiritual counsel, helping the poor, and in all ways trying to make present in the world the charity of Christ, they hoped to show that love of God did not mean neglect of neighbor. Indeed, the logic of their service was that a twofold witness, to the primacy of God and the goodness of one's neighbor, was the best way to express the balance of Christian faith.

The Jewish rabbis have carried much of the burden of proclaiming to their people the primacy of God. They have used the precepts of the Torah to structure the sanctification of all creation. These precepts are not ascetical, in the sense of deliberately curbing the flesh to help the spirit wax fat. But they do inculcate discipline, regularity, self-restraint. They do drive home the point that God's will ought to shape how people use their time, use their money, configure their values, honor their creaturehood. Often it has been demanding to be a rabbi, responsible for teaching the hallowed tradition while carrying a full quota of family responsibilities. Often nearly heroic women have freed rabbis (who until very recently were all males) to study and teach. The centrality of Torah in Jewish life has meant that study has been the primary spiritual discipline. As much as prayer, study has been a lifting of the mind and heart to God that hallows the personality. The love of learning that such study encouraged spread to secular scholarship, once traditional Judaism entered upon modernity. The notion that learning is the mark of a holy person continued to make learning about Torah the prime analogate, but any learning deserved respect, because it exercised a great gift of God: human intelligence.

Christian spirituality again has been more ambivalent. While there were famous rabbis like the Baal Shem Tov who relativized the importance of learning, there were more Christian saints. The instinct was the same in both cases (love is more important than knowledge), but Christians had less need of study because their Law was simpler. Certainly, the Church honored its outstanding teachers. Being named a "Doctor" of the Church added eminence to any canonization. But the Pauline view of wisdom, the crux of which was that Christ crucified abashes all human wisdom, had great influence in Christian spirituality. If Christ on the cross was a stumbling block to Jews, and to Gentiles foolishness, Christians had to be careful about their embrace of learning. They had to be sure that the wisdom to which they aspired was compatible with Christ's having challenged, if not overturned, many worldly values. Paul's words to the Corinthians rang eloquently in the memory of many Christian spiritual masters:

> When I came to you, brothers and sisters, I did not come proclaiming the mystery of God to you in lofty words or wisdom. For I decided to know nothing among you except Jesus Christ, and him crucified. And I came to you in weakness and in fear and in much trembling. My speech and my proclamation were not with plausible words of wisdom, but with a demonstration of the Spirit and of power, so that your faith might rest not on human wisdom but on the power of God (I Corinthians 2:1–5).[3]

From texts such as these influential church fathers such as Tertullian asked rhetorically, "What has Athens to do with Jerusalem?".

Pagan learning, represented by Athens, seemed irrelevant to the revealed wisdom associated with Jerusalem, the city of God's peace.
Even when the issue was not pagan learning but Christian understanding of revelation and human existence, the attitude that Tertullian represented could qualify the importance given to scholarship.
Throughout the history of Christianity, many unlettered preachers
and teachers have based their ministries on such a qualification, arguing that it is more important to possess the power of the Holy Spirit
(to which their ecstatic experiences might testify) than to have mastered books.

Judaism has had few equivalents to such a supposed exemption from
learning (if not outright despising of learning). Even Jewish fundamentalists have often been scholarly in their fashion, mastering great portions of biblical or Talmudic literature. The notion of an ignorant rabbi
has generally been abhorrent. Christians have agreed, every time that
the education of their clergy has sunk low and been seen to abet low
morals. During the reform of the Church in the sixteenth century, for
example, both Protestants and Catholics focused on the low quality of
the clergy. Still, that has not meant taking learning into the bosom of
Christian spirituality, at least to the extent that learning has been taken
into the bosom of Jewish spirituality. On another occasion, it would be
interesting to reflect on the varying effects that this difference has
produced in the Christian and Jewish mysticisms.[4]

Modern Western Atheism

In modernity the spirituality developed from the beginnings laid down
by Jesus derailed. The opening to the Father, the intimate transcendent, closed up. The leading modern thinkers preferred a program
of self-salvation. In part due to the success of researches in science, and
in part due to the lack of spiritual vigor in the churches, many intellectuals thought that humanity had come of age and no longer needed
religion. The churches seemed to be obstacles to progress. Theological
doctrines seemed abstract, arbitrary, compared to scientifically proven
truths. Many literate people looked on the Bible as an outmoded

collection of myths. Perhaps it had been suitable when humanity was in its infancy, still subject to a nature that it did not understand. With the advent of great power over nature, however, the Bible seemed an anachronism. Secularizing tendencies within the Bible itself, unleashed by de-divinizing nature and worshiping a divinity transcending the world, came to fruition. The God of the Deists had little to do with the world, and the Bible seemed a collection of myths.

When Francis Bacon (1561–1626) proposed a second organon (methodology), to replace that of Aristotle, the contemplative depth of the classical philosophers' view of science broke away from its moorings. Bacon expected that knowledge would yield power over nature, to improve the human condition. He had less interest in contemplating God than in clarifying empirical approaches to "natural philosophy." Natural philosophers such as Descartes and Newton continued to speak of God, but reason, rather than faith, was their great interest and reliance. Michael Buckley has studied the rise of modern atheism from these beginnings. His main lament is that those responsible for safeguarding Christian truth were so untheological in their responses. They accepted the problematic introduced by the natural philosophers, moving from the traditional grounding of Christian spirituality in Scripture and religious experience.[5]

Modernity was a complex phenomenon, of course, with numerous subsidiary movements. The Renaissance, the Reformation, the Enlightenment, the Romantic movement, the political revolutions, the Industrial Revolution, the explorations of the New World, and many other factors contributed to the characteristically modern confidence that human reason and energy would remake the world. Not only would technological skill refashion physical nature, making it the servant of human needs, human beings would transform human nature as well. Alchemical investigations and political mysticisms are only two of the substreams of the latter conviction. By the time of the Marxist and Nazi regimes, it had become clear that concrete human nature was less important than those regimes' convictions about how to bring about a new messianic age—one founded not by divine grace but human ruthlessness.

What Eric Voegelin has called the "gnostic" character of modern totalitarian regimes has its roots in the precarious balance that Christianity had tried to strike between the immanence and the transcendence of divine grace.[6] Inasmuch as Marx and Hitler tried to bring the eschatological energies of Christian spirituality to bear on this-worldly projects of reforming human nature and establishing this-worldly utopias, they lost the traditional balance and with it mental health. It became permissible in Nazi Germany and Stalinist Russia to murder people in the name of helping the next generation. It became legitimate to export millions to concentration camps because they did not fit into the reigning ideology. Ideology itself (the veneration of a set of ideas not necessarily tied to experience) replaced common sense. The facts that all human beings die, are ignorant of where they came from and where they are going, and can never fulfill themselves or others completely made no difference to the totalitarian ideologues. Their project was to make humanity its own God. To ignore the manifest absurdity of such a project became a bizarre badge of courage. True Nazis or Soviet Communists would skirt the finitude of humanity, attempting thereby to show that they were true believers in National Socialism or Marxism-Leninism.

The best opposition to this debased spirituality of the totalitarian atheisms has boiled down to simply telling the truth. Alexander Solzhenitsyn, the paradigmatic opponent of Soviet Communism, relied on this tactic to protect himself against the Soviet leaders and make the world appreciate the horrors of the Gulag Archipelago to which Stalin sent millions of dissidents. When we realize the implications of this tactic, we have the blueprint for a postmodern critique of modernity. Moving from the disastrous end point of modernity in the middle of the twentieth century, and drawing on both Christian humanism and classical Greek philosophy, analysts such as Solzhenitsyn and Voegelin have shown that transcendence (reaffirming that human beings cannot save themselves, cannot be their own God) is implied in the very makeup of the human being, as this makeup manages to survive Nazi death camps and Soviet gulags. The implication of simply telling the truth, facing down the lies of the totalitarian regimes, is that truth is not the captive of human beings but their master. One might say the same about love, as exceptional prisoners in the camps discovered that love was absolutely necessary if they were to continue to feel like human beings.

The interesting thing is that this method of critique—displaying the inbuilt postulates of the human spirit, the necessary conditions for its health—applies as much to Western, supposedly free culture, as well as to Nazi Germany and Stalinist Russia. It is not only the totalitarian regimes, European and Asian, Latin American, and African, that have (in our opinion) arisen atop a basic lie, a fundamental misstatement about human nature. The vulgar materialism and atheism of the capitalist West have done the same.

Such an analysis of modern atheism clearly has to be qualified on many counts. First, religion has continued to be influential in many countries, especially among the common people, raising the question of how seriously we ought to take the atheism that has been doctrinaire among intellectuals. Second, atheism can be a form of both honesty and "negative theology" (reflection on how the transcendent is unlike all our human analogies), sincerely expressing people's inability to find credible spiritual pathways in the religious institutions or credible images of a transcendent, holy Being. Third, modernity brought many advances in technology and greatly expanded our understanding of both natural and human realities. Modern science, technology, and medicine greatly improved the health and material standard of living of millions, while modern political ideas allowed millions to assume greater responsibility for their own destinies. So a fair tally of the modern age, and even of modern atheism, would find much to call progress and incorporate into a viable postmodern spirituality.

The deficiencies of modernity, though, still prove formidable. By bracketing or trying to remove the human orientation to transcendent meaning—in our view, communion with God, participation in a universe that human beings did not create and have to reverence as given by a transcendent Other, on penalty of ruining their own natures if they do not—modernity erred at the most fundamental level. It said that humanity could be the measure of reality, and that saying has proven ruinously false, culpably untrue. As one of Dostoevski's characters puts it, "If God is dead, everything is permitted." Modernity collapsed when the totalitarian reforms of the twentieth century showed that statement to be horribly true.

Islam, Judaism, and Christianity

There are obvious and profound similarities between how Muslims have thought about God and tried to live holy lives and how Jews and Christians, basing themselves on the Bible, have thought about God and tried to live holy lives. The *Qur'an* and the Bible both speak of a single God. Muslims, Jews, and Christians have all been monotheists, convinced that only God has complete sway in the rightly ordered human personality. Idolatry has been a great wickedness in all three religious cultures. The spiritualities of Muslims, Jews, and Christians have all sought to free people to serve God alone. That has meant deprecating what any this-worldly authorities might counsel, and deprecating as well the value of any this-worldly treasures.

Another similarity has been that all three traditions have thought themselves realistic. Acknowledging the complete sovereignty of God has been the first step toward realism, but a second step has been acknowledging the goodness of creation. The world has not been an illusion. Material nature has not been a deception or something to be despised. The rocks and the trees, the animals and the birds, came from God as surely as human beings. The spirituality of human beings never meant that their bodies were not precious. The mortality of human beings and animals did not mean that they should be despised. Certainly the flux and uncertainties of creatures showed that they were not God. Certainly no sane people put their trust in any creature, least of all in human rulers. But this limitation in any realistic estimate of the world did not cancel out God's presence.

For Islam, the things of creation have been portents of the divine will. For Judaism, God loved the world and wanted people to hallow their existence in space and time. For Christianity, the love of God went to the extreme of the divine Word's taking flesh and dwelling among us human beings, making himself subject to the conditions of creation just as we are. Unlike some Eastern traditions that have been suspicious of the reality of the world, mainstream Islam, Judaism, and Christianity have thought that realism, wisdom, means planting one's feet solidly in space and time. One's relationship with a God existing outside space and time ought to enhance one's sense of responsibility for the world, not diminish it. The deeper people go into their own depths or penetrate the beauty of the world, the closer they come to God. The ascetical strains of these traditions (especially Christianity) not withstanding, mature Muslim, Jewish, or Christian faith has meant becoming comfortable in the world, learning to appreciate the world as God's wonderful, ongoing work.

A third similarity among these three traditions is that they have all revered prayer. Prayer is the direct approach to God that true faith requires. Turning to God in prayer is the best way to express one's complete dependence on God. Traditional Judaism might place study of the Torah, God's word, at the center of rabbinic spirituality, but genuine study was little different from prayer. Only the rabbis who pondered the text from the heart became true masters. Similarly, all Muslims have looked to the *Qur'an* for the sources of their prayer, so all Muslim prayer has been marked by a profound sense of God's majesty. Mainstream Christian prayer has passed through Jesus to the Father, in the supportive presence of the Holy Spirit. Traditional Christian liturgies were Christocentric, addressing true worship to Jesus Christ, who with the Father and the Holy Spirit has been thought to be one God, now and forever. Whatever the modalities or cultural overtones, then, the three spiritualities have counseled people to pray to God passionately, with utter honesty, and with great gratitude for the divine goodness.

If we reverse the order in which we have taken these three similarities among Muslims, Jews, and Christians, moving from prayer through a realistic assessment of the world to the oneness of God, we glimpse how the traditions have also differed. The Christocentrism of Christian prayer, which cannot be separated from the Christian conception of God as a trinity of divine "persons" (centers of consciousness but, unlike human persons, ones not deriving their identities from limitation), sets it apart from Jewish and Muslim prayer. Relatedly, Christians have not feared representations of divinity, as Jews and Muslims have. If the Word of God took flesh, then flesh could represent God. Iconography is at the center of the Christian doctrine of the Incarnation—the ultimate significance of Jesus. The controversies over the proper status of icons that raged in Eastern Christianity turned over every aspect of this matter.

Under Jewish and Muslim influence, the iconoclasts argued that the uniqueness of God (based on the divine infinity) meant that any representation of God was bound to be fallacious. The iconodules, who defended worshiping God through images, argued that Christ himself was a great Icon of God, and that representations of Christ participated in his representation of divinity. In siding with the iconodules, Christian orthodoxy underscored its differences from both Judaism and Islam. It said that matter was not foreign to the inmost nature of God, and that God was self-expressive, both in the eternal life of the trinity and in God's actions in time.

Inasmuch as Christians were not forced to focus all their worship upon the Incarnate Word, but could address the Father or Spirit directly, Christian prayer could be like Jewish and Muslim prayer in bowing low before the ineffable spirituality of the infinite deity. But even this Christian prayer not explicitly focused on Jesus occurred in an economy of salvation pivoted on the Incarnate Word, so one could never rightly oppose prayer that dealt with God blankly, suppressing any finite images, and prayer that deliberately used images of Christ. (We prescind from the question of Christian prayer to Mary the Mother of God and the saints as taking us afield, except to note that this sort of prayer, if orthodox, was never worship [latria]. However, it did further distance Christian prayer from Jewish and Muslim prayer, and both Jews and Muslims tended to consider it idolatrous. For orthodox Christians it merely expressed the solidarity of ordinary believers with the holiest of their fellow believers, who could intercede with God on their behalf.)

Jewish prayer differed from Muslim prayer inasmuch as the Jewish sense of election and covenant was rooted in the Mosaic legacy. While Jews venerated Abraham, they treated Moses as their greatest teacher. Naturally, they did not venerate Muhammad, and Muslims' veneration of Muhammad placed Abraham, Moses, and Jesus in a secondary status. Jews and Muslims were alike, however, in going directly to God. Muslim prayer has stressed the majesty of God even more than Jewish prayer, while Jewish prayer has been willing to badger God, haggle with God (on the models of Job and Abraham), with an intimacy and boldness foreign to Muslim prayer.

The sense of the material world, of realism about creation, that one finds in Christian prayer is colored by the central place of Christ and so differs somewhat from Jewish and Muslim senses. Some of the deepest Christian theology depicts physical creation as fulfilled in the communication of divinity to the human nature of Jesus. Relatedly, it incorporates creation into the eschatological fulfillment that it thinks began with the incarnation, death, and resurrection of the divine Word in Jesus. One finds the richest seeds of this theology in Pauline and Johannine texts. When Christians became preoccupied with the eschatological dimensions of their spirituality, they tended to denigrate the significance of the world. The effect in some eras (for example, the fifteenth century) tended to be counsel to consider "this world" passing and endure its trials by thinking of heaven.

Jews were seldom so world-denying as Christians shaped by such a spirituality could become, though in times of persecution Jewish faith in heaven (the world to come) could run to similar conclusions. Muslims also had a strong doctrine of judgment and heaven, but only in time of war, when it was helpful to counsel soldiers that by dying in a holy cause they would go immediately to the Garden, did this tend to make the significance of the world pale. Muslim convictions about the primacy of God's will, with their dangers of fatalism, could induce a kind of despair about the significance of human actions in the world, but this attitude only appeared when Muslims felt culturally depressed. In the golden age of Islam, faith was a source of great energy for action in the world.

Last, the differences that we can note in prayer and attitudes toward the material world colored the three traditions' senses of God. The Christian God was the Father of Jesus, to whom Jesus, as the eternal Word (enfleshed), was identical except that he derived all that he was from the self-understanding of the Father while the Father was underived. The Spirit was equally divine, deriving from the love of the Father and the Word or Son but otherwise being all that they were. Christians claimed that this understanding of God did not make three Gods. It was a monotheism, not a tritheism. There was only one divine nature. The three persons shared this nature equally, in a way that did not divide it. Each person was divine wholly and infinitely. When comparing their sense of God with that of Jews and Muslims, Christians said that there was only one God, and that their explication of God as a trinity was merely a better symbolism for the one God than what Muslims had fashioned in speaking of Allah or Jews had fashioned in speaking of their divine Lord.

Naturally, Jews and Muslims disagreed. Both could say that, as One, the Christian God was the God whom they worshiped. Both also had to add, however, that Christian trinitarian symbolism was more dangerous than helpful. True, the Hebrew Bible spoke of the Word of God and the Spirit of God. But it had no Incarnation of the Word. Inasmuch as the Incarnation of the Word was the mainspring of the Christian understanding of God as trinitarian, Jews had to repudiate the Trinity. In rejecting the Christian claim that Jesus was the Son of God incarnate, as well as the claim that he was the Messiah that Jewish faith longed to see, Jews put considerable distance between their own theology and that of Christians. Muslims reacted similarly, with the advantage that the foundation of their rejection of Christian claims for Jesus was present in their scripture itself. In the *Qur'an* Allah says that God has no Son, and that claims for a Son must be rejected. They are a blasphemy, leading to an idolatry, and Muslims have to repudiate them. Muslims feel that Christians share much theology with them, and Muslims greatly revere Jesus. But neither Jesus nor Muhammad was divine. God does not share divinity with anyone or anything. The godness of God makes that impossible. Relatedly, God is quintessentially One, and trinitarian symbolism tends to obscure God's oneness. God cannot be represented (Jews agree), so Islam is aniconic, in theology as well as spirituality. How this is possible, granted the dependence of human thought on images (insight, Aristotle said, is the grasp of form or meaning in phantasms), is a further question, but one that doesn't obscure the main thrust of Muslim or Jewish theology proper. God is not to be represented, because God stands beyond all finitude, in a splendor that is not isolated but is unique and self-sufficient.

Contemporary Religious Fundamentalism

Muslims, Jews, and Christians have all been liable to fundamentalism, but so have Hindus and others not considered monotheists. Fundamentalism can spring from supposedly doctrinal roots, or it can be mainly a matter of social self-identification: defending the traditions that make "us" who we are. Either way, it includes a tendency to think about God and scripture literally. The mystery of God fades, while the metaphorical quality of scripture goes by the board. Fundamentalists want a pellucid map of reality. They want to have God in his heaven (there are few feminist fundamentalists in the religious assemblies, though no doubt there are feminists fundamentalist about feminism), and they think scripture gives them a heavenly view. Fundamentalists also tend to be exact and rigid in moral matters. They seek a certain, unwavering delineation of right and wrong, good and bad. The great advantage of fundamentalism, psychologically, is that it offers stability and security. The great disadvantage is that fundamentalism purchases these at the price of oversimplification, so they break down under the pressure of a reality that refuses to fit into fundamentalist categories. Above all, God, the foremost reality for religious people, refuses to fit into fundamentalist categories. One cannot meet the God of the mystics and saints—those who have directly experienced the divine holiness suggested in scripture—and come away thinking that any human categories could capture God. The best we can manage are frail analogies.

What, then, are we to make of the contemporary phenomenon of religious fundamentalism? Above all, how are we to evaluate its kinship with violence, physical or psychological? The answer depends on how we read the history of religions, what theology we extract from this history, and how we interpret the religious psychology of great founders like Buddha, Confucius, Jesus, and Muhammad. Though it is difficult to construe any of these founders as a fundamentalist, they all believed passionately in the truths disclosed to them, and their passion can make fundamentalists think them kindred spirits.

Such a conclusion is unwarranted. The great founders, in our opinion, were highly sophisticated, precisely because they had been overwhelmed by ultimate reality. No simpleminded expression of what ultimate reality is like or requires of human beings could do justice to the Way of the Buddha or Confucius, to the Father of Jesus or the Allah of Muhammad. The Way is the creator of significance, and the significance that human beings find in the Way is always less than the Way itself. The Father is the source of the Torah, not the captive. Allah is the source of the *Qur'an*, and no human exegesis of the *Qur'an* can ever capture his richness.

It is advisable, then, to pay as much attention to psychology and sociology as to theology, when trying to understand contemporary Muslim, Jewish, or Christian fundamentalists. What are they trying to protect? What scriptural texts do they rely upon, and what texts that would challenge their theology do they overlook? Who are the enemies against whom they rail, and why are these people so despicable? How do they respond to the argument that God wants peace, justice, love, friendship among human beings, all of whom are God's children— what shields do they erect against its force? How do they legitimate their authority to act in God's name? Why are they so confident they know the exact meaning of given scriptural texts or, for that matter, the will of God?

The list of questions could go on and on, but the drift should be plain. Revelation is not so simple as reading a few choice words from a privileged text. Where did these words come from? (How did we get them?) How did the text become privileged? The "text" of itself is simply squiggles on a page. Its meaning is culturally conditioned. People can find such meaning so persuasive and helpful that it seems more than human (divinely inspired). But they cannot shortcircuit the cultural processes that produced the scriptural texts, nor can they deny, in awareness of the facts and good conscience, that these processes produce other texts not considered sacred. Meaning is what human beings make, day in and day out. God can be with them in this work, can direct certain phases of this work in special ways, but no meaning can bypass language, traditioning, and the other processes that human beings have created to communicate with one another. There is no unmediated divine revelation in history.

So fundamentalism is a tough row to hoe on hermeneutical grounds (on the basis of how human beings make meaning). It is also tough to defend psychologically. The division of the world into right and wrong, good angels and bad angels, grace and sin is necessary, but it cannot be simpleminded. To make it simpleminded is to show oneself adolescent: still growing toward the realization that human beings must submit themselves to a mysterious God and live by faith, not certitude.

However, the worst problem in defending fundamentalist Muslims, Christians, Jews, or other religionists occurs when they become violent. In our view, to commit terrorism in the name of Allah is a contradiction in terms. To hate other people and move to destroy their homes, schools, and other cultural institutions in the name of God's grant of holy land is to default on any covenant with a God compassionate and merciful, slow to anger, and abounding in steadfast love. Violent Christian fundamentalists ignore the example of Jesus, who suffered the onslaughts of evil in love. Indeed, Jesus told his followers to love their enemies and pray for those who persecute them.

These analyses are not likely to persuade violent fundamentalist Muslims, Jews, or Christians, because all three groups can point to scriptural texts depicting God as wrathful toward sinners, unbelievers, people outside the community of the elect. Still, the question of where the Muslim, Jews, and scriptural theologies center—what images of God hold primacy of place and what are secondary—remains troublesome for fundamentalists. While nonfundamentalist believers can admit the presence, perhaps even the limited legitimacy, of texts that portray God as profoundly just, utterly opposed to evil, and so punitive toward the wicked, all the while holding that God is more basically loving and forgiving, fundamentalists have a hard time making the love and forgiveness of God basic and still continuing to brim with hate or arrogate to themselves the vengeance of God.

In the final analysis, God cannot be as the violent fundamentalists picture divinity, if we read any of the scriptures whole. God has to stand beyond our neuroses and hatreds, be a lover of all that divinity has made. Evil has to be a surd that God suffers, with a patience that human beings have to struggle to imitate. To set ourselves in the judgment seat of God is to open ourselves to harsh judgment in return. The deeper currents of the great world religions run into the sea of the divine mercy. In the light of the living God, the theisms say, all people have sinned and fallen short of the divine measure. All need forgiveness, mercy, and love, so all ought to extend forgiveness, mercy, and love—even to those outside their camp, those by human title their enemies. That is the outreach of the wisdom we find in the great religious founders. Only if God is merciful can human beings continue to hope for peace, summon the heart to search for new beginnings.[7]

Sages and Prophets

The last "further question" that we consider is the relation between sages and prophets. Buddha and Confucius are sages. Jesus and Muhammad are prophets. Phenomenologists could say more about each of the four, but their contemporaries tended to think of them in these terms. The sage, in fact, is the most honored figure in Eastern religious history and psychology. The prophet ranks high in Western religious estimation. Granted, Buddhists who came to think of the Buddha as the embodiment of the Dharma went beyond characterizing him as a sage, just as Christians who came to think of Jesus as divine went beyond characterizing him as a prophet. (On the whole, sage and prophet were enough for the followers of Confucius and Muhammad, though each founder underwent a canonization that verged at times on apotheosis.) Nonetheless, if we compare the spiritualities of sages and prophets, we create a fertile cross-pollination.

The sage is after wisdom. Wisdom is the long view, the most realistic assessment, the noetic and moral stance (the two cannot be separated) that shows people how to live well—as best human beings can. The prophet is after divine guidance. Prophecy is an interpretation of what God is doing in history, what God wants human beings to do. The prophet receives the Word of God, and so the hallmark of prophecy is receptivity to God. God must be able to play the prophet like a musical instrument. What the prophet proclaims is not his or her own. For the prophet to substitute human vision or hearing for divine revelation is a ruinous deception.

Granted this initial description, one can see how the sage is oriented differently from the prophet, yet not wholly so. The sage wants to know how ultimate reality has ordered the world. To know this, the sage has to encounter ultimate reality, be formed by ultimate reality. By the time that Confucius was seventy, he had no will of his own. What he wanted had become identical with what the Way prescribed. We might also say that by the time he was seventy Confucius had no mind of his own. He had the mentality of the Way, the vision that the Way granted. His wisdom was that of the ancients who had pioneered study of the Way. Such study was not academic. It involved an immersion in the patterns of nature, the trial and error of governing people, the hard work of ordering one's own soul. But it could lead to a tradition, and Confucius prided himself on standing in that tradition. Still, standing in that tradition did not absolve one from the need to open one's soul for direct formation by the Way. The Way was a present reality, more than an ancient doctrine. The Way could be heard in the morning, allowing the sage to die in the evening content.

The Way that the Buddha walked and taught was similar. It depended on direct contact with ultimate reality. Wisdom could not be separated from meditation and morality. Wisdom was holistic, the formation of one's entire being by the Dharma. The Dharma was not an academic teaching. It was the expression, the self-revelation, of ultimate reality. Buddhanature was the source of buddhahood. The knowledge that the enlightened person gained was of the knowability of all reality. The light that flashed in the sage's mind was the light that all beings carried. To gain the wisdom that Gautama enjoyed and relied upon when he taught, one had to pass beyond the partiality of human wisdom and be formed by the nonduality of *nirvana*. *Nirvana*, the beyond in human beings' midst, could not be explicated by discursive reason. But it could be grasped in enlightenment, by a non-discursive intuition. And, when grasped, it turned out to be the grasper. The experience of enlightenment took the human being into the perspectives, the reality, of the beyond.

Jesus also depended on personal experience of ultimate reality. Whatever he had learned by studying Torah paled compared to his direct experience of his Father. The Father was the measure attuning Jesus's soul. The Father was the divine beyond come into Jesus's midst and so promising the Reign of God. Jesus could not induct people into his sense of the Reign of God unless they gave him faith. Giving him faith, they opened their souls as he had, so that the Father could form them. The formation worked by the Father, through the Holy Spirit, brought people to right order. Then they could believe that God was real, loving, and concerned to redeem them from the disordered, unjust situations in which they found themselves. Then they could believe that God was at hard labor healing their sicknesses, physical and spiritual.

Jesus made all this credible, through his own teaching and healing, but when people believed in Jesus, they opened their souls to the source of Jesus' power, his divine Father. Thus the wisdom that Jesus possessed, and the prophecy that he brought to his people, were like the gifts of Confucius and the Buddha. They were not his own. They came to him from a beyond present in his midst, his soul and milieu. The modality in which they came was faith: complete openness to the Father, full trust that the Father would be as the Torah and the Israelite prophets had said.

This modality is not so prominent in the spiritualities of Gautama and Confucius, but it is present nonetheless. One had to take refuge in the Buddha, the Dharma, and the Sangha to enter upon the noble eightfold path. Taking refuge was giving them faith—entrusting one's entire being and destiny to them. Analogously, one had to join Confucius in honoring the sages of yore, if one were to enter upon the Way of traditional Chinese wisdom. Such an honoring had to come from the heart. It could not be mere lip service, for that would work no changes in the disciple's substance. When Confucius himself became the great exemplar of traditional Chinese wisdom, the honor necessary for a successful discipleship began to focus on him. He was now the Master in whom one had to believe, to whom one had to entrust the substance of one's character. So Christianity, Buddhism, and Confucianism all depended on both experience and faith, if one ventured after the heart of their spiritualities. All three asked disciples to entrust themselves to a wisdom, a goodness, that could not be proven true at the outset. At the outset, one had to make an act of faith. Only through the experience of believing could it become reasonable to make Jesus, Gautama, or Confucius the exemplar of ultimate wisdom, the fully trustworthy exponent of what human beings had to do, if they were to prosper at the deepest levels.

Much the same holds true for Muhammad and Islam. The prophet did not announce his own wisdom, but that of Allah. To receive the wisdom of Allah, one had to open one's soul, be a believer, a submitter to the divine Word. One could not separate obedience of the intellect from obedience of the will. No mere lip service would suffice. The experience of being ordered by the Word of Allah only came through longstanding absorption in the *Qur'an*. To grasp the significance of Qur'anic revelation and become a saint, an authentic doer of the Word of Allah, a real walker on the straight path of those whom Allah favors, one had to make the *Qur'an* the substance of one's soul. The measure given by Allah was the measure that nourished the soul, brought the soul to harmony with the music of the spheres. Muhammad was the model for such a harmony. God had attuned Muhammad so perfectly to the divine measure that what came forth from the mouth of the Prophet and was compiled into the earthly *Qur'an* was infallible guidance. The more deeply one submitted to this guidance, the better Muslim one became. The better Muslim one became, the more clearly one saw that being a Muslim was the essence of being human. The human vocation was to serve Allah, obey the divine will in all circumstances. That was the message that Muhammad had proclaimed. That was prophecy and wisdom in one.

Christians, Buddhists, and Confucians can all respond positively to such Muslim convictions. The experience of Muhammad and devout Muslim believers is cognate to the experience of their founders and saints. There is only one God, ultimate reality, Way. God has many names, and God can bless many pathways. But the substance of God is one, and the Way is always an attunement to the substance of God. Human beings are radically equal in their need for such attunement. All have souls that perish if not opened to, formed by, the divine measure. The love of God poured forth in people's hearts by the Holy Spirit is the crux of human fulfillment. To miss the light that dawns in enlightenment is to miss what one's spirit has been made to enjoy. Sages and prophets have little difficulty communicating. As soon as they focus on the experiences that brought them into harmony with the unseen, divine measure, they know intuitively that they agree on essentials. The gist of both wisdom and prophecy is the primacy of the holy otherness that made the world and constitutes human fulfillment.

NOTES

1. Philip Kapleau, *The Three Pillars of Zen* (Boston: Beacon, 1965), p. 205.
2. D. C. Lau, trans., *Lao Tzu: Tao Te Ching* (New York: Penguin, 1982), p. 91; see also Arthur Waley, *Three Ways of Thought in Ancient China* (Garden City, NY: Doubleday, 1956).

3. *Holy Bible: New Revised Standard Version* (Nashville: Cokesbury, 1990), pp. 166–167.

4. See *Christian Spirituality*, three volumes (New York: Crossroad, 1985, 1987, 1989), and *Jewish Spirituality*, two volumes (New York: Crossroad, 1986, 1987).

5. See Michael J. Buckley, *At the Origins of Modern Atheism* (New Haven: Yale University Press, 1987).

6. See Eric Voegelin, *Science, Politics and Gnosticism* (Chicago: Regnery, 1968).

7. See V. S. Naipaul, *Among the Believers* (New York: Vintage, 1982).

CHAPTER 7

A FOUNDATIONAL
SPIRITUALITY

Ecological Sensitivity

In this chapter we turn from the legacy of the great religious founders to what a spirituality viable for the twenty-first century might entail. Using what we have learned from the Buddha, Confucius, Jesus, and Muhammad, and from considering further questions about the spiritualities of the major world religions, what can we say about the spiritual program that the next generations of human beings will require?

First, we can say that the willingness of the great religious founders to accredit the physical world, material creation, can be a good stimulus to reflections on the ecological dimensions of future spirituality. Certainly, the founders did not approach the physical world with anything like the information that modern science has given us. They did not know how intimately linked the various ecosystems are, and they had not glimpsed the immense damage that human technology would wreak on the global ecosystem. Still, their sense of the divine reality moved sufficiently within the cosmological myth to make them feel that material creation could be instinct with the holiness of ultimate reality.

The Buddha thought that the world was burning, but when one had quenched the flames of desire, the world became congenial. One did not have to fear material nature or the human body. Food and sex were not huge problems. The Way was a middle path, avoiding the excesses of extreme asceticism and self-indulgence. Zen masters and others

208

developed this tradition into a naturalistic aesthetic that helped people move toward enlightenment. Rock gardens and reflecting pools could remind people of the priority of nature, the unreality of self-centeredness.

Confucius accepted the reality of the physical world as a manifestation of the Way that could order human affairs. He approved of the rites offered in the Spring for fertility, the rituals performed in the Fall for harvest. The songs from the rites celebrated the beauty of birds, the splendors of sunrise and sunset. These helped the Master to center his soul, and when his soul was centered he knew that human beings could move through the world gracefully.

Jesus accepted the biblical view that creation comes from God and is good. The lilies of the field and the birds of the air spoke to him of divine providence. He neither indulged the body nor abused it. Food and drink, sex and farming, were obvious necessities and occasions for blessing God. People were foolish to concentrate on the wealth that nature could provide or neglect the greater wealth that came from pleasing God. But God was no despiser of creation or beauty. If used properly, the gifts of creation provoked thanksgiving for the bounty of God.

Muhammad spoke in similar tones. Creation came from Allah. Human beings were the vice-regents of Allah, entrusted with the husbanding of creation. The goods of creation were portents of the goodness of Allah. If people abused these goods, they displeased Allah and headed toward the Fire. If they used food and drink, sex and money well, they headed toward the Garden. The central point was the priority of Allah. Anything that detracted from this priority was problematic.

Contemporary ecological science shows us new dimensions of the question of how we ought to treat material nature, but some of the basic attitudes expressed by the great founders remain germane. First, expressing matters in Western theistic terms: unless we find reasons to reverence creation, we are not likely to amend our destructive ways and treat nature wisely. A powerful reason to venerate creation is to see it as a free work and gift of God. When we realize that nothing in creation had to be, everything appears gracious. The Source of being went out of its way to share being. Creation is as it is because of a divine desire. Certainly we have to question this desire, when we find creation painful or problematic. We want to ask the Creator to defend the world. "Well and good," confident spiritual masters say. "Ultimate reality has nothing to fear from honest human questioning. Questioners who maintain their honesty soon find that their own assumptions also come up for scrutiny."

For example, who are we to say that creation ought to run in such and such ways—so that there would be no earthquakes, no floods, no volcanic explosions? Creation is as it is. We did not make it, we do not understand it, and there are severe limits on our power to change it. The first plank in any realistic ecological platform is to acknowledge that we are dealing with a mystery. The more that we learn about nature, the more questions arise. Creation is far more intricate, delicate, confounding than we ever thought. For religious people, this dawning realization evokes further praise of the Creator. For any people who are honest, it inculcates humility. We are the pots, not the potter. It is hubris to think we can refashion nature to our own liking.

Three paragraphs from a recent report on the state of the environment suggest the problems that result when respect for the environment or the material limits on our standards of living languishes:

> Consumption has become a central pillar of life in industrial lands, and is often embedded in social values. Opinion surveys in the world's two largest economies—Japan and the United States—show consumerist definitions of success becoming ever more prevalent. In Taiwan, a billboard demands, "Why Aren't You a Millionaire Yet?" The Japanese speak of the "new three sacred treasures": color television, air conditioning, and the automobile.
>
> The affluent life-style born in the United States is emulated by those who can afford it around the world. And many can: the average person today is four-and-a-half times richer than were his or her great-grandparents at the turn of the century. Needless to say, that new global wealth is not evenly spread among the earth's people. One billion live in unprecedented luxury; one billion live in destitution. Even American children have more pocket money—$230 a year—than the half-billion poorest people alive.
>
> Overconsumption by the world's fortunate is an environmental problem unmatched in severity by anything but perhaps population growth. Their surging exploitation of resources threatens to exhaust or unalter-

ably disfigure forests, soils, water, air, and climate. Ironically, high consumption may be a mixed blessing in human terms, too. The time-honored values of integrity of character, good work, friendship, family, and community have often been sacrificed in the rush to riches. Thus, many in the industrial lands have a sense that their world of plenty is somehow hollow—that, hoodwinked by a consumerist culture, they have been fruitlessly attempting to satisfy what are essentially social, psychological, and spiritual needs with material things. [1]

By neglecting the limits of the ecosphere, and confusing material (consumerist) indices of success with truly human fulfillment, the recent generations have produced a twofold crisis. On the one hand, we are now close to exceeding the carrying capacity of the earth. On the other hand, many of our most fortunate people feel spiritually bankrupt. Their lives seem bereft of meaning. Meanwhile, the rights of their children and grandchildren have fallen into abeyance. Inheriting a diseased, dysfunctional ecosphere, how will the generations of the twenty-first century enjoy a truly good life? How will they respect their immediate forebears, who handed them so many crises?

The great need, then, is for wisdom like that of the four great religious founders. It is inconceivable that any of them would have led or approved a consumerist movement. It boggles the mind to think that any would have countenanced the modern destruction of the environment or the modern substitution of material possessions for spiritual riches. Each would have stood up for the rights of creation as something that human beings did not bring forth and so must not deface or destroy. Each said, repeatedly and eloquently, that only by attunement to a more than human Way, a truly transcendent God, can human beings find either the balance necessary to handle this-worldly responsibilities or the complete fulfillment intimated in their depths.

Social Justice

If considering the current state of the earth leads to a call for environmental restraint and the reform of consumerist cultures, considering the current state of the nations leads to a call for a restructuring of wealth. The one billion affluent live in the same ecosystem as the one billion destitute. Increasingly, they live in the same economic system. For the great religious founders, they live in the single providential order created by God, the single system of "the ten thousand things" that provide all human beings their natural milieu. As intelligent and mortal, they share the same paradoxical human nature. They are more like than different, if we consider the mysteries of their coming into being and passing away.

All these are titles to basic equality of opportunity and material conditions. If the differences among people—in history, geographical location, physical or spiritual endowment, and the like—justify some differences in their material standards of living, the likenesses among people postulate severe limits on such differences. Thus, Muhammad instituted the alms, in token of the solidarity of all members of Islam. Each Muslim had the responsibility to help others. A destitute Muslim in the midst of plenty shamed the community.

Early Christian instinct ran in the same direction. The Fathers of the Church taught that charity toward the poor was a solemn duty. They said that the goods of the earth existed for all the earth's people. For some to arrogate extra portions to themselves was a radical injustice—a species of theft. In the same tradition, Christian social ethicists have said that no one has the right to luxuries as long as anyone lacks necessities. Human beings are members of one another. In Christian theological perspective, they are all at least potential members of the Body of Christ. Social justice requires economic and political arrangements that respect these realities and reflect them. People cannot in good conscience call others "brother" and "sister" on Sunday and not care whether such people starve during the week.

The equivalents for the Eastern spiritual masters are hard to determine. Social justice is nowhere near so prominent a theme in Buddhist and Confucian writings as it is in Western texts. Buddhists have tended to say that the enlightened personality will be benevolent toward all living things. Nonviolence is at the core of Buddhist ethics, and nonviolence can be interpreted as a mission to oppose poverty, sickness, ignorance, and the other forces that twist the lives of the unfortunate. Buddhist monastic literature counseled a stripped life-style, free of concern for material possessions. Monks were to beg their food, learning humility and tasting the lot of the poor. All these Buddhist traditions could be turned in the direction of social justice. For the twenty-first century, Buddhist detachment could promote simplicity and nonconsumption in ways that helped both the environment and the world's poor. If the wealthy nations learned that true prosperity requires freedom from material possessions, they might more readily give from their abundance to the poor. Equally, they might be willing to reconfigure the patterns of the global economy that have established the poor in their wretchedness. A new world order, not predicated on greed, might emerge as more than a dream.

The Confucian fascination with social dynamics could be put to good use in the twenty-first century. What are the rituals, the rites of mutuality, needed to educate people into solidarity? How do human beings have to think and feel about one another, if they are to act decisively against world hunger, illiteracy, desperate poverty? Confucius thought that the example of political leaders was crucial to the establishment of peace and prosperity. He was convinced that only truly virtuous leaders could get the job done. Have matters changed completely today, due to the great expansion of global population and the development of a manifold interconnectedness? Could the example of the leaders of the United Nations, or of the great powers, make a major difference in how the wealthy nations treated the poor, how the powerful nations laid down their arms?

We have seen the enormous impact of Russian figures such as Gorbachev and Solzhenitsyn. In their very different ways, each has changed the shape of Soviet culture and clarified the new world order needed in the twenty-first century. The reform of political processes in the most powerful nations would give emerging nations better models. No sane analyst would expect this to overcome tribal animosities or substitute for the immense labor of creating traditions of democratic government. On the other hand, it could provide the hope, the vision, now clearly lacking in many third-world countries.

When people think they can govern themselves civilly, they do better than "every man for himself." Many more things become possible. The limits of our progress are in significant part the limits of our imaginations. Questions about the limits of human goodness (our willingness and ability to live for the common good, which includes the long haul, rather than selfishly) certainly would remain, but they would not seem utterly crushing. A Confucian approach to providing good example, wisdom and goodness incarnate, could be enormously helpful in combating cynicism.

None of this is offered simplemindedly. The centuries separating us from the great religious founders have altered humanity's social problems considerably. Freud and Weber have shown how thoroughly our world views reflect psychological and sociological needs. Yet we modern Westerners have not become a completely different species. We retain most of the virtues and vices that the founders assumed. The parts of their portfolios dealing with cooperation and solidarity are well worth recalling. Taken together, such stocks of wisdom suggest that human beings are as deeply social as they are individual. In the view of the Way or God, they belong together, though not as ants or bees. If they hear the Way in the morning together, by the afternoon they can be working out practical agreements.

Many current social problems are so obvious that argument about nonessentials seems sinful. When there is an excess of food in one nation and a great lack in another, the response is clear to any with eyes: make a transfer. How such clarity gets lost in practice is a case study in the great deficiencies of human nature—what Christians call original sin. But abuse need not take away proper use. The fact that politicians and agencies find it hard to accomplish simple, obvious transfers does not mean that such transfers are not eminently sane. It means that the people involved need conversion to the bigger picture supplied by the Tao or God. It means that along with arbitrating practical disagreements we have to keep supplying vision and motive.

Without people to represent the viewpoint of the Way and God, practical affairs will always bog down. The separation of religious idealism from pragmatic politics has always proven disastrous, but the principled separation attempted in the modern West has compounded such disaster. Now it is no longer legitimate in governmental circles to argue that many things should be done simply because they are right—an imperative laid upon the honest conscience by God. The great religious founders would say that until that does become legitimate, social justice will remain a matter of rhetoric more than efficient action.[2]

Personal Integrity: Sex and Money

Thus far, we have reflected on the ecological and social dimensions of a viable future spirituality. With debts to the great religious founders, we have tried to be responsible when it came to nature and society, two of the four major aspects of reality. In this section we reflect on the guidance the founders offer for the personal aspect of reality. What will be asked of the self in the next century? What orientations are likely to prove most helpful? Obviously, we cannot treat this question exhaustively. Here it will be enough to deal with two obstacles on the way to integrity: sex and money.

Sex has always fascinated human beings. The difference between male and female is probably the most significant in our species' repertoire. Race and economic station certainly diversify people, but sex is the difference that has proven most intimate, delightful, and problematic for religion. The puzzle of the unity and diversity of the human race is epitomized in sexual differentiation. Men and women are equally human, holding matter and spirit in common. Yet their relations are so dialectical that all their interactions are stamped by difference. How much of this is cultural and how much biological is impossible to determine. There is no unacculturated biology and no bodyless culture.

The religions have mirrored the cultures in which they have arisen, usually being patriarchal or egalitarian as their host environments were. That has meant second-class status for women, at least concerning official power and leadership. For example, the Buddha is said to have been reluctant to admit women into the Sangha, Confucius would not take female students, Jesus admitted no women into the circle of the twelve (his official disciples), and Muhammad put women into the care of men. On the other hand, the Buddhist ideal of wisdom, traditional Chinese imagery for the Tao, and Christian images of wisdom and saintliness all suggest that the kinship between femininity and ultimate reality has been close. Muhammad, the *Qur'an*, and Islam show fewer openings toward the feminine, but they make it clear that women can be as good Muslims as men.

Here, though, we are most interested in rethinking the interplay of the objective, procreative aspects of sexual difference and the romantic aspects. There is no easy formula linking the two, but when one considers them in light of the order disclosed by the Way or God, it becomes clear that each has formidable rights. To overlook the objective orientation of sexual differentiation toward reproduction is to make a mistake laughable to most traditional peoples. To them the obvious use of sexual differentiation was the continuance of the species, the furtherance of the tribal line. Subjective, personal aspects of sexual interaction were secondary.

In our modern efforts to defend the subjective side of sexual interaction, we have sometimes forgotten the objective side. Certainly love is the catalyst for the healthiest sexual interactions, and romance seems an evolutionary necessity. Love is at the core of human creativity, including the creation of the most powerful analogies for God. But sexual love that ignores its capacity for procreation hides its head in the sand. The wisdom of the great religious founders suggests how to reconcile the potential conflicts between procreation and personal, romantic love. When people are formed by the Way or God, they can move to a higher viewer that makes procreation an expression of romantic love. Relatedly, it makes romantic love a beautiful mechanism for procreation. Providentially, procreation can occur as the fruit of the best of human experiences. What blocks this possibility becomes an enemy of both human survival and human fulfillment.

For example, treatments of abortion that limit it to the context of environmental problems (population control) slice away the truly human dimension.[3] Personal integrity requires much more. The great religious founders say that our sexuality is a modality of our selves. Only when we discipline our sexuality from within can we expect to be free of its threat to disorder our lives, both individual and social.

This implies that sexuality will be no less challenging in the future than it has been in the past. The great founders spend relatively little time on sex, because they assume that openness to the transcendent measure will bring it into proper perspective. It is delightful, a gift of God, but nothing to dominate human consciousness. For it to dominate would be idolatrous, or the feeding of karmic desire. Few contemporary Westerners make this assumption so simply. When one adds to the traditional challenges the current statistics on AIDS, other sexually communicated diseases, abortion, and population growth, to say nothing of consciousness raised by feminist and men's studies, gaining a sane view of sex looms as no mean achievement.

Fortunately, the contemplation that Eastern and Western masters have lauded continues to be therapeutic in the domain of sex. If people have regular access to the transcendent, they are unlikely to lose their balance badly—for more than short stretches. If they realize that their love for the transcendent is cognate to their best human loves, they can make genuine love—both delight in and willingness to sacrifice self for the beloved—the thread through the labyrinth.

The question of money is simpler. Money is much more obviously only a means, never an end. Where love can claim to be the heart of the religious matter, and so sexual love can become a legitimate preoccupation, only irreligious people can think that money is the be-all and end-all of life. One cannot serve God and mammon. All monasticisms have inculcated poverty of spirit, which is aided by frugality if not outright material poverty. Money is the source of many evils, because it takes away perspective, flattens people to two dimensions. So the management of money, for the great religious founders, ought to be relatively simple.

One can only manage money well, even for religious purposes, if one stays detached. To begin to love money for its own sake, or for the sensual satisfactions it can purchase, is to close one's spirit to God. Any other analysis of attachment to money is a delusion—a capitulation to the evil spirit (to use the language of Christian discernment). Money is good to the extent that it helps people live well: centered in God. It is a blessing, when it enables people not only to live peacefully but also to aid the unfortunate, alleviate suffering, sponsor good works.

Otherwise, money is a miserable master, feeding the fires of greed. Greed is a low, primitive vice, warping the human spirit. Thus the concern with money, profit, and affluence that one finds in many contemporary nations is a sign of spiritual disease. Such concern disorders personalities, if not whole cultures, and from disorder one never gets peace or joy—the marks of the divine Spirit. Therefore, when they address individuals serious about spiritual reform, future masters will do well to make the bottom line brutally clear: we cannot let ourselves become entrapped by money. Mammon is the realm of spiritual death.

Transcendence: Prayer and Meditation

Important as perspective, right order, about nature, society, and the self is, the crucial question in any serious spirituality is how to relate to ultimate reality. Even amateurs know that how one regards the self, or other people, or the world depends on how one relates to God. God, the Tao, Allah—whatever the name, the reality claims to be the most important factor in establishing meaning. Here we deal with this factor under the formality of transcendence. Here we are interested in views of what lies beyond human capacities, draws people forward for their fulfillment, that might make men and women capable of functioning well in the next century. Indeed, we are interested in what might take them beyond functionalism, to the entirely new level of being spoken of by the great religious founders: nirvana, goodness, heaven, the Garden.

We can assume that, in addition to naming states outside of human understanding, the terms that the founders used for transcendent reality expressed something experiential. Eternity and God mean nothing to human beings without a reference to experience. Sometimes that reference is only negative: the denial of the limitations that we find in all that human beings enjoy or suffer. Other times the reference is positive: intimations of a love, a peace, a joy, an understanding that would fulfill the human heart utterly.

Either way, the reference of human beings to ultimate reality, God, springs from actual experience. The longing for God is something documentable in all ages. People may not know how to name what they want, the completion for which they long, but they make clear their desire. Indeed, often their very unhappiness with life is the most eloquent evidence. Thus Teresa of Avila, going to the extremes characteristic of mystics, said that she died because she did not die. Her suffering was to have to continue to live and so be without her beloved Lord. She intuited that only when she had left the body, her mortal state, would she find complete fulfillment—full union with her Lover. This is an unusually clear statement of the pathos in religious love, or simply human longing for fulfillment, but one not foreign to the experience of artists, human lovers, or even ordinary human beings in moments of peak experience. At such moments, life seems insupportably beautiful, or crucifying. The person knows that earthly existence can never meet the need, the desire, the love that is brimming in his or her heart.

Conversely, moments of great trial, when everything seems black and the soul feels emptied of all consolation, spell out the same message. We do not find in space and time the explanation, let alone the fulfillment, of our human constitution. *Pace* the secularists who deny the significance of all profound human longing, the fact that our reach exceeds our grasp is a fundamental datum, perhaps *the* fundamental datum, in any adequate analysis of human nature. Even when we cannot pin "human nature" down so as to satisfy logical positivists, the fact remains that most human beings recognize the longings expressed in great art and literature, the passions that bring people alive and challenge them, only to raise the question of why we have been made with such profound need and hope.

Moreover those human beings who don't recognize such longings seem to the rest of the population repressed, flattened, deprived—less human than we wish they were, less willing and able to unfold their wings and fly to the extremes of their potential. They cannot sense the full dimensions of their pathos, perhaps because it would seem unbearably painful, so they try to constrain human potential to what is manageable, if soon felt to be boring. Without transcendence, they lack interest. In the perspective of the great religious founders, they are more to be pitied than blamed. They have been made to contemplate ultimate reality, truly holy being, and they refuse the invitation. The knock has come at the door, and they have pretended to be absent, uninterested.

The way to contemplate ultimate reality is to pray or meditate. One can distinguish between prayer and meditation, but no useful distinction is hard and fast. Prayer addresses ultimate reality directly, usually assuming that it is personal. Meditation thinks about ultimate reality, sometimes so as to stop thinking—to reach a thoughtless, imageless, holistic appreciation. At that point, it much resembles contemplative prayer, which also leaves words and images behind, to content itself with a simple gaze at or attendance upon the beloved divinity. The utility of prayer or meditation is that it gives people a means to deal with transcendence—contact it, open the soul toward it, formalize its importance in their lives.

But prayer and meditation soon leave utility behind. They are not exercises for self-improvement so much as stages on the way to worship. Worship is the adoration of ultimate reality. Ultimate reality deserves to be acclaimed, thanked, praised simply for being what it is. Worship gives ultimate reality its just deserts. Certainly, such an acknowledgment fulfills the worshiper, but that is not the main motivation. The main motivation is more spontaneous and selfless: acclaiming the beauty of God, the goodness of God, the mercy of God; letting the mind and heart exult in the perception of how wonderful is the mystery of creation, the mystery of the Creator.

However much colored by the beliefs of the given tradition in which the worshiper stands, true worship reaches beyond anything parochial to praise divinity, ultimate reality, as such—on its own terms. The effect is to secure the worshiper in the primacy of ultimate reality. People who worship regularly and from the heart have virtually no temptation to make sex, money, or anything else that is limited their God. They stand free of all practical idolatry, and with their freedom comes considerable wisdom.

For the great religious founders, transcendence is the telltale lift of the human spirit beyond its material limitations. The human side of dealing with ultimate reality is keeping going beyond present attainments, present fears, anything that would stop us from placing human destiny in the keeping of the holy mystery we sense at the beginning and the term of our journey. The divine side of transcendence is the limitlessness of this beginning and term. There is no starting point in God, and no end. Infinity is precisely having no term, no boundary, in any direction. The godness of God is this infinity, which is holy: so real that it becomes the judge of everything less than itself.

Language breaks down, but the movements of the human spirit that take it beyond itself remain. The source of order in human affairs comes from beyond those affairs. The attunement of the human spirit that makes for wisdom is the inreach of the divine Beyond. God carries people forward, under the species of an unlimited goodness. Once drawn beyond this-worldly judgments, we find all things made new. God can be the recreator of human affairs, whenever human vision becomes transcendent.

But human beings cannot make this happen as they wish. It depends on the movements of divinity toward them—the reaching into their souls of the divine Spirit who lives beyond them (as well as in their inmost precincts). In that sense, everything significant about humanity is grace—a gift from the Beyond that makes us more than we can be on our own. On our own we cannot be human. That is our strange condition, the bedrock of our suffering. Only by agreeing to the drift of the best in us toward transcendence do we escape from such suffering. Only by letting ourselves be carried by ultimate reality are we immortalized.

None of this makes any sense, unless we pray or meditate regularly. All of it seems mystical babble, until we experience not only the limitlessness of the human spirit but also how the divine Spirit draws us. The great religious founders were great because they knew how to name these things. From the order put into their spirits by the Beyond, they could legislate how we human beings can become fully human— can realize the "more" that our best intuitions sketch.

Light and Warmth

Nature, society, self, and ultimate reality will be as present and pressing in the twenty-first century as they have been in all the prior centuries of human existence. Prayer and meditation will continue to be the privileged ways to wisdom and formation by transcendence. And light and warmth will continue to be the signs by which we can know that a spirituality is healthy. Saints will continue to be people who clarify our situation and so love us that we want to do right by their light.

Light is a religious symbol. East and West, among shamans, prophets, and sages, light comes to mind when the business of becoming human gets serious. Light is paradoxical, though, because the light of the Beyond can be darkness for human beings. Human beings have to lose the tiny light of their own wisdom, if they are to gain the great light of transcendental wisdom. What we can know apart from God leads us astray as often as it brings us home. So the process of enlightenment includes stretches of unknowing. We pass through dark nights. Clouds drift over our minds, making us wonder whether we understand anything at all. We lose our customary, commonsensical bearings, because we are taken from our customary harbor to the sea of ultimate reality. Through that exodus, ultimate reality starts to become real, and customary realities start to lose their reality. "Reality" itself becomes a paradoxical term, as do "goodness," "wisdom," "success," and the many other terms we use facilely to describe our goals.

Still, the process of enlightenment does bring us light. We do learn more and more about our own makeup, the true build of the world, what makes for community among human beings. We do see how small we are, in the total scheme of things, and how mottled by ego. We do feel, increasingly, that the great problem is our impurity. Nothing in us escapes selfish desire. At first realizing this disgusts us, but then we realize that it is mere self-knowledge, and so something we should accept without fuss. Indeed, we realize that it is ground for humor. As egocentricity and self-concern fade, humor grows. We find that enlightenment discloses dozens of ironies. We sometimes think we can see the Buddha smile. The cant and pomposity of human beings is so ridiculous that we begin to feel sorry for our kind. With such sorrow, such compassion, our light becomes distinctly warmer.

Can we speak about light becoming warmer? Of course. Even the natural analogy allows it: the light of a summer day is warmer than the light of dead winter. But the more significant experience is the warming of interior light. Less and less do our insights seem sharp or cutting. More and more are they rounded, bent by compassion. The great compassion of the Buddha was his realization that human beings are wounded by ignorance. To live in the darkness that is not God's over-shadowing of our minds but the over-shadowing caused by our own vices is deadly pain. Any person with a common measure of humanity would want to alleviate this pain. The solidarity that Confucius and Mencius associated with *jen* moves us to want to touch the hurt, wipe away the tear. The sinner seems more to be pitied than condemned. Now and then, more and more, our first reaction of anger at injustice or evil changes to a surge of compassion.

The saints most lament the hurt that sinners do themselves, and the feeble attempt of sin to injure God. If they could, sinners would assault the divine beauty, take a hammer to the symmetry of creation. But God lives beyond the assaults of sinners. Only inasmuch as divinity takes flesh, as ultimate reality chooses to lodge in human beings, does what made the world allow the world to wound it. Still, such an allowance makes God merciful, compassionate, long-suffering. God wants the return of the sinner to health, not the sinner's punishment. God is light, in whom there is no darkness at all. Even more, God is love, in whom there is no coldness at all.

These are faltering analogies, feeble metaphors, of course, but what else do even saints possess? The fascinating thing is that, even though they disavow such a claim, saints come to represent the divine light and love, to make it present in our midst. Gautama, Confucius, Jesus, and Muhammad did not found their religions by doctrine. They themselves were the teaching that launched the movements we now associate with their names. The light that delighted their followers shone from their faces. The love that made their Ways seem possible radiated from their hearts. Without losing the limitations intrinsic to their being fully human, the great founders put divinity into their followers' midst. What they said was pale and two-dimensional, compared to what they did and were. People said no one had ever spoken as they had, because people heard them with complete receptivity. Somehow they galvanized the full equipment that human beings have for receiving the self-communications of the Beyond, the divine. With a look, a gesture, a joke, the founders made their hearers feel loved, and so able to open themselves without fear. The ordinary barriers to hearing, being seized gently, having one's life turned around, dropped away. What the Western traditions have called faith swung into action, as though someone had turned a switch or stimulated a new system of healing.

Light and warmth converge, flow back and forth, support one another. Like wave and particle, they can be different, or equivalent, or so primordial that we cannot define their relations. In human affairs, we first think that warmth follows upon light. It seems clear that we have to know something or someone before we can love it, him, or her. We have to be aware, discern its goodness, rebut fears that this attractive other will let us down. Then we can open our hearts, extend our wills, let ourselves identify with it. Then we can feel its warmth and give our warmth in return. But more experience leads to further awareness. Then we realize that only by loving something or someone do we really come to know it, her, or him. Only when we have been warmed can we begin to understand. Knowledge becomes connatural, marital, as we live with the things and people we love. Warmth generates light as much as light generates warmth.

The analogy extends to our relations with the divine, which are the crux of any significant spirituality. We love God more as we grow more enlightened. But our love, in turn, makes our appreciation, our enlightenment, brighter. In maturity, we have become one with the Way, so to love it is to love ourselves, and to love ourselves is to love it. It is our love, and we can feel that we are its love. The knowledge we have of it seems reciprocated: it knows us to our depths—to places we don't even suspect. We embrace it, with both mind and heart, but it embraces us more comprehensively, more strongly. For it is the greater and we the lesser. We could not even seek it, had it not already found us. We could not be, had it not been first and from its being drawn us forth. We owe all that we are to it. All things, all words, all affections are its property. Of ourselves we have nothing, because on our own we would not be. What light we have, what warmth we feel, are gifts it bestows upon us. The wisdom that has gone beyond our illusions of self-sufficiency, that sends forth light from *nirvana*, shows us that without it we are completely empty. Yet with it, in it, we are full. There is no being we do not possess, when we possess Being. God and we are a majority, because God is everything but our nothingness.

How can this be, what does it mean, why should we have such gifts? God knows, and God alone. The most basic question in Western philosophy is, Why is there something rather than nothing? The wisest answer is that we cannot know, unless the source of all somethings should vouchsafe to tell us. The saints, our exemplars of light and warmth, do not pretend to know. They are ardent believers, but they do not claim to know. They possess God in faith, hope, and love, and from their possession comes a connatural knowledge. But that does not remove the divine mystery. Nothing can. God is intrinsically, constitutionally, beyond human understanding. We can know that God is, but we cannot know what God is. And when we know that God is, we do not know prepositionally. We accept the drift of our spirits away from the contingency of all things, into the transcendence of a Beyond that is no thing, and in our drifting we become certain that an Other runs the show, orchestrates the music, pulls the strings of all the puppets.

In the twenty-first century, the show, the music, the puppetry will continue. Since God is God, that is certain. Equally certain is the centrality that light and warmth will hold. Human beings will find nothing more telltale or decisive than knowing and loving. No better criteria for authenticity, maturity, or saintliness will emerge. Those who know enough not to speak about ultimate things except very humbly will still be the best exponents of the Tao. Those who bow low in prayer, awed by the ineffable majesty of Allah, will still be the best Muslims. And those who love to the extreme of embracing their enemies will still be the best Christians. The Buddha will smile, as he always has, because all life will continue to be suffering that helps, nearly forces, people to seek a foundational spirituality—one equal to the task of showing people the Way to the Light and Warmth that cannot fail. Believing this, we ourselves cannot fail to bless the lives we have been given and be benefactors of all the seekers after a viable spirituality whom providence puts in our way.

NOTES

1. Alan Durning, "Asking How Much is Enough," in *State of the World 1991*, ed. Lester R. Brown (New York: W.W. Norton/Worldwatch Institute, 1991), pp. 153–154.
2. For some equivalents in American religious history, see Denise Lardner Carmody and John Tully Carmody, *The Republic of Many Mansions: Foundations of American Religious Thought* (New York: Paragon House, 1990).
3. See Jodi L. Jacobson, "Coming to Grips with Abortion," in *State of the World 1991*, pp. 113–131.

INDEX

Index